The Missing News:
Filters and Blind Spots in Canada's Press

TABLE OF CONTENTS

The Authors

Robert A. Hackett, professor of communication and co-director of NewsWatch Canada, has been researching, writing and teaching on political communication and the news media since 1980. He is on the editorial board of **Journalism Studies,** and has been active in grassroots media reform initiatives. He is co-author of **Sustaining Democracy? Journalism and the Politics of Objectivity.**

Richard Gruneau, professor of communication, has written widely over the past 25 years in social and cultural theory, political economy, media and popular culture. His most recent books include **Class, Sports and Social Development** (2nd edition, 1999); **TVTV: The Television Revolution—The Debate** (co-edited with Robert Anderson and Paul Heyer, 1997); **Hockey Night in Canada: Sport, Identities, and Cultural Politics** (co-authored with D. Whitson, 1993), and **Popular Cultures and Political Practices,** (edited, 1989).

Donald Gutstein, co-director of NewsWatch Canada, teaches in the areas of documentary research, journalism studies and information policy, edits the **Newswatch Monitor,** and has recently published ***e.con: How the Internet Undermines Democracy.***

Timothy A. Gibson is a doctoral candidate in communication, focusing on media and cultural studies. He is currently writing his dissertation, a study of the cultural politics of homelessness and gentrification in Seattle.

All four authors are based in the School of Communication at Simon Fraser University in Vancouver, B.C., where they can be contacted at newswtch@sfu.ca

THE MISSING NEWS:
FILTERS AND BLIND SPOTS
IN CANADA'S PRESS

Robert A. Hackett & Richard Gruneau
with Donald Gutstein, Timothy A. Gibson,
and NewsWatch Canada

Canadian Centre for Policy Alternatives/
Garamond Press

Canadian Cataloguing in Publication Data

Hackett, Robert A.
  The missing news: filters and blind spots in Canada's press

ISBN 0-88627-173-8 (CCPA) - ISBN 1-55193-027-7 (Garamond Press)

1. Journalism--Censorship--Canada. 2. Reporters and reporting--Canada.
I. Gruneau, Richard S., 1948- II. Canadian Centre for Policy Alternatives

P92.C3H33 1999   302.23'0971   C99-901335-1

Printed and bound in Canada

Published by

Canadian Centre for Policy Alternatives
410-75 Albert St
Ottawa ON K1P 5E7
Tel 613-563-1341   Fax 613-233-1458
www.policyalternatives.ca
ccpa@policyalternatives.ca

Garamond Press *Canada's leading independent academic book publisher*
63 Mahogany Court, Aurora,
Ontario L4G 6M8
Tel 905-841-1460   Fax 905-841-3031
www.garamond.ca
garamond@web.net

Acknowledgements

NewsWatch Canada's work, including the production of this book, has been wide-ranging and collective from the start. Robert Hackett directed a grant from the Social Sciences and Humanities Research Council of Canada (SSHRC) that funded much of the collaborative research. He took a lead role in assembling the materials and shaping the book into chapters; he also wrote initial drafts of the Introduction and Chapters One, Two and Eight.

Drawing upon a variety of studies conducted by NewsWatch over the past several years, Timothy Gibson wrote early drafts of Chapters Three, Four, Six and Seven under Hackett's supervision. Donald Gutstein edited many of the synopses that form the nucleus of Chapter Five, and he was the primary author of a NewsWatch report on the *Vancouver Sun* which is incorporated into Chapter Seven. With Hackett, Gutstein co-taught the annual seminar whose work has been the project's backbone.

Richard Gruneau edited and extensively revised every chapter, adding new ideas and materials in numerous places throughout the manuscript; he was also a consultant to the project under the terms of our SSHRC grant.

This book itself is only the tip of the NewsWatch Canada iceberg. Many dozens of people have contributed substantially to the project since 1993. First, and foremost, we salute the dozens of journalists and writers who produced the underreported stories "found" by NewsWatch researchers between 1993 and 1995 and the editors and publishers who published them. Collectively, they are evidence that independent journalism in Canada is alive and kicking.

We also want to thank Bill Doskoch for taking the public-spirited initiative to launch this project and to help nudge it along in various ways since 1993. For their inspiration and guidance, we also thank our colleagues at Project Censored (U.S.A.) at Sonoma State University, notably founder Carl Jensen (now retired), former associate director Mark Lowenthal, and current director Peter Phillips.

Special thanks are due to our colleague James Winter at the University of Windsor for his friendship and moral support, and for his own and his students' participation in this project from 1994 to 1997. Jim contributed to our successful grant application to SSHRC that helped get Project Censored Canada—the earlier incarnation of NewsWatch—off the ground. In addition, Jim worked with students at the University of Windsor to assemble the "junk food news" lists noted in Chapter Eight and to research underreported news stories for 1994 and 1995. While our formal association with Jim lapsed at the end of the research grant, we continue to value his unwavering moral commitment to democratic discourse, and we look forward to his forthcoming study of blind spots in local Windsor media.

In addition to the SSHRC, we received vital initial funding from the Goodwin's Foundation, as well as subsequent grants or contracts from the Council of Canadians/Campaign for Press and Broadcasting Freedom, the B.C. Federation of Labour, the Communications, Energy & Paperworkers' Union, the B.C. Teachers' Federation, and other concerned individuals. A grant from Simon Fraser University's publication fund, administered by Vice-President of Research Dr. Bruce Clayman, made possible the indexing of this book, a task ably completed by Mark Coté.

In addition, we want to thank our colleagues and support staff in our School of Communication, notably former director Bob Anderson, current director Brian Lewis, professor Pat Howard, and the School's remarkable administrative assistant, Lucie Menkveld.

The project could not have accomplished anything without the research conducted by the dozens of senior undergraduate students in the Project Censored Canada seminars at Simon Fraser University and the University of Windsor. From Simon Fraser these student researchers include: (1994) John Brosseau, Gloria Drynock, Chad Galitsky, Tanya Hamade, Joanne Kulicki, Todd Manuel, Isaac McEachern, Tricia Milne, Tarina Palmer, Robyn Shillito, Magda Szulc, Karen Tomblin and C. John Wakefield; (1995) Diane Burgess, Laurie Dawkins, Chantal Ducoeurjoly, Bill Duvall, James Duvall, Shoni Field, Rita Fromholt, Tony Fusaro, Dale Gamble, Madelaine Halls, Clayton Jones, Cheryl Linstead, Kirsten Madsen, Lauren Maris, Carmen Pon, Elizabeth Rains, and Karen Whale; (1996) Angela Austman, Ron Bencze, Christoph Clodius, Nicole de la Roche, Lisa Harding, Clayton Jones, Suzanne Maier, Bernie Melanson, Jacqueline Mosdell, Susan Wilson Murray, and Seana Wright.

From the University of Windsor, student researchers included: (1995) Cameron Dempsey, David Fittler, Tony Fusaro, Ava Lew, Jennifer Morrison, Steve Rennie, Humaira Shah, and Tracy Workman;(1996) Donna Bazzi, Lee Dunford, Dave Ertle, Jennifer Ganton, Mara Geleynse, Jeremy Gillies, Lanie Hurdle, Dave Krishnamurthy, Dawn McLean, Brad Milburn, Jennifer Morrison, Andrea Neufeldt, Darren Osborne, Michelle Pisani, Brendan Rooney, Alysia Sepkowski, Nick Shields, Linda Stroud, Caaleb Trott, Luke Van Dongen, Kevin Wickham, and Cindy Wolin.

At Simon Fraser, NewsWatch research has also been conducted by: (1997) Jan Anderson, Rob Finlayson, Sarah Galasso, MyLe Lai, Benjamin Letts, Mavis MacMillen, Emira Mears, Janet Ready, Kirstin Simmons, Brent Stafford, Jason Watson, and Trisha Wilson; (1998) Louise Barkholt, Dianne Birch, Wendy Fister, Michele Green, Trevor Hughes, Ilona Jackson, Lee Johnston, Christine Krause, Paul Krueger, Darren Seath and Scott Uzelman.

We also want to thank the many undergraduate and graduate students at Simon Fraser who have worked for the project as part-time research assistants or office managers. Since 1993, these have included James Compton, Kathleen Cross, Bob Everton, Moneca Faircrest, Rob Finlayson, Michele Green, Larissa Gunther, Michael Jones, Michael Karlberg, Patsy Kotsopoulos, Christine Krause, Cheryl Linstead, Mark Lowes, Katherine Manson, Isaac McEachern, Jacqueline Mosdell, Lenore Ogilvy, Tarina Palmer, Michele Platje, Brent Stafford, Karen Tomblin, Scott Uzelman, and Jack Walton, as well as Cindy Rozeboom in Windsor.

Integral to the project's first several years was the panel of judges: Canadians who had made notable contributions to public life, academia or journalism. The following are the judges who participated once or more in selecting our lists of top ten underreported stories for the years 1993-1995: Donald Benham, journalism professor, Red River Community College; Lise Bissonnette, publisher, *Le Devoir*; Sandra Bernstein, journalist; June Callwood, journalist and author; Sharon Carstairs, former leader, Manitoba Liberal Party; Michael Clow, sociology professor, St. Thomas University, Fredericton; David Cohen, Faculty of Law, University of Victoria; John Crosbie, former federal cabinet minister (Progressive Conservative); Peter Desbarats, Dean, University of Western Ontario Graduate School of Journalism; Clark Davey, former managing editor, *The Globe and Mail*; Francois Demers, Dean of Arts, Universite Laval; Rita Shelton Deverell, senior producer and host, Vision TV; Tom Flanagan, former research director, Reform Party; Fred Fletcher, political science professor, York University; the late Joe Ghiz, former Premier of Prince Edward Island (Liberal); Judith Haiven, author and filmmaker, Saskatoon; Deborah Jones, freelance journalist; Laurier LaPierre, broadcaster, journalism professor, Regina; Lawrence Martin, journalist/author, former *Globe and Mail* correspondent; Linda McQuaig, journalist and author; John Miller, chair, School of Journalism, Ryerson Polytechnic University; Pierre O'Neill, former journalist and press secretary to Prime Minister Pierre Trudeau; Howard Pawley, former Premier of Manitoba (New Democrat); Shirley Sharzer, former assistant managing editor, *The Globe and Mail*; Maggie Siggins, author; Richard Starr, freelance journalist; Gillian Steward, former managing editor, *Calgary Herald*; Lindalee Tracey, journalist and author; Michael Walker, director, the Fraser Institute, Vancouver; Bruce Wark, journalism professor, former producer of CBC Radio's *Media File*; and Barrie Zwicker, publisher of *Sources*.

———

Foreword

The type of story that Canadian news media would be almost certain to miss would be something like this: the inauguration and survival of an organization devoted to drawing attention to stories that Canadian news media would be almost certain to miss. That explains why many Canadians still haven't heard of Project Censored Canada or, as it is now called, NewsWatch Canada, although it has been surveying Canadian news media since 1993. I hope this book will alert more Canadians to the existence of NewsWatch Canada and to persuade them of its importance.

The reasons why news media tend to ignore this kind of critical activity, while blithely criticizing everyone else, are fairly complex. For obvious commercial and professional reasons, journalists probably can't be expected to leap at opportunities to publicize their own shortcomings. On a deeper and more significant level, however, journalists are primarily and legitimately concerned about constant attempts by others to conceal information from them, and to prevent its publication. Their preoccupation with this makes them impatient with critics who accuse journalists of ignoring or concealing information, even if it may be sometimes unintentional.

Despite this, Canadian journalists in recent decades have accepted such agencies of accountability as provincial press councils, broadcast standards councils, and ombudspersons. In fact, the growth and scope of this kind of self-regulation in Canada stands in sharp contrast to the experience of similar agencies that have been attempted in the United States.

But these Canadian agencies deal with published or broadcast material, and act only in response to audience complaints. This is why NewsWatch Canada and its U.S. model, Project Censored, which goes back to 1976, are so important. They deal with the many stories that have not been published, the many developments that are ignored by the major media, and they ask why.

It takes a great deal of expertise to undertake this type of exposé, which is why Project Censored and NewsWatch Canada have involved media experts with both professional and academic experience. It also takes a thick skin because identifying these "missing" stories involves assessing their importance, and that brings subjective and political factors into play. The organizers of Project Censored and NewsWatch Canada are regularly assailed from the right and the left for some of their annual brickbats—but that, as they say, goes with the territory.

Despite the problems inherent in doing this, it is a vital task. All of us instinctively recognize the importance of mass media in our personal, social, business and political lives. How well the news media are fulfilling their obligation to give us all the news that we need is of concern to everyone. You don't have to agree with all the findings of NewsWatch Canada to appreciate how these findings, and the debates that they instigate, are in the public interest.

This book not only reviews these findings since 1993, but also describes related research that has taken place under the NewsWatch umbrella. This research has originated in the valid assumption that blind spots in the media don't occur haphazardly, but tend to fall into patterns related to ownership of news media, the structure of media organizations, the type of personnel they employ, the conditions under which these journalists work, the type of products they are expected to produce and, last but not least, the way in which all of us consume these products. These are all subjects complex enough to often frustrate the most persistent researchers but, as this book shows, answers can be found.

In fact, as readers of this book will discover, these "black holes" of stories missing from the media universe, as in the real universe, often tell us more than the media "stars" do about what is really happening out there.

Peter Desbarats
London, Ont.

Peter Desbarats retired in 1997 as Dean of the Graduate School of Journalism at the University of Western Ontario, a position that he assumed in 1981 after three decades in print and electronic journalism. He continues to live in London, Ont., and is active as a freelance journalist, author, speaker and participant in many media organizations. His most recent book is *Somalia Cover-up: A Commissioner's Journal.*

Preface

When at its best, journalism in a liberal democracy holds government and other power-holders accountable by investigating their actions and decisions, thus truly informing people. It fosters participation in public life by providing a forum for civil debate (one definition of democracy is "government by discussion"). It helps clarify policy and value choices, and effectively filters information (using criteria of public relevance, interest and significance) so that citizens are not overwhelmed by infoglut. At the same time, it must fairly reflect the diversity of reasonable voices, viewpoints, and often competing political perspectives in Canadian society.

All that is a tall order. Generally speaking, Canada's news media do a reasonable job of living up to these high standards. Still, there are enough examples of media failings to warrant a systematic examination of the Canadian news media. How do newspapers and TV stations decide what news we will receive, whose letters will be published, or who will be accorded credibility? Are all the socially important stories that *might* be told actually making it into the mainstream? If not, why not? Finding answers to those questions is what NewsWatch Canada is all about. But, before learning about it, we should first learn something about an American research group, "Project Censored."

Watergate, the early 1970s U.S. political scandal that led to the unprecedented resignation of a president, has achieved mythical status in American journalistic culture. The exploits of *Washington Post* reporters Bob Woodward and Carl Bernstein turned on a generation of young journalists to the notion of being investigative reporters. But what is often forgotten is that the *Post* was almost alone on the story until after Richard Nixon was re-elected president in 1972. Many senior pundits thought Watergate was a non-story.

At one point, Katherine Graham, the *Post*'s legendary publisher, asked her equally legendary editor Benjamin Bradlee, "If this is such a hell of a story, where is everybody else?" This question caught the attention of Carl Jensen, a professor of communications at Sonoma State University in California, and prompted him to do some digging of his own. Jensen found that many alternative publications were breaking stories on Watergate that the mainstream media were ignoring. From that, he developed the idea that someone should survey the alternative and mainstream press to see whether other socially important stories were failing to get the attention they deserved.

The result was the creation of Project Censored, a research group dedicated to studying under-reported stories in the U.S. news media. In 1976, Project Censored produced its first top 10 list of underreported stories, and it has been producing these annual lists ever since. I first encountered the work of Jensen and his colleagues in 1990 while working as a reporter for a Regina newspaper. I was browsing in a Montreal magazine stand, flipping through a copy of the *Utne Reader*, a *Reader's Digest* of the U.S. alternative press. An article about the work of Project Censored caught my attention, but I just filed the information away at the time.

Over the next three years, several things happened that reawakened my interest in Jensen's work. First, the CBC was hit with the first in a series of massive cutbacks. Then, in the wake of a significant recession in 1991-92, the Canadian news media were battered by successive rounds of reorganization and cutbacks. In addition, Conrad Black bought a minority stake in Southam News, a company that had to go before a Bureau of Competition tribunal over its plan to buy most of the community newspapers in the lower mainland of B.C. That move threatened to give Southam control of about 95% of the print advertising market in the region (given what has happened since, that now seems like very small beer).

In my capacity as a board member of the Canadian Association of Journalists (CAJ), I began to raise the possibility with colleagues of launching a Canadian version of Project Censored to see if all the cutbacks and ownership changes were having an impact on the news. While the CAJ sponsors professional development for its members, and offers awards for the best investigative reports, I wondered if it wouldn't be a useful exercise to examine what the media might be doing wrong and to ask questions why.

The CAJ has its roots in an earlier organization, the Centre for Investigative Journalism, whose mandate included the following: To reveal "the concealed, obscure or complex matters that significantly affect the public." I believed it wasn't a distortion of the CAJ's own mandate to include an examination of why issues that significantly affect the public may have been undercovered.

With the board's permission, I wrote to all the major journalism and communications programs across the country to search for an academic partner. From that, one emerged: the School of Communication at Simon Fraser University in Burnaby, B.C. (the University of Windsor joined later). Bob Hackett, an associate professor, and Donald Gutstein, a lecturer, split the job of research director. They were later joined by their colleague, professor Rick Gruneau, who became a consultant to the project.

Some initial funding from the Goodwin's Foundation, followed by a major grant from the Social Sciences and Humanities Research Council of Canada (SSHRC), provided the budget, students provided much of the labour, and Project Censored Canada was up and running. It sought to use the methodology pioneered by Jensen: find important stories in the alternative media and see if they were duplicated in the mainstream.

Efforts to publicize Project Censored Canada in the early years provided some interesting lessons. Only one major newspaper, the *Toronto Star*, which has a full-time media writer, published any sort of in-depth article on the project and the issues it hoped to raise. Other newspapers came up with creatively bureaucratic reasons on why they couldn't do anything on it. One alternative magazine refused to run a story on it because it felt the CAJ's involvement tainted the project (too mainstream). It seems left, centre and right alike can all find reasons not to cover something when the spirit moves them.

One journalism professor, Chris Dornan of Carleton University, was quite busy in the spring of 1994 critiquing the project in commentaries for CBC Radio and the *Globe and Mail*. At the conclusion of a seminar devoted to the project held at an academic conference in Calgary, Dornan looked startled when I thanked him for his input, saying wryly that if it wasn't for his critical broadsides, "the CBC's listeners and the *Globe and Mail's* readers might never have heard of Project Censored Canada."

PCC started out by producing a working list of under-reported stories—their methods for selection are described elsewhere in this book—which were then sent to a national panel of judges. The judges were people who have had distinguished careers in either journalism, politics, public service, or academia. They were given a set of criteria and asked to select the ten stories they felt were most notable. Following this, the individual ratings were added up to produce a national top ten list of under-reported stories, which was then made public.

When Jim Winter of the University of Windsor joined the project, he started producing a "junk-food news" list, another creation of Jensen's, the term referring to news that is heavy on entertainment value but low on intellectual nourishment. The top junk-food news story for 1995 was the incredible hype behind the launch of Windows 95—a "story" where the lines between advertising and news were blurred beyond recognition.

Over the years, as the project has evolved and as the individuals involved have evaluated its impact, Project Censored Canada's role has changed slightly. The name was changed to NewsWatch Canada in 1997 to reflect this re-evaluation. Rather than simply compiling lists of the top ten under-reported stories, the NewsWatch team began more systematic analyses of major "blind spots" in Canadian news coverage.

For example, one NewsWatch study, released in 1997, found that big business has received more favourable treatment in the media than it cares to admit. Another finding was that major media corporations tend to be gentle when doing stories on themselves.

Why should the public care about all this? Mainly because information is the lifeblood of a democratic society, and the news media are a very major part of the circulatory system. Ideally, we should all function as citizens in addition to our roles as workers, managers, parents, spouses and golf buddies. To be an effective citizen, you must be informed about the issues and events of the day. Then you can decide if you want to do something, like lobby your elected representatives, or help pressure businesses whose practices with respect to employment, environmental or ethical standards might be found wanting.

The problem is that, to make good decisions about effective forms of civic involvement, we need thorough information and a diversity of opinion. If we collectively make bad decisions, we have a worse country as a result. In the end, do the findings of NewsWatch Canada suggest that Canadians are getting inadequate information about key stories? Is there anything systematic or socially-structured about patterns of under-reporting found in Canadian media in the 1990s?

To get detailed answers to these and many other questions about Canadian news media, keep reading this book.

—Bill Doskoch

Introduction

On August 27, 1980, the Southam and Thomson Newspaper chains simultaneously closed two major city dailies and consolidated their holdings in several others. Competition within the newspaper industry seemed to be disappearing overnight. Jolted into action, Pierre Trudeau's Liberal government soon created a Royal Commission on Newspapers, chaired by Tom Kent. Later, federal competition policy watchdogs charged Thomson and Southam with collusion.

Ultimately, however, the chains won the day. The legal challenge failed, and the policy follow-up to the Kent Commission was virtually nil. Kent's proposals to restrict ownership concentration and to protect editorial independence in papers owned by big chains or conglomerates ran into a wall of outraged opposition from well-connected media owners.

Preoccupied with other priorities, the federal government hastily retreated.

By 1996, in the wake of Conrad Black's stunning takeover of Southam Inc., the level of corporate concentration in Canadian newspapers was arguably higher than in any other major democracy. But this time officials in Ottawa reacted to Black's takeover with a yawn. No Royal Commission. No legal challenge from the competition policy bureaucrats. On the contrary, the takeover was pre-approved.

Meanwhile, through the 1990s, as newspaper chains consolidated and struggled to increase profits during an economic turn-down, there were huge cutbacks in newsroom resources, especially in the area of investigative journalism. Newspapers across the country began to look more and more similar. In a world increasingly saturated by visual media, newspapers were under pressure to become a medium more complementary to commercial television.

One result was a greater emphasis on "news" from the worlds of popular culture and entertainment, on headline-grabbing scandals, and dramatic and spectacular stories about celebrities and celebrity-politicians. At the same time, newspapers began to devote more attention to news "features" and to special sections on "homes," "electronics," and "travel," where the lines between news and advertising became increasingly difficult to draw.

Canadians now live in a highly complex media environment where newspapers are not the stand-alone, sometimes iconoclastic media that they once were. But they are still immensely important vehicles for democratic communication. At present, no other mass medium offers the same combined possibilities for accessibility, in-depth analysis, potential diversity of viewpoints, and sustained reflection on important political and economic issues.

That is why we can't ignore them or take them for granted. And that is why the current lack of government interest in newspapers as an important part of public policy in a democratic society is troubling.

More troubling, for many people, is the manner in which the news media in general currently operate. Criticism of the media has become a knee-jerk reflex for large numbers of Canadians, especially over the past decade. Such criticisms are varied: included are complaints, from both the political left and right, about the "bias" of journalists; the news media's over-emphasis on trivial issues rather than the great political issues of the day; the seeming obsession with scandal and "negative" reporting; and the apparent concern for the bottom line more than anything else.

Journalists have often been the primary targets of many of these criticisms, and this has prompted a certain amount of defensiveness on the part of journalists, as well as considerable soul-searching. Whatever the reason, over the past two decades, more and more journalists have felt a need to better understand the social, economic and political forces affecting their craft. And, in some instances, journalists have felt compelled to take an even more activist stance as reformers, educators and critics.

Bill Doskoch, a former reporter with the Regina *Leader Post* and executive member of the Canadian Association of Journalists (CAJ), is one of these activists. Concerned about cutbacks in newsroom resources and corporate concentration in the news industry, Bill had the idea of involving the CAJ in a plan to start a Canadian version of a U.S. media watchdog group known as "Project Censored." Donald Gutstein and Robert Hackett in the School of Communication at Simon Fraser University accepted the CAJ's invitation to create this watchdog group, and began to assemble a research team. The result was "Project Censored Canada" (PCC), created in 1993.

At Simon Fraser, we saw the CAJ's proposal as a pedagogical opportunity to teach students methods of media analysis in a project relevant to the real world we kept hearing was out there somewhere, as well as an opportunity to bring journalists and academics together in a much-needed public conversation. Press owners, certainly, were not about to initiate it.

The project was also a chance to provide an alternative to the Fraser Institute's National Media Archive (NMA), probably the only ongoing public media monitoring in Canada. While NMA reports are sometimes useful, they have a consistent spin hostile to the CBC and, in our view, they are too quick to imply that journalists lack balance when they don't share the Institute's own brand of free market evangelism.

In its first few years, the research team at PCC focused on uncovering under-reported stories in the news, and we produced "top 10" underreported story lists annually, following the model of our U.S. counterpart. In 1995, the project received a three-year collaborative research grant from the Social Sciences and Humanities Research Council of Canada (SSHRC), with Hackett as principal investigator, and Richard Gruneau and James Winter as co-investigators.

Gruneau came on board as a consultant, and Winter ran a seminar at the University of Windsor to help locate and select both undercovered stories and overhyped "junk-food" news. Our lists of under-reported stories were not intended as ends in themselves. Rather, they were a tool for broader purposes. We hoped that, cumulatively, the lists could suggest not just individual stories, but larger topics or issues that were under-covered by the news media. Once that was done, we could then think about why such blind spots exist.

By interviewing journalists and reviewing the academic literature, we intended to draw links between influences on the process of selecting news, on the one hand, and the actual "content" of news, on the other. In effect, we are trying to infer the media chefs' recipes by repeatedly tasting their dishes and by asking a few discreet questions of the waiters and other diners.

At the same time, we offered the under-reported story lists as a way not just to explain the news system, but to evaluate it. Is it comprehensive and diverse, or are significant stories and viewpoints falling between the cracks?

So, from the start our project had a double purpose: to contribute to scholarly research on the news, and to stimulate well-informed debate among the broader public. In this regard, we have never claimed to offer the last word about blind spots in the news; rather, we mean our work only as a modest contribution to an ongoing conversation about the media.

We say "modest" because the exercise of finding news blind spots poses huge methodological challenges. In effect, it is like looking at a picture and asking what should be there but is not. How do you decide what is a relevant and significant omission? Where do you locate under-covered stories if not in the press itself? How do you decide whether a story has been under-covered relative to its importance? We have never had the resources necessary to explore these issues as deeply as we'd like. Instead, we have undertaken a range of smaller, more preliminary projects over the years, with tantalizing but not definitive results.

Even at best, the very idea of identifying blind spots in the news is an unavoidably subjective enterprise, influenced by our own values and underlying assumptions, and open to differing interpretations. It's not simply a neutral exercise in observation and description—such as bird-watching, for example— and it would be misleading to claim otherwise.

Recognizing this, we have tried to put certain checks and balances in place throughout our research to ensure that it does not simply reflect our own prejudices. For instance, in our initial search for under-reported stories, we sent out a call for nominations to a wide variety of individuals and groups, representing highly divergent values, causes, and political positions. We then selected short lists of stories according to exacting criteria and subjected them to extensive discussion in student seminars.

These short lists of under-reported stories were sent to a national panel of judges of prominent Canadians, selected for regional, gender, and political diversity. Our top ten lists of under-reported stories were based on the judges' rankings. The 31 judges who participated are listed in the acknowledgments section of this book, and a more detailed discussion of the criteria for story selection and other methodological issues can be found in Chapter Five.

Through the early to mid-1990s, our top ten lists certainly stimulated debate at several CAJ conventions, bolstered the morale of advocacy groups whose issues we publicized, and even received a respectable amount of attention in the news media. At the same time, though, by 1996 we were becoming intrigued with the more general blind spots that might lie behind the individual stories. To study these blind spots required a broader, more systematic focus, something that was also mandated by our SSHRC research grant. Accordingly, we switched from researching under-reported stories, and preparing annual top ten lists, to more systematic content analyses of specific aspects of news coverage in Canada.

To reflect this broader focus, we changed the name of our research group to NewsWatch Canada. The new name was also intended to minimize confusion with the U.S. Project Censored. Although Project Censored USA was our initial inspiration, the two projects are entirely separate. Moreover, some people took our earlier name to imply (wrongly, very wrongly) that we held a conspiracy view of the media. After one too many phone calls from folks telling tales of CIA or Russian plots, we made the name change official in 1997.

As a way to research news blind spots, content analysis has two advantages. First, it enables us to answer particular questions about general patterns of news coverage. You don't have to review every newspaper or TV newscast to answer questions like, "How much coverage does business receive, compared to trade unions, and how favourable or negative is it?" Or "What kinds of people are quoted in the news?" Instead, much like opinion polls or market surveys, content analyst uses sampling and data-reducing coding procedures.

Second, content analysis is a more rigorous technique than top ten lists. In principle, two researchers, working independently but following the same coding rules, should come up with the same results. To that end, the content analyst tries to devise clear definitions of the categories of news "content" that are being recorded, and to record them consistently. Inter-coder reliability tests are conducted: basically, two or more people would code the same articles separately, and calculate the percentage of agreement. As a general rule, we discarded or recoded data that did not achieve at least 80% consistency on inter-coder reliability tests.

Still, even the seemingly "hard data" of content analysis entails decisions about what categories of content are meaningful to record, what patterns in the news content so categorized are noteworthy, and what benchmarks are appropriate for comparison against those patterns.

To take one example: Assuming that there were recognized criteria for what counts as "negative" coverage, suppose you discovered that 70% of media coverage about the current provincial government was negative. Would you then argue that the media were "biased" against the government? Suppose it turned out that the previous government had received 90% negative coverage? Does that mean that in fact the current government is getting "kid glove" treatment? It's a version of the old question: Is the glass half full or half empty?

At the end of the day, even the most seemingly "objective" news media research, like the news media themselves, is unavoidably value-laden. We make no bones about our moral and political positions: we took on this project because we believe that journalism's most important tasks in a democratic society include holding those in power accountable, and giving voice to those who can't automatically command attention through money or political power.

Given such a value standpoint, several critics, apparently oblivious to their own ideological assumptions, have dismissed this project out of hand as an ideological exercise. Perhaps it's a sign of the times—like the bumper-sticker that reads, "I respect your opinion, I just don't want to hear it." More fair-minded readers, though, may want to evaluate the arguments and evidence we offer before passing judgment.

The first chapter of the book begins with an exploration of some of the reasons why, in theory, significant news stories might not receive sufficient coverage, starting with heavy-handed censorship of the traditional, brutal and authoritarian type. By contrast with many less fortunate countries in the world, Canada is free, more or less, from this kind of censorship. However, there may be other, more subtle ways in which power inequalities, economic pressures, and other factors constrain the selection of news. In the latter half of the opening chapter, and in Chapter Two, we review some of the main arguments in the academic literature about such influences on the news.

In Chapter Three, we turn from a review of academic literature to see what Canadian journalists themselves have to say about blind spots and filters in the news, based on interviews with journalists in major Canadian news media in 1996, and a 1997 NewsWatch survey of CAJ members and other working journalists.

Chapter Four offers a different perspective on filters and blind spots in the news media, based on a 1995 mailout survey of about 300 media relations officers representing government, business, industry, policy think-tanks, professional groups, military/defense organizations, and advocacy groups concerned with gender, labour, social welfare, environmental, religious and ethnic/race issues. These are people who sometimes feel the need to deliver messages to broader publics through the media; conversely, the media often rely upon them as "sources" of information. We were particularly interested in the similarities and differences between "establishment" and "advocacy" groups, and we compare and contrast the views of interest groups with those of journalists.

Chapter Five features summaries of what we consider to be the most significant and enduringly relevant 20 under-reported stories from our lists for the years 1993, 1994 and 1995. In addition, the chapter provides shorter capsule summaries of the remaining top stories identified by NewsWatch researchers and our panels of judges.

Interested readers can locate longer versions of these latter stories on NewsWatch's web site at http://newswatch.cprost.sfu.ca.

Finally, Chapters Six and Seven turn to a discussion of arguments and research focused on discovering broader patterns in the news: systematic blind spots, as it were. Do these blind spots matter? And what, if anything, can concerned Canadians do about them? These are questions that are explored, in a preliminary way, in Chapter Eight.

Chapter One

Is Canada's Press "Censored?"

News is one thing in Canada that seems to be in abundant supply. We have two English-language national TV networks, two all-news cable channels, the Internet, 105 daily newspapers, and literally hundreds of community papers and special-interest magazines. You'd think, with this wealth of news media competing for our attention, that it would be pretty hard for significant stories to be overlooked, significant opinions to be ignored, or important or controversial ideas to be suppressed.

If the sheer number and diversity of news media are taken as a measure, Canadians seem closer to a truly free marketplace for public information and opinion than ever before. Equally important, news media today are engulfed in a broader media system that generates a seemingly infinite plurality of images, identities, arguments and ideas. In a world of communications satellites, digital media, and an accompanying proliferation of media tailored to specialized audiences, there appears to be more than enough information and opinion to suit every possible taste.

As the old saying goes, however, appearances can be deceiving. We believe that, when you take a closer look at Canadian news media, you find a lot less freedom and diversity of information and opinion than at first sight. What are the factors most involved in limiting or shaping Canadian public expression in the media?

GOVERNMENT CENSORSHIP?

In many parts of the world—and earlier in Canada's own history—the most obvious answer to the question posed above would be easy: repression and censorship by governments. In the name of national security, public morality, or social order, many governments have restricted freedom of speech and press. Often the real motive, of course, has been to stifle information or viewpoints that could embarrass the authorities or provoke political opposition.

Such state censorship is easy to impose when the state owns the media: dissident journalists, editors and managers can simply be fired and replaced. Authoritarian governments can effectively control privately-owned media, too.

They can apply economic pressure—by withholding government advertising, for example. They can use relatively moderate legal coercion, such as Singapore's stringent libel laws. Or they can use more brutal forms of intimidation.

The New York-based Committee to Protect Journalists (CPJ) confirmed that, at the end of 1997, 129 journalists in 24 countries were being held in prisons on charges related to their work, with Turkey, Nigeria, Ethiopia and China heading the list.

Even worse, 26 journalists in 14 countries were killed while on assignment, or as a direct result of their professional work. One of the most poignant of the murders involved a Cambodian-born Canadian citizen, Michael Senior. Orphaned during Pol Pot's terror and adopted by a Canadian family, he returned to his birthplace in 1995 and began to work as a journalist. Suddenly, on July 7, 1997:

> Michael Senior was shot dead by soldiers—before the eyes of his wife and brother-in-law—because his outrage moved him to photograph their looting in the aftermath of the coup two days earlier that brought Hun Sen to full power. "He had put the camera down and was apologizing," his anguished mother told CPJ from her home in Port Moody, British Columbia, "but they shot him, anyway."[1]

Usually, foreign governments are not *directly* responsible for these crimes. Political opposition groups and drug dealers have also used murder to silence troublesome journalists. Nonetheless, critics often produce compelling evidence that the assassins have links to the authorities. And rarely have authoritarian governments vigorously investigated and prosecuted those responsible: only five of the 26 murders of journalists noted above have led to arrests, and even in those cases those believed to have ordered the killings have not been charged.[2]

Canadians can count themselves lucky that such atrocities are almost unheard of at home. This isn't to say that Canadian journalists have never faced threats or violence related to their professional duties. In some instances, reporters covering organized crime or questionable business activities have been targeted. For example, in the early 1990s, *Vancouver Sun* business reporter David Baines received death threats, as did Vancouver CBC reporter Greg Rasmussen after his 1998 investigation of the Hell's Angels.

Other cases have arisen from bitter conflicts within some of Canada's "ethnic communities." *Vancouver Sun* reporter Kim Bolan and a number of Indo-Canadian journalists received threats in 1998 related to their reporting of tensions between "fundamentalists" and "moderates" in B.C.'s Sikh community. Most tragically, those tensions appear to have triggered the murder in

November of 1998 of outspoken moderate Tara Singh Hayer, the editor/publisher of a Vancouver-area Punjabi language newspaper. Hayer had been the target of three previous assassination attempts, one of which left him confined to a wheelchair.

It's no detraction from the considerable courage of journalists such as Hayer to point out that such brutal attempts to silence journalists are mercifully rare in Canada, and they certainly have not been instigated by Canadian governments. Even much milder forms of state censorship are typically viewed with great concern in liberal-democratic societies, such as Canada.

At the same time, governments and citizens in liberal democracies also accept the principle of certain limits on freedom of expression. We generally agree that press freedom needs to be balanced against important social interests (such as military security or public decency), as well as other individual rights, such as the right not to have your reputation unfairly damaged by false and libelous statements, or the right to a fair trial when accused of a crime.

The problem is that the line between *the right to free expression* and *the right to protection from injurious expression* has always been difficult to draw. Democratic citizens of good faith can easily disagree on the appropriate balance between these two rights. For that reason, most forms of state censorship of information, images or opinion are surrounded by controversy.

One of the most agonizingly contentious grounds for the censorship of opinion is the avoidance of negative racial stereotyping, and beyond that the incitement of hatred towards identifiable groups, which is a criminal offence. In 1994, for example, three books by the well-known Canadian writer W.P. Kinsella were pulled from a Catholic high school after a complaint that they insulted First Nations people. In Toronto, the Board of Education asked for the removal of William Golding's novel *Lord of the Flies* because it contained the word "nigger."

In 1997, Doug Collins, a controversial right-wing columnist with a North Vancouver community newspaper, was summoned before a B.C. human rights tribunal for a column casting doubt on the Holocaust and alleging Jewish control of Hollywood. Controversy swirled: most editorialists took the position that, while Collins's views were clearly objectionable, it was not the role of a government body to censure him. In the end, the tribunal agreed that Collins's views were repugnant, but he was not found to be guilty of infringing B.C.'s legal provisions for the protection of human rights (Collins was later fined, however, after a second complaint focused on a longer track record of intolerant columns).

Even more celebrated controversies during the 1990s concerned the government regulation of speech in respect to sexual politics and standards of public decency. In 1993, after one listener complained about sexually explicit gay poetry on an "All Day, All Gay" program, the CRTC slapped the wrists of CKDU-FM, the Dalhousie University radio station in Halifax. In Toronto, artist Eli Langer and gallery director Sharon Brooks were charged under a new child pornography law for exhibiting Langer's depictions of children and men in sexual situations.

Provincial censors sometimes restrict or even ban the distribution of films. Ontario restricted the Japanese film *Tokyo Decadence* in 1994. In 1996, the Maritime Film Classification Board banned Anjelica Huston's critically acclaimed directorial debut, *Bastard Out of Carolina*. Generally regarded as a powerful and well-crafted exploration of child sexual abuse, the Board deemed one graphic scene of a young girl's rape as unacceptable.

In British Columbia, Surrey's school board voted to ban three children's books about same-sex parents from the classroom, provoking a court case pitting the teachers' federation and the provincial government against conservative parents' groups. Similarly, Christian groups such as the Parents Against Corrupt Teachers attempted to ban from Ontario high schools *Foxfire*, a novel by Nobel Prize nominee Joyce Carol Oates, depicting violence, drug use and sexuality (the main character is a lesbian) among working-class girls involved in urban gangs.

Vancouver's Little Sisters Bookshop, specializing in gay, lesbian and bisexual art and literature, has been fighting state censorship since 1986. Canada Customs officials have sometimes seized and even destroyed material imported by Little Sisters, including titles that have been imported by more "mainstream" bookstores without hindrance. Glad Day Books in Toronto has faced a similar problem, receiving more than 400 seizure notices since 1985.

Given the costs of law-suits filed and inventory seized or destroyed, such censorship has affected the distribution of literature in Canada. Canadian bookstores are becoming more reluctant to order sexually explicit gay and lesbian material, while some American distributors are becoming wary of Canadian orders; at least one no longer handles them.

After various law-suits and appeals, Little Sisters was finally able to gain a court hearing on the constitutionality of the law permitting such censorship in 1994. While prominent witnesses—including authors Jane Rule and Pierre Berton—testified on behalf of Little Sisters, the bookstore won only a partial victory. In 1996, Justice Kenneth Smith found that Canada Customs had applied the law in an arbitrary and discriminatory way, awarding $170,000 in special costs to the store; but he rejected the argument that the law itself was unconstitutional.[3] As we write this, in 1998, the censorship continues, and the dispute seems destined for Canada's Supreme Court.

Besides newspapers, books, films and art, the so-called new media have also been the site of ongoing censorship controversies. In particular, the Internet, the loosely connected global network of millions of computers, has come under government scrutiny. Although some consider the Net's structure too anarchic to regulate its content effectively, the U.S. Congress passed the most ambitious attempt to do just that in 1996. The U.S. *Communications Decency Act* sought to make it a criminal offence to use interactive computer systems to transmit patently offensive sexual material to minors, or to specific individuals.[4] The Act's constitutionality was immediately challenged in court by civil libertarians and other groups, initiating an extended legal struggle.

Despite the occasional exception, such as Doug Collins, the mainstream news media do not consciously incite racial or ethnic hatred. Nor do they push the envelope on matters of decency or sexual politics. Thus, the news media's big players were not directly affected by the cases noted above. Still, the mainstream press do not escape direct state controls over information altogether. On a daily basis, limits on court reporting are probably the most notable form of overt government regulation of newsworthy information. Canada's most controversial court publication ban during the past decade was undoubtedly the 1993 trial of Karla Homolka, who was charged with manslaughter for assisting her then-husband Paul Bernardo to rape, torture and murder two teenaged girls. The judge imposed a gag order on reporting details of Homolka's sensational trial until Bernardo could have his own day in court.

By early 1994, though, the ban had turned into a theatre of the absurd. The *Washington Post* and other newspapers in the United States, where the ban could not be enforced, ran extended stories on the trial and the ban. Copies were smuggled into Canada. Canadian librarians, forced to act as scissor-wielding censors of U.S. periodicals, objected. Editorials cried out for the public's right to know. A retired Canadian police officer, trying to force the courts to reconsider the ban, was arrested for distributing British and U.S. articles about the case. An American deejay also broke the ban by walking to the centre of a cross-border bridge and broadcasting trial details.

Though Customs seized truckloads of U.S. newspapers at the border, cyberspace eluded them. Canadians with access to the Internet could indulge in gruesome trial details with the tap of a mouse—triggering more debate about obscenity and censorship on the Net.

Once the Bernardo trial started, though, the Homolka trial ban became irrelevant and all but forgotten. Given the American examples of publicity-fuelled media circuses— the O.J. Simpson criminal trial, for instance—many commentators defend the need for courts to impose restraint. During Bernardo's trial, when Justice Patrick LeSage disallowed the public viewing of horrific, sexually violent videotapes made by the notorious couple, there was little dissent. The restriction was widely acknowledged as legitimate and necessary.

ALTERNATIVE FORMS OF CENSORSHIP?

In summary, a certain amount of government censorship of free public expression, including news media, is not unknown, even today. Canadians are certainly wary of government censorship, but they tend not to get overly vexed about it if they can be convinced that censorship is justifiable in order to protect other important rights and values. Indeed, throughout our history, Canadians have shown much greater tolerance of government restrictions on certain forms of public expression than Americans have.

More notably, government censorship as it exists in Canada today hardly compares with the brutal repression in countries such as Turkey, China, Indonesia or Cambodia. In Canada, the exercise of censorship is infrequent and its effects marginal in the day-to-day decisions that shape the selection of news and define the terms of public debate. Because most media are privately owned rather than state-owned, and because the Canadian Charter of Rights and Freedoms offers constitutional protection against government censorship, it seems reasonable to expect Canada's media to be more accountable and diverse than the media in authoritarian regimes. Canada's media clearly have more freedom to report the truth in the public interest, and to provide access to unofficial and alternative voices as well as official perspectives.

Still, government is arguably not the only Big Brother that can suppress or limit publicly relevant information and opinion. Without prejudging the merits of the arguments at this point, consider the following examples—few directly involving government—that various observers have described as instances of censorship:

1. Writing in the *Toronto Star*, Naomi Klein argues that there is a disturbing trend towards censorship by powerful distributors in the entertain-

ment industry that threatens to leave artists who create controversial works out in the cold.[5] For example, in 1996, Cineplex Odeon had Toronto film-maker John Greyson arrested at the opening of his own film (*Lillies*) for the unauthorized act of handing out pamphlets for a protest action against the Ontario government's cutbacks.

In the U.S., author Michael Moore was banned from reading at Borders bookstores because he requested during one in-store reading that union activists who were picketing outside be allowed to speak at the microphone.

Disney-owned Miramax refused to distribute Larry Clark's film *Kids* without an NC-17 rating, which would have kept most of the film's intended audience from seeing it. Instead, Clark distributed it unrated through a smaller company, thereby reaching a smaller audience. Indeed, some studios won't even make NC-17 films any more, according to Klein, because big video rental stores such as Blockbuster refuse to carry them. This makes such films unprofitable unless directors make large cuts to avoid the NC-17 rating.

2. In May 1996, *Financial Post* journalist Michael Coren showed up at the CBC program *Coast to Coast* for a pre-arranged interview on current leadership issues, only to find that his appearance had been cancelled. This sudden change of heart, according to Coren, was prompted by a column he had written several weeks earlier about a potential CBC strike; he had quoted one CBC host who described CBC's technical staff as behaving like "oppressed coal miners, when in fact they are well-paid suburbanites who do not work particularly hard." Apparently CBC technicians took exception to the article and refused to allow Coren on air. While Coren acknowledged that his past dealings with the same studio had been handled professionally, he argues that this was a case of politically motivated censorship.[6]

3. At the other end of the political spectrum, leaders of the activist group Citizens Concerned About Free Trade (CCAFT) claim that their views have been consistently censored by the mainstream media. In *New City* magazine, David Orchard describes how, during the 1993 federal election, CCAFT's national organizer Marjaleena Repo called Toronto's *CBC Radio Noon* open line show to respond to the question "Are you getting the information you need in this election?"[7] When she told CBC staff in the pre-interview that she wanted to discuss the media's under-reporting of free trade, Repo was not allowed on air. Calling in to another *CBC* phone-in show a year later, Repo was informed that her name was on a list of people not to be let on.

4. Some observers argue that the fashion of "political correctness" is stifling free expression in art and literature that may offend minority sensibilities. In *Media* magazine, Robert Roth notes examples of black activists in

Toronto trying to ban the 1927 musical *Show Boat* and a museum exhibit about Africa containing arguably outdated and offensive portrayals of blacks.[8] Paintings of black women with fruit on their heads were removed from a Montreal university for similar reasons.

Controversy erupted at the University of Victoria after a female professor and several students denounced other professors for creating a "chilly climate" for feminist analysis. Ottawa protestors tried to ban Holocaust denier David Irving from a public podium on grounds that he was spreading hatred. The Ontario NDP government enacted provincial guidelines curbing anything spoken, read or displayed on campus if it "creates a negative environment for individuals or groups."

All these examples raise issues worthy of consideration, argues Roth, but too often activists are overzealous and try to suppress opposing viewpoints in such debates.

5. Guy Bertrand, the Quebec lawyer who initiated the Supreme Court case on the legality of Quebec secession, is a former separatist who reached the conclusion that independence would probably ruin Quebec. As head of the group Citizens for a Democratic Nation, he has been campaigning for federalism in recent years. One of his tactics has been to call attention to facts rarely reported in the francophone media: Quebec's high rate of unemployment, suicide and bankruptcy. He considers these problems to be reflections of social and economic instability that would only worsen after separation. Bertrand is highly critical of the francophone press, accusing it of being predominantly separatist, and his rallies and statements receive little coverage except in the English-language *Montreal Gazette*.

6. Allegations of censorship also extend to what happens inside newsrooms. For example, according to Kim Goldberg, corporate policies towards freelance journalists are effectively silencing an entire group of voices in the media.[9] Newspaper chains such as Thomson and Southam have started to require freelancers, who would otherwise have full copyright protection, to sign away re-use rights to their stories. This policy enables the chains to republish an article in other papers or in electronic form after paying only an initial (and often Scrooge-like) fee.

In addition to threatening freelancers' precarious livelihoods, Goldberg argues, this new policy can be used to politically censor particular journalists. Citing her own experience at B.C.'s *Nanaimo Times* (then owned by Thomson), she points out that two politically dissident freelancers had their columns cancelled after refusing to sign the free re-use contracts. Other less controversial freelancers were retained, despite their refusal to sign away their rights.

7. Another report from Kim Goldberg suggests that such silencing occurs at larger papers, too.[10] She reports that pressure from *Vancouver Sun* management in 1992 caused environment reporter Ben Parfitt and native affairs reporter Terry Glavin to accept a buy-out offer from the paper. Parfitt had written a piece identifying the multinational public relations firm Burson-Marsteller as the orchestrating force behind many of the forest industry's PR campaigns, including the creation of the pro-logging B.C. Forest Alliance and the Share B.C. movement. Parfitt had to sell the story to another local paper to get it published in full, but *Sun* editors told Parfitt that the story had compromised his ability to cover forestry for the *Sun*. Glavin noted that pressure from the logging industry on *Sun* management made serious environmental coverage difficult: "Every time we touched on a story that in any way cast doubt on the ability or the intent of B.C.'s major forest companies to provide secure, stable, safe jobs to working people and to provide a viable, environmentally sound, well-managed forest industry on public lands in British Columbia, the amount of grief that would result was--well, it was pretty hard."

Goldberg writes that the same day that the *Sun* itself hired Burson-Marsteller to boost sales was the day that David Suzuki's environmental column was dropped. (Interestingly, these events sparked a public "Take Back the News" symposium in downtown Vancouver which drew an unprecedented 700 people expressing concern about environmental coverage. This symposium was one of the catalysts for the creation of Project Censored Canada.)

8. At the *Ottawa Citizen*, another Southam-owned paper, a more recent drama played itself out in the story of Chris Young, a respected veteran journalist at Southam who had held many senior editorial positions. In 1996, Joan Fraser resigned as editor of the *Montreal Gazette,* unwilling to be part of the new regime after Conrad Black took control of the company in 1996. Young wrote a piece lamenting Fraser's departure, and criticizing Black's views that English Canada would be better off under new "arrangements" with the U.S. in the event of Quebec's separation. Black responded with a rebuttal in the *Citizen,* one described by Young as a "ferocious, vicious personal attack." Shortly thereafter, the *Citizen* dropped Young's column, and refused to print Young's response to Black's attack. Commenting in a *CBC National Magazine* documentary on Black's press empire, Young concluded that "the chill is on."[11]

The examples of alleged "censorship" itemized above tell us several things. First, not only governments but also interest groups and media corporations can be accused of censorship. Second, those who make accusations of censorship, as well as the alleged practitioners of censorship, come from across the political spectrum. In addition, the word "censorship" in these examples is typically used as a politically loaded "hiss-boo" word; people use it to discredit actions they dislike, rather than to describe something analytically.

Finally, censorship as it is normally used in everyday language is not only a loaded concept; it is a narrow one. Every example we've mentioned involves a *conscious* act of suppression: to fire a journalist, to ban a book or painting, to prevent a caller from speaking on air. Is it not possible, though, that such things as *unconscious* biases, laziness, tradition, organizational routines, self-censorship, institutional inertia, or a dozen other factors might lead to the silencing of certain stories and voices, without necessarily any conscious intention to censor them?

It is certainly true that instances of outright censorship can occasionally be found in Canadian news media. One particularly notable recent example occurred in the fall of 1998 when David Black, the publisher of dozens of B.C. community newspapers, ordered his editors not to run any commentary supporting the land claim deal negotiated between B.C.'s NDP government and the Nisga'a people.

Such examples of overt corporate censorship appear to be infrequent, however. Most academic research in recent years has emphasized how news is limited and shaped in more subtle ways. This research suggests a need to move beyond the idea of overt censorship in order to explore what some scholars call "filters" in the news system. These filters are factors that more or less systematically weed out certain kinds of potential news, but typically operate far less directly than conscious censorship.

NEWS FILTERS: JOURNALISTS AS NEWSWORKERS

In a more innocent time, it used to be said that news simply reflects or mirrors what happens in the real social and political world. Even today, this position is still sometimes used to deflect criticisms of media sensationalism or negativity.

"If you don't like the news," media spokespeople might say, "hey, don't blame us. We're just the messengers bearing bad news."

But in the cynical 1990s, the notion that news simply reflects raw events seems almost quaint—on a par with the belief that politicians just represent the voters who elect them, or that the free market gives people what they deserve. Perhaps rightly so, because, as dozens of media scholars point out, *news is a manufactured product.*[12] It is both selected (from a huge range of potentially reportable events), and constructed. That is, events are transformed into stories, and a story must have both an audience (which interprets the story according to its values and experience) and a story-teller (who selects facts, arranges their sequence, and chooses the language with which to describe them).

All this does not mean that news is fabricated out of thin air. Clearly, traffic accidents do happen, politicians and princes sometimes behave scandalously, and O.J. Simpson was indeed charged with murder. The point is, rather, that news is an active representation of the world, not a passive reflection of some pre-given reality.

Nonetheless, the most important issue for understanding the production of news goes beyond simply recognizing that the media act to filter the infinity of events into a manageable bite-sized chunk. The key questions are: how well do the media filter reality, for what purposes, through what processes and structures, and in whose interests? And, in the process, do particular kinds of publicly-significant information about the world get systematically filtered out, producing notable omissions—let's call them "blind spots"— in the news.

An obvious place to start a search for news filters is with journalists themselves—the reporters, researchers and editors who are responsible for generating news on a daily basis. Perhaps, if we know about journalists' personal backgrounds and values, we can better understand the "biases" of news. This is how the question of news filters is often approached: as a question of conscious or unconscious bias on the part of journalists.

For example, one line of criticism—expressed by certain members of the political left—suggests that journalists are simply middle-class professionals, and are thus hostile to, or largely ignorant of trade unions. This allegedly produces a highly-significant blind spot: lack of balanced or informed labour coverage.

A similar view suggests that, as journalists move up in their careers, they sometimes become celebrities in their own right (especially the daily stars of network television). Because these celebrity-journalists begin to move in rarefied social circles, the argument runs, they lose touch with ordinary citizens. As a result, news that connects with the concerns and values of everyday life and ordinary people is in short supply.

The most politically influential critique of journalists' biases, though, comes from more conservative critics, especially those of the political right. In this view, the good old days were the 1950s, when news simply reported on "reality," and political journalism treated politicians and authority figures with enough respect that they could communicate with their publics. But (so the story goes) those days are gone. Instead, with the rise of adversarial—or attack or "gotcha"—journalism in the 1960s, the news has adopted a pervasive "left-liberal" or anti-authority bias. Adversarial media have become active players in the political process, sowing seeds of cynicism towards business and political leaders.

This narrative has become a familiar refrain in recent years, a favourite of many politicians, neo-conservative think-tanks, evangelical free marketeers (who focus on perceived media hostility to free enterprise rather than to government), and a handful of media scholars and journalists.

Several factors are supposedly to blame for this allegedly new brand of destructive, biased, and negative journalism. One widely-noted corrosive force is television, a medium driven primarily by visual and entertainment imperatives. Television is found guilty of a wide range of sins: most notably, helping to lose the Vietnam War (by allegedly casting doubt on the likelihood of winning and by showing more bloodshed than the U.S. public could stand); and helping special interest groups hijack the political agenda by over-covering staged but visually exciting disruptions and protests, or victim-oriented sob stories high in human interest.

Another favoured neo-conservative target is "Watergate envy," referring to the famous role of *Washington Post* reporters Bob Woodward and Carl Bernstein in uncovering scandal in the White House and thus toppling Richard Nixon in 1973. Since then, the argument runs, journalists have been schooled on the Watergate model, encouraging them to pursue professional awards and social status by uncovering scandal in high places and bringing down politicians. This kind of scandal-mongering, the argument continues, makes life impossibly difficult for elected officials in the United States.

According to veteran journalist and educator Anthony Westell, this post-Watergate style of journalism has spread to Canada, where it is even less appropriate, because Canada has organized opposition parties that are supposed to be the watchdog on public affairs.[13]

The primary villain in the neo-conservative theory of "adversarial media" is the new generation of critical journalists who began their careers in the 1960s and 1970s. Neo-conservative critics argue that many of the new journalists of the time were products of the "counter-culture" and that their hypercritical approach to journalism simply reflected the counter-culture's anti-establishment and nihilistic tendencies. The result was a generation of journalists less interested in reporting on "the system" than in opposing it.

Here, the story divides into two versions. The more credible version sees journalists as hostile to authority in general, not motivated by any particular ideology, but rather part of a culture of aggression and mindless negativism. For example, in an influential recent essay in *The New Yorker* magazine, Adam Gopnik argues that aggression has become an abstract value in U.S. culture and entertainment. Journalists act aggressively not to accomplish something, "but simply in order to be seen to be aggressive."[14] After all, aggression sells. News stories adopt an adversarial posture, but an empty one, divorced from any analytical standpoint that could propose positive alternatives.

While this theory hardly offers a complete picture of journalism, there is nevertheless something to it. Even if it has more to do with style than substance, there is undoubtedly a certain adversarial ethos in journalism. Furthermore, this adversarial ethos has a long history. The early popular press in Canada and the U.S. often featured populist critiques of the wealthy and the powerful. One of the best known early examples is the "muck-raking" journalism that became prominent in the U.S. in the early years of the 20th century.[15]

A key question, however, is whether journalism's adversarial ethos has now been largely severed from any significant commitment to collective public purpose and social responsibility. The answer to this question is by no means clear, but you don't have to be a conservative to see troubling signs. For instance, one Vancouver reporter interviewed by NewsWatch Canada researchers a few years ago responded to questions about his paper's news coverage by bragging that his reporting had caused a cabinet minister to resign: as if that were the pinnacle of professional achievement.

There is another, more self-consciously politicized version of the "Adversarial Media theory"—again, advanced mainly by conservatives— which sees journalists as politically biased against capitalism and individual freedoms. Borrowing some key ideas from the U.S. sociologist Daniel Bell, this view portrays journalists as part of a "new class" of bureaucrats and intellectuals with a value-system at odds with true individualism and the achievement-orientation of business. This supposed "new class" has a vested interest in expanding the regulatory activity of the state, at the expense of individual freedoms, especially in the sphere of private business. Neoconservative critics argue that the media act as an instrument of the "new class" and promote its anti-capitalist and anti-individualistic world view.[16] According to this theory, journalists tend to be morally and politically more liberal or left-wing than the rest of the population, leading to a host of double standards and blind spots in the news, favouring liberal over conservative causes and viewpoints.

This neo-conservative attack on the supposedly "left-liberal" media has been widely publicized, and in some quarters it is more or less an unquestioned article of faith. In the United States, in particular, it is a view that has adapted well to a renewed populist suspicion of educated "experts" in political and cultural life—a suspicion fuelled by reactionary radio talk-show hosts and typified by bumper stickers with slogans such as "I Don't Believe the Liberal Media." As a rigorous explanation of what's in the news and how it got there, however, this fusion of "new class theory" and "adversarial media theory" has serious problems.

Most notably, it exaggerates the extent of journalists' leftism. For example, academic studies of U.S. journalists have found that journalists do tend to have more schooling and are less religious than average (especially compared to rural and older people). But a careful look at aggregate tendencies in the research also suggests that journalists' views do not depart radically from mainstream values and assumptions.[17] In other words, newsrooms are not likely to be oases of aggressive nihilism, nor are they hotbeds of political radicalism. In any case, many of the journalists allegedly radicalized during the 1960s counter-culture have retired, moved on to other occupations, and/or have become more conservative.

By the same token, the "left-liberal media" hypothesis exaggerates the like-mindedness of journalists. It is easy, but often misleading, to treat journalists, or "the media," as a monolithic group. For instance, there may be significant differences between journalists in élite national media and those in the small-town press.

In addition, conservative critics sometimes seem to extrapolate too carelessly from (selected) surveys of journalists' political views to news content. "If most journalists are lefties," they say in effect, "then the news itself is tinted pink." But bias that *makes a difference* must be on the screen or page, not just in newsworkers' heads. So there is an additional problem with the conservative critique: a missing link between journalists' consciousness and actual news content. Not surprisingly, a well-funded industry has arisen to supply the missing link—to "prove" that news is indeed slanted to the left, and to provide the research ammunition to pressure the media to become more "balanced"—i.e., to move to the right.

In the United States, conservative media institutes range from the wildly polemical group Accuracy in Media (whose director, in one critic's view, "tolerates double standards that would make a Stalinist blush")[18] to the more reputable Center for Media and Public Affairs. In Canada, the political right's cudgels have been taken up by the Fraser Institute. Since 1974, the Fraser Institute has consistently promoted the free market as the solution to all manner of public policy issues. By the mid-1980s, the Institute had an annual budget of over $1 million and a staff of eighteen, thanks to the backing of over

400 corporations and prominent right-wing Canadian businessmen such as Peter Pocklington and Conrad Black.

One of the branches of the Fraser Institute is its National Media Archive (NMA), founded in 1987 with an annual budget of about $200,000. The NMA conducts content analyses, reported in its monthly newsletter, puportedly to put the "objectivity, balance and fairness" of media coverage of public issues to "scientific scrutiny". The NMA has consistently failed to acknowledge that, no matter how scientific it may seem, content analyses—including the NewsWatch Canada studies summarized in later chapters in this book—always rest upon certain assumptions: What kind of content conveys meaning, and deserves to be noticed and recorded? What are appropriate benchmarks against which to compare patterns of news?

In practice, the NMA systematically highlights and contextualizes its research findings selectively. In other words, there is a consistent spin, described aptly by columnist Andrew Coyne, himself an enthusiastic free marketeer: "Ostensibly, it's just disinterested empirical observation, like bird-watching, but the intention is clear: to gather proof of the leftist conspiracy conservatives are convinced is running the media."[19] Judging from the double standards in its reports, as well as the free market evangelism of its parent institute, the NMA seems especially keen to demonize the publicly-funded CBC.[20]

This brings us to a final flaw in the conservative critique of media: the evidence that news itself actually has a consistent left-wing bias is questionable, to say the least. For instance, one of the oldest right-wing articles of faith about the media—that U.S. television network coverage cast the Vietnam war in an unfavourable light, and showed too many American casualties, thus undermining public support for the war—has been demolished in recent years by careful scholarly study.[21] Yet the myth persists, perhaps in part because it serves useful political purposes: during the U.S. interventions in Grenada, Panama and the Persian Gulf, it helped to legitimize military restrictions on independent media coverage.

At the same time, the ongoing "flak" from conservative think tanks continually makes journalists look over their shoulders to avoid being accused of left-wing bias.[22] For example, the NMA's studies, however flawed, have nevertheless had an impact on the climate of discussion among CBC managers and directors.

In the end, the "biased journalists" argument simply sidesteps too many important issues. Even if some journalists begin their careers with strong political viewpoints, their working conditions do not make it easy to keep them. After years of observing political gamesmanship, journalists tend to become as cynical about left-wing views as anything else—or, as one TV reporter told Newswatch researchers, after years of interviewing sources and hearing arguments on both sides of various issues, journalists tend to move towards the middle-of-the-road politically.

Even more importantly, apart from a handful of commentators given a soapbox on radio talk shows or the op/ed columns, newsworkers have few career incentives to display strong opinions. Moreover, newswork is still influenced in subtle ways by journalists' beliefs in the value of objective reporting. Objectivity has always been an elusive, and somewhat tarnished, value in news media; but as an abstract ideal, objectivity remains one of the hallmarks of professionalism in North American journalism.

There are also strong institutional and economic pressures that arguably play a greater role in news production than do the opinions of individual journalists. News, after all, has to be produced daily, even hourly; it involves collaboration and cooperation to efficiently process continually "new" events; and it is produced within complex hierarchical organizations which face ongoing political and economic pressures to generate news that audiences will regard as credible and unbiased.

For all these reasons, the production of news has become highly routinized. Journalists learn to work within the framework of demands and perspectives imposed by these routines—routines which in turn help news organizations to adapt to their external environment.

In their book, *Mediating the Message*, Pamela Shoemaker and Stephen Reese conclude a thoughtful review of the scholarly research on the likely influences of journalist's social backgrounds and values with these sensible observations:[23]

1. Whether the personal characteristics of journalists influence news content probably varies a lot between organizations, depending on such factors as the numbers of like-minded people, and the power of an individual's position. A person in a key role, and one relatively immune from pressure from above, can affect news judgment and content. This point was underlined by a *Globe and Mail* editor who told us: "A lot depends on who's the editor on duty on a given day." For example, word at the water-fountain passed on to us by various sources has it that a senior editor of one important Canadian newsroom is a gay man who is in the closet, but whose sexual orientation has positively influenced the organization's coverage of gay rights.

2. A significant shift in the demographic composition of a newsroom— say, a critical mass of women, ethnic minorities or younger people—may well

affect the newsroom's culture. But it is difficult to generalize about this from the available literature. In addition, it is difficult to assess how resistant an alternative newsroom culture might be to larger institutional pressures toward conformity.

3. The *professional* orientations of journalists—their professional training and experiences, role conceptions and ethics—are probably more likely to influence news content than their *personal* attitudes, values and beliefs. It probably makes a difference whether journalists think of themselves as mirrors or conduits whose main role is to passively report events and statements, especially from the powerful; as watchdogs or adversaries whose main role is to hold the powerful accountable; or as entertainers and celebrities whose main role is to attract an audience.

Many observers believe that the culture of professionalism in North American journalism has been changing over the past two decades, away from an ethos of public service and civic responsibility, and towards the imperative of attracting audiences through entertainment and the culture of celebrity.

Depending on the substance—the content—of journalists' sense of professionalism, this too could lead to blind spots. For example, if "adversarialism" is a hallmark of professionalism, then journalists who produce too many "good news" stories about government actually working could be scorned by their colleagues as flacks or flunkies. Likewise, advocacy or analytical journalism might be regarded as an unprofessional departure from the ethos of objectivity, a departure permitted only in specialized niches like the op/ed pages, which are off-limits to most journalists.

Still, it is important, once again, to conclude with a note of caution about explanations that focus exclusively on journalists. For a more complete understanding, it is necessary to know more about the cultural, institutional and organizational dynamics that shape the news process.

MEDIA ROUTINES, NEWS VALUES, AND ORGANIZATIONAL DYNAMICS

On the surface, news might seem to be unpredictable and ever-changing, constantly in need of updating as waves of potentially newsworthy events crash around us every day. Yet, as any news consumer knows, there is a certain predictable sameness to the events and places in the news. CBC veteran Don Herron captures the essence of this simple wisdom in a line from one of his old *Hee Haw* comedy sketches: "The news today is the same as it was yesterday. It just happened to different people."

The joke can be taken even further. More often than not, even the people in the news remain the same: a handful of the famous, the infamous, and the powerful.

If today's on-the-scene, hot-off-the-press news seems all too familiar, it is mainly because news organizations themselves typically want to make news production as predictable and routine as possible. Why is this the case? In *Mediating the Message*, Shoemaker and Reese suggest three kinds of reasons.[24]

First, there are supply considerations. News organizations need a predictable, manageable, and newsworthy supply of news. They also need rapidly to compress the unpredictable and infinite number of events in the world into a finite "news hole." For such reasons, news organizations develop a "news net" of bureaux, beats and news services. That news net depends heavily on the information-producing routines of other bureaucratic organizations such as governments, opposition political parties, corporations, universities, and those interest groups that can afford offices, paid staff, and in-house experts.

There is a "bureaucratic affinity" between media organizations that need a supply of news, and source organizations that seek to publicize their messages through the media. This does not mean that media and source organizations always indulge in mutual back-scratching. Journalists can react against what they perceive as excessive or clumsy attempts at manipulation by sources. Sources often feel that they are forced on the defensive by the media's appetite for scandal, sensation, and simplification. Still, most news consists of institutionally-sponsored information disseminated through routine channels (press releases, news conferences, interviews, etc.). Enterprising or investigative reporting that operates outside or against official channels is the exception rather than the norm.

Second, production considerations encourage news media to routinize the news. That is, news organizations need not only a secure supply of usable news; they also need to process the news efficiently. Management always needs to deploy staff, technology, budgets, and other resources with an eye to the bottom line. Reporters and editors need to cope with constant time and space constraints, and to work with colleagues without costly supervision or conflict over basics.

These factors help explain the prevalence of predetermined story angles (to meet deadlines and to harmonize the efforts of the different newsworkers—reporters, editors, graphic artists, etc.—who may be collaborating on a given story). These constraints also help explain why news focuses on pre-scheduled events, and why news is "typified" into different types or genres: for instance, the hard news, soft news, opinion columns, and features found in the daily paper.

The impact of organizationally-rooted routines on content is particularly evident when you compare TV newscasts with the daily press. TV newsrooms have a smaller staff and their video-based news-gathering technology is more costly and complex. So it is no surprise that TV typically covers a smaller range of events than does the press, giving greater play to those with visual interest.

In addition to considerations of *supply* and *production*, there is a third set of constraints related to the *consumption* of news—namely, that there is no point producing news unless somebody is reading or watching it. News has to attract an audience. Presumably, it must appeal to audiences' tastes, interests, values, or needs, and avoid consistently offending them. The journalistic methods of objectivity or fairness, such as quoting both sides in a controversial story, can be seen partly as ways of minimizing complaints from media audiences. Similarly, the criteria of relevance that journalists routinely use to select news stories, often called "news values," can be seen in large part as devices to appeal to the interests of news consumers.

What are some of the dominant news values in Canadian journalism? They are difficult to define precisely, and they vary somewhat between news organizations. Generally, though, the more of the following qualities a story has, the more likely it is to be considered newsworthy: timeliness; relevance to an ongoing topic or theme; political significance; consistency with journalists' expectations, or conversely, novelty, shock or scandal; drama; clarity and unambiguity; conflict; negativity (harm, threat, death, destruction); scope or scale of impact; human interest; and the involvement of individuals, especially celebrities and power-holders. When a story embodies almost all of these news values, you have a blockbuster: the death of Princess Diana was a notable recent example.

Our point is that considerations of supply, production and consumption can all lead to the omission of significant news. Organizational pressures seem especially important in the practice of "pack journalism;" reporters and editors are aware that their news judgment will rarely be challenged when they publish safe "follow-the-leader" stories. Stories, however, that dispute conventional wisdom and that are not being pursued by other media are more likely to be buried.

Similarly, important information sometimes doesn't make the news because it might bore or offend readers, and doesn't fit conventional news values. For instance, the news media may overlook important long-term trends or conditions, such as the increase in male sterility, the decline in America's public education system, or the auto industry's refusal to mass produce electric cars—all under-reported stories identified by Project Censored in the U.S. during the 1990s. Instead, the media more typically focus on short-term events that are high in the news values discussed above.

Likewise, potential stories that are outside the established news net of sources, beats and daily schedules are less likely to make the news. News organizations may think twice about running stories that are likely to offend powerful sources to the point of inviting retribution or disrupting the supply of news from them—unless the story has already become widely reported, or is so newsworthy that the news organization is willing to burn its bridges with the source. Conversely, a story promoted by people or groups who have not yet become recognized as reliable and routine sources is less likely to make the news.

Taken together, the considerations of supply, production and consumption mean that news is in large part an organizational product. David Taras, a University of Calgary media scholar, puts it this way:

> The structure and purpose of the organizations within which journalists work condition how the news is produced. Events and issues are like light being filtered through a prism, the prism being the news organization; how the light is reflected depends on the particular characteristics of the organization through which it passes...News, in short, is recontextualized to fit the product needs of the institution presenting it.[25]

News may be an institutional product, but that does not mean it is merely fabricated out of thin air, or that it is merely propaganda or a variety of fiction. Rather, like any systematic way of telling stories (including scholarly books), it is a selective version of reality. Most thoughtful observers of the media would agree with this claim. The more difficult questions are these: Who (or what) imposes or enforces organizational priorities in the media? And what are those priorities or purposes in the first place?

In the case of the publicly-owned CBC, the organization's formal purposes are explicitly defined in the 1991 Broadcasting Act. These include providing a wide range of predominantly and distinctively Canadian programming in both French and English, reflecting Canada and its regions to national and regional audiences, contributing to shared national consciousness and identity, and reflecting Canada's multicultural nature.

Few other news organizations have such an explicit mandate. For example, what is the purpose of a commercial news operation? The answer to this question depends on who is answering it. For example, in 1981, the Kent Commission on Newspapers identified key stakeholder groups in the industry, each with its own expectations of newspapers, and its own understanding of freedom of the press. Kent argued that members of the general public "need news and information which help them make sense of their lives."[26] Canadians regard newspapers and other media as having responsibilities to the public different from those of other businesses, and a majority of them are prepared to accept certain restrictions on freedom of the press in the interests of morals and good taste. For their part, journalists tend to see press freedom as the foundation of democracy. They like to see themselves as "righter of wrongs, watchdog of political integrity...a pure seeker of truth" who should "assume the responsibility of finding and publishing what the public should know, rather than seeking to satisfy the lowest common denominator of popular demand as determined by market studies and advertising surveys."[27]

Journalists' unions, in particular, defend the notion of the media's social responsibility. They regard journalists as the best defenders of the public's right to information and of diversity in the press, and they are "the severest critics of newspaper ownership."

By contrast, while they sometimes admit that the press fulfills essential functions in a democratic society, newspaper owners and publishers tend "to think more of profit as the criterion for evaluating a newspaper than of conformity to ethical and intellectual principles." Press baron Pierre Peladeau was extremely forthright when he told the Kent Commission, "Profit is the name of the game." Peladeau was not alone. Other owners also stressed that a newspaper's first duty is to survive economically; otherwise, it could not provide any kind of public service. Owners may often pursue objectives like public service, political influence and public prestige, in addition to business interests and, sometimes, even at the expense of them. But—as numerous inquiries into the workings of the press have shown—for most news organizations in a commercial media system, "the primary goal is economic, to make a profit."[28]

The media's bottom-line orientation to profit has intensified since the Kent Commission reported nearly two decades ago. Increasingly, the family-owned media firms of yester-year, like the Southam newspaper chain, are being swallowed by huge multi-media conglomerates owned by stockholders looking to maximize short-term profits. Shoemaker and Reese note some of the implications of this shift:

When a company is privately owned, the owners can operate the business as they see fit. But most large media firms are owned by stockholders. This form of ownership intensified the purely economic objectives of the company. Managers of publicly traded companies can be replaced if they fail in their responsibility to the stockholders to maximize profit. The stock market cares little for public service if it means sacrificing profitability.[29]

Other structural shifts can also enhance the profit orientation. For instance, Shoemaker and Reese note that media corporations have gotten larger. Larger media firms "take fewer risks than smaller ones, which includes exerting their power where possible to obtain economic and political advantage. These corporate goals can permeate the entire firm."[30]

More and more critics, including a growing number of former journalists, are concerned that the "corporate goals" of profiting and marketing are overriding the public service traditions of journalism—and they point the finger squarely at owners and senior management. In the final analysis, says James Winter, a Windsor professor and a co-founder of Project Censored Canada, news is a "management product." Organizational goals are ultimately determined and enforced by ownership, whose powers include those of hiring, firing, promoting, allocating resources, and in a general way setting the standards, priorities, precedents and policies that constitute a corporate culture. Owners hire publishers who reflect their views, Winter points out, and these publishers in turn "hire and promote managers, who then hire and promote editors and managers...Journalists who do not demonstrate "the right stuff" simply are not going to go anywhere."[31]

David Radler, president of Hollinger International and a close associate of Conrad Black at the pinnacle of Canada's largest newspaper empire, has made the point starkly:

> I don't audit each newspaper's editorials day by day, but if it should come to a matter of principle, I am ultimately the publisher of all these papers, and if editors disagree with us, they should disagree with us when they're no longer in our employ. The buck stops with the ownership. I am responsible for meeting the payroll; therefore, I will ultimately determine what the papers say and how they're going to be run.[32]

Radler has a particular reputation for making his presence felt in newsrooms; his regular telephone calls to *Vancouver Sun* editors are the stuff of newsroom gossip. Management influence can trickle down to the micro-level of news content in less obvious ways, as well: through senior editors' ability to assign stories, veto those that reporters themselves initiate, decide headlines, story angles and story placement, demand rewrites, or drop stories altogether.

Even if the newsroom is unionized, reporters have little power to intervene in editorial decision-making; usually they can at best remove their byline if they object to editorial changes in the story. Ultimately, the most effective form of ownership influence on news content is through self-censorship, as journalists simply abandon the attempt to pursue stories they know management will veto.

Still, we need to take a broad view of all this. Commercial media are part of a complex system of economic, organizational, social, and cultural interdependencies that set a variety of limits and exert differing kinds of pressures on the production and dissemination of news. This complex system of interdependencies does not always provide effective checks to the power of individual news owners, but it mediates their interventions in subtle ways and complicates the news filtering process.

To illustrate this point further, let's consider some news filters in more detail, beginning with the relations between news sources and news organizations, and returning to questions about state policies that variously influence the production of news.

Sources, the State, and the Production of News

Sources—the people and institutions who supply newsworthy information—are an essential part of journalism. After all, much of the news consists of what people have told reporters. Indeed, some scholars see the journalist-source relationship as the defining moment of news, its most essential ingredient.

"News is not what happens, but what someone says has happened or will happen," writes Leon Sigal, professor of government at Wesleyan University.[33]

News media tend to concentrate their resources where news predictably and routinely occurs. Legislatures, government offices, city hall, police departments, courts, business corporations, and other bureaucracies all turn out a regular, reliable volume of frequently self-serving but credible and easily accessible stories. Officials from such institutions are quoted with considerable and recurring frequency in the news. Why?

First, the practice of striving for objectivity requires journalists to ground their reports in statements attributed to presumably relevant, authoritative, and accredited sources. It's an efficient, economical way to produce credible, acceptable news stories. Moreover, such sources are convenient. They are generally articulate and available, they have offices and cell phones, they return your calls promptly. Furthermore, the information is usually free. Large bureaucratic organizations often have the resources to subsidize the production of information— press releases, interviews, research studies, and even video clips—which is at once self-serving and newsworthy.[34] To be sure, journalists do not always act as uncritical transmission belts for official information, and there is often tension between reporters and sources. Still, there is also a mutually beneficial relationship between them: media need stories, sources (sometimes) need publicity.

Who has the upper hand, the media or source institutions? We noted earlier how sources themselves often feel that the media set the agenda, frequently ignoring or distorting their intended messages, and on occasion, generating unexpected whirlwinds of hostile publicity.[35] Others see the relationship as generally symmetrical, a kind of tug-of-war in which each side has its own "weapons"—for example, the media's access to mass audiences, versus (some) sources' control over newsworthy information.[36]

A third view sees a narrow set of key institutions dominating the media, and setting the frames and limits of media discussion of public issues.[37]

Whatever the merits of these competing views, what is clear is that not all sources are created equal. Sometimes grassroots advocacy groups or independent experts can become news sources, but unless they have the power to shape future events, or the resources to subsidize and package credible information, they are often fighting an uphill battle. If they stage disruptive events in order to gain media attention, their actions are likely to receive more coverage than their views. For the media, it is safer and easier to rely on conventional institutional sources—a dependency reinforced by the ability of governments, corporations, and other wealthy institutions to use public relations professionals to mount sophisticated media campaigns.

Their tactics can make it easy and seductive for journalists to present a tailor-made image, and difficult to present a more balanced picture. In addition, centralized, hierarchical organizations may restrict the flow of publicly relevant and potentially dramatic information to the media for long periods of time.

For example, sexual harassment in Canada's military occurred for years, apparently, before *Maclean's* magazine and other media helped bring it to public light.

For news media, governments are the most important source institutions of all. In addition—to return to an issue raised earlier—governments enforce a variety of laws and regulations that influence news selection. Laws affect the press at two levels. At one level, a number of federal and provincial laws provide a legal framework for the operation of newspapers as a business. Some of these laws provide support for the power and profits of press corporations; others place restrictions on them.

The supports have included certain tax exemptions and concessionary postal rates, as well as two key income tax provisions. One allows Canadian companies to deduct the cost of loans used to buy shares in another company, which helps large media corporations to take over other ones. Another clause disallows tax deductions for advertising in foreign-owned periodicals that are directed to Canadian readers. Effectively, this clause precludes foreign ownership of newspapers in Canada (thus protecting the home markets of Canadian-owned print media conglomerates).

The most important restraint on newspaper owners—in principle, at least—is the Competition Act of 1986. Like anti-trust law in the U.S., its essential purpose is to protect competitors in a given market from unfair trading and other practices, and to ensure that consumers receive the presumed benefits of competition, and do not suffer from the evils of monopoly. Under this law, large-scale corporate mergers are subject to the federal competition bureau's review and approval.

That's the theory. In practice, the Act has not slowed the process of concentration in the press. In part, that is because the Act does not mandate the Bureau, when it reviews takeovers, to consider editorial diversity, only the impact on markets—which the Bureau generally defines exclusively as markets for advertising. When the Council of Canadians filed a legal challenge to the Hollinger takeover of the Southam newspaper chain in 1996 on grounds of its threat to editorial diversity and Canadians' rights of expression, the Federal Court dismissed the case out of hand.

Also, one suspects that the absence of political will to apply the Act more vigorously is a factor. The only major case in which the Bureau ordered a partial rollback of a newspaper merger (Southam's takeover of Vancouver-area community and real estate weeklies in the early 1990s) was subject to years of legal appeals by Southam.

While the terms of the Competition Act are hardly the stuff of every-day conversation, people are likely to be far more familiar with the way the Canadian state provides legal support for press freedom through the Charter of Rights and Freedoms. The Charter provides for "freedom of thought, belief, opinion and expression, including freedom of the press and other media of communication," subject to "such reasonable limits prescribed by law as can be demonstrably justified in a free and democratic society."

It is precisely this tension between freedom and the exercise of "reasonable limits" that makes the Charter itself the source of so much controversy. A number of our earlier examples of restrictions on speech in respect to matters of human rights, hate literature and obscenity provide demonstrations of such controversies. Other notable legal regulations that affect the press include laws against defamation, contempt of court, and the unauthorized transmission of official state secrets.

All of these restraints are intended to balance freedom of the press with other rights and needs, such as individuals' right to protect their reputation against untrue allegations or to receive a fair trial when accused of a crime, and the right of government and courts to function without obstruction and to keep some information confidential on such grounds as national security.[38]

Two other significant governmental constraints on news production are worth noting. One is the constitutional tradition of secrecy in governmental deliberations, particularly cabinet meetings. Again, there are often sound reasons in theory for such restraints: the need for secrecy to insure full and frank discussion, for example. But sometimes—this will come as no great revelation— governments withhold information for no other reason than to cover up their own mistakes or deceptions.

Critics feel that "access to information" legislation, which the federal government and most provinces have enacted, has had only mixed success in producing more "open" government. A host of blockages, from formal exemptions in the laws themselves, to access fees, bureaucratic attitudes, and delays in fulfilling information requests, hamper the opening of the windows of government.[39]

One of the most important legal constraints which sometimes filter out public information are the provincial laws of civil libel. These laws are intended to protect individuals against the publication of untrue (or at least, unproven) statements which may damage their reputations. Civil defamation proceedings against the media are initiated not by the state—this is not part of criminal law—but rather by aggrieved individuals. Even the threat of a libel suit can result in "libel chill" in the press, as media lawyers often advise extreme caution in stories that reflect negatively on particular individuals.

"Libel chill" is not mere paranoia. The *Globe and Mail* spent $200,000 on legal fees in 1987, even though no defamation cases went to trial. Reporters and editors may have second thoughts about tackling persons known to be litigious. It is worth noting that it is the wealthy and the powerful who have both public reputations to protect and the resources to engage lawyers to "chill" their critics.[40]

Like the dog in the Sherlock Holmes mystery that failed to bark at a nocturnal intruder, sometimes something that does *not* happen can be significant, too. Researchers for the Kent Commission regarded it as important that no Canadian government had passed laws to protect editorial diversity and independence from mergers and conglomerates, to tax excess profits, to establish journalism as a self-regulating profession, or even to prevent newspaper companies from using child labour to deliver their product to doorsteps (technically, paper boys and girls are "independent contractors").

Consequently, Canadian law has "assisted in making the proprietors the key element in the world of the daily newspapers...[It] has permitted a proprietor to determine the character of his papers. It has permitted, or encouraged, proprietors to consolidate their holdings. It has also encouraged them to stay Canadian."[41]

Toronto law professor Harry Glasbeek goes even further, arguing that in effect the courts are defining freedom of the press as a property right of media owners, rather than a human right of individual citizens. Only a few years after the 1982 adoption of the Charter of Rights, Glasbeek predicted that its guarantee of press freedom would be used "to defend individuals generally and the media in particular from state controls, but not individuals or their defender, the state, from private interests," thus helping the private press "to retain its sovereignty as a purveyor of information and opinion."[42]

Canadian courts have not given a similarly strong endorsement to other possible definitions of press freedom: the right of citizens to inform themselves (part of the Kent Commission's vision of press freedom); the right of journalists to express themselves without editorial intervention from corporate management; a right of reply for individuals or groups attacked in the media; or a right of access to the press for those whose voices are currently excluded.[43]

In principle, the legal situation in radio and television is somewhat different. Since the 1930s, the air waves have been legally considered public property; broadcasters are granted licences by an independent regulator (since the 1960s, the CRTC) to use in the public interest. The current Broadcasting Act requires broadcasters, among other obligations, to "provide a reasonable opportunity for the public to be exposed to the expression of differing views on matters of public concern." In practice, commercial imperatives affect private broadcasters as strongly as newspapers, and the CRTC has been very reluctant since the 1970s to become embroiled in controversies over news content. Still, it does at least provide an avenue for public complaints and a form of moral pressure on broadcasters. In the print media, by contrast, the law currently provides few means for counterbalancing corporate power or the blind spots that may result from it.

ENDNOTES

1. *Attacks on the Press in 1997* (New York: Committee to Protect Journalists, 1998), p. 11.
2. *Attacks on the Press in 1997*, pp. 6, 10.
3. Martina Jimenez, "Little Sisters Loses Customs Appeal," *Vancouver Sun*, June 25, 1998.
4. For more information see "Communications Decency Act," *Ready Reference: Censorship*(Pasadena: Salem Press, 1997).
5. *Toronto Star*, Nov. 25, 1996.
6. *Financial Post*, May 22, 1996.
7. *New City*, Summer, 1995.
8. *Media*, April, 1994.
9. *Canadian Dimension,* November/December, 1996.
10. *This Magazine*, August, 1993.
11. *CBC National Magazine*, October 22, 1996.
12. On this point see Pamela J. Shoemaker and Stephen D. Reese, *Mediating the Message: Theories of Influences on Mass Media Content*, 2nd edition (White Plains, NY: Longman, 1996). Our discussion of news filters in this chapter is heavily indebted to Shoemaker and Reese.
13. Anthony Westell, "The Press: Adversary or Channel of Communication?" in H.D. Clarke, C. Campbell, F.Q. Quo, and A. Goddard, eds., *Parliament, Policy and Representation* (Toronto: Methuen, 1980), pp. 25-34.
14. Adam Gopnick, "Read all About It," *The New Yorker*, December 12, 1994, p. 42.
15. Some Canadian examples are discussed in Paul Rutherford, *The Making of the Canadian Media* (Toronto: McGraw-Hill Ryerson, 1978).
16. S. R. Lichter, S. Rothman and L.S. Lichter, *The Media Elite* (Bethesda, Md.: Adler and Adler, 1986); Edith Efron, "The Media and the Omniscient Class," in *Business and the Media*, ed. Craig E. Aronoff (Santa Monica, Cal.: Goodyear, 1979), pp. 3-32; Irving Kristol, "Business and the 'New Class'," *The Wall Street Journal* (May 19, 1975), p. 8. Our discussion here draws from Robert Hackett and Yuezhi Zhao, *Sustaining Democracy? Journalism and the Politics of Objectivity* (Toronto: Garamond, 1998), pp. 136-141.
17. See Herbert Gans, "Are U.S. Journalists Dangerously Liberal?" *Columbia Journalism Review*, November/December, 1985, pp. 29-33.
18. Alan Wolfe, "The Real Aim is Ideological," *The Nation*, September 13, 1986, pp. 215-219.
19. Andrew Coyne, *Financial Post,* August 9, 1989, p. 11.
20. See Hackett and Zhao, *Sustaining Democracy*, pp. 101-105.

21. For an example, see Daniel Hallin, *The "Uncensored" War: The Media and Vietnam,* (Berkeley: University of California Press, 1986).

22. For a more detailed discussion see Edward Herman and Noam Chomsky, *Manufacturing Consent* (New York: Pantheon, 1988), ch. 1.

23. Shoemaker and Reese, *Mediating the Message,* ch. 5, especially pp. 101-103.

24. Shoemaker and Reese, *Mediating the Message,* pp.105-137.

25. David Taras, *The Newsmakers: The Media's Influence on Canadian Politics,* (Scarborough, Ont.: Nelson Canada, 1990), p. 19.

26. Canada, Royal Commission on Newspapers, *Report* (Ottawa, 1981), Ch. 2.

27. *Royal Commission on Newspapers,* p. 27.

28. Shoemaker and Reese, *Mediating the Message,* p. 145.

29. Shoemaker and Reese, p. 145.

30. Shoemaker and Reese, p. 145.

31. James Winter, *Democracy's Oxygen: How Corporations Control the News* (Montreal: Black Rose, 1997), p. 86.

32. Peter C. Newman, "The Inexorable Spread of the Black Empire," *Maclean's,* February 3, 1992, p.68; cited in Winter, *Democracy's Oxygen,* p. 86.

33. Leon V. Sigal, "Sources Make the News," in Robert Karl Manoff and Michael Schudson (eds.), *Reading the News* (New York: Pantheon, 1986), p. 15.

34. Oscar Gandy, *Beyond Agenda-Setting: Information Subsidies and Public Policy* (Norwood, NJ: Ablex, 1982).

35. Richard Ericson, P. Baranek, and J.B.L. Chan, *Negotiating Control: A Study of News Sources* (Toronto: University of Toronto Press, 1989).

36. Edwin Black, *Politics and the News: The Political Functions of Mass Media* (Toronto: Butterworths, 1982).

37. Stuart Hall et al., *Policing the Crisis: Mugging, the State, and Law and Order* (London: Macmillan, 1978).

38. See Robert Hackett, *News and Dissent: The Press and the Politics of Peace* (Norwood, NJ.: Ablex, 1991), pp. 88-89.

39. See Arthur Siegel, *Politics and the Media in Canada,* 2nd ed. (Toronto: McGraw-Hill Ryerson, 1996), pp. 41; 52-55.

40. Peter Desbarats, A *Guide to Canadian News Media,* 2nd ed. (Toronto: Harcourt Brace, 1996), p.183.

41. Colin Wright, "Issues of Law and Public Policy," in Walter Tarnopolsky, Colin Wright, Gerald A. Beaudoin, and Edith Cody-Rice, *Newspapers and the Law,* vol. 3 of Research Studies on the Newspaper Industry in Canada (Royal Commission on Newspapers: Ottawa, 1981), pp. 68-69.

42. H. J. Glasbeek, "Comment: Entrenchment of Freedom of Speech for the Press — Fettering of Freedom of Speech of the People," in *The Media, the Courts and the Charter,* ed. Philip Anisman and Allen M. Linden (Toronto: Carswell, 1986), pp. 100-103.

43. Hackett and Zhao, *Sustaining Democracy?* p. 191.

Chapter Two

Paying the Piper

When you ask people who work in news media about the factors that most influence the selection of news, they often point to the power of the audience. Audiences have power, the argument runs, because their purchasing and viewing habits ultimately determine the kind of news content the media offer. No commercial news organization could survive without attracting viewers, listeners, and readers, and this supposedly makes consumers the "sovereign" elements in the media system.

At one level, this observation is a truism. There is no doubt that any commercial media system has to be attentive to the interests, desires—and, arguably, even the opinions—of its audience. But again, when you look more deeply, the issue is not quite so clear-cut. The problem comes when the banal observation that commercial media are dependent on their audiences is treated as if it were a full and adequate explanation of the factors that shape the news. For one thing, the "consumer sovereignty" argument often has a self-serving ring to it. Over the years we have heard many comments from owners, editors and journalists that sound something like this: "If there's too much bad news, or if news is too sensational or politically biased, it's because that's what sells. That's what people want. And if there aren't enough investigative reporting, foreign news, or analytical features, it's because people find it offensive or boring. Who are we to argue? What could be more democratic than allowing people to shape media content through their viewing and buying decisions?"

In this kind of argument, "giving the public what they want" is presented as an inherently democratic act, a rejection of the élitism of editorial policies designed to, say, force the public to read more international news than they might necessarily want. More notably, this populist approach to "democracy" sells, especially at a time of high public skepticism about the role of "experts" and opinion- makers in contemporary politics and social life. Still, it might not be a bad idea to redirect some of this skepticism in order to question the idea that consumers are simply barking orders to obedient media corporations.

One thing we might be skeptical about is the implicit assumption underlying consumer sovereignty arguments that the audience actually has some
kind of coherent collective voice. Against this view you can find a wealth of
market research and scholarly studies that emphasize the diversity, and often
contradictory nature, of media audiences in the 1990s.[1] These studies suggest
that it is now very difficult to sustain any kind of argument for a broad, collectively shared, conscious, and well-ordered set of preferences that shape contemporary media consumption.

Media consumption today does not appear to reflect deeply held preferences and values, so much as well-established habits: routine choices made
between the most readily available alternatives that media corporations find
profitable and convenient to offer. Even in the 100-channel universe—and
we speak as confirmed late-night channel surfers—sometimes you just end up
watching whatever is least objectionable.

Moreover, audience pressures on the media have always been selectively
interpreted, deflected, and even resisted within media organizations. In many
instances, owners, editors and journalists have felt the need to provide a broad
spectrum of news "in the public interest," in addition to following public taste.
As a result, the major news media have sometimes included materials that
may be of only passing interest to many readers, viewers and listeners— for
example, detailed discussions of trade agreements, constitutional amendments,
aspects of international law, or political issues in places far away from North
America.

At its worst, this self-assigned editorial gatekeeping by news media has
lent itself to paternalistic hectoring: an "élite" editorial voice that chastises
"the people" for voting a particular way, failing to see the need to "tighten
their belts," or remaining overly parochial in a world that requires a more
global perspective. But, at its best, the result of editorial choices and selec-
tions in news coverage has been to help audiences learn more about important
issues in their own society, as well as to expose them to ideas, places, events
and issues from around the world. In this respect, news media have arguably
played an important educational function in democratic societies, not least by
creating opportunities for more cosmopolitan perspectives in political discourse.[2]

The question is whether the best-case scenario noted above is likely in
an era where consciously market-driven journalism seems to be increasingly
shaped by surveys and polling—surveys designed to make the news reflect
consumer tastes and preferences more directly. It is certainly true that you
can read these surveys to suggest that many people really do want a steady

diet of "infotainment." Nonetheless, there are other equally credible inter-pretations.

Doug Underwood, a newsroom veteran of 13 years who now teaches in Seattle, puts it this way:

> The new corporate-minded editors say they are just giving readers what they want. Yet they do not really know what readers want. Surveys can be read in any number of different ways, and that is why they have done the newspaper business so little good...The read-ers of newspapers...look to journalists to define for them what is interesting and important. Readers can't find it a pretty picture to see journalists looking out at them, asking plaintively, "What in the world can we do to please you?"[3]

THE CORPORATE PRESENCE IN THE PRESS

Quite apart from the ambiguities of audience preferences, several economic characteristics of the media system itself threaten diversity, audience choice, and public control. These characteristics include high entry costs, concen-trated and conglomerate ownership, minimal competition within important markets, and the commercial pressures associated with dependence on ad-vertising revenue. High entry costs mean simply that it is very expensive, for example, to buy or start a television news station or large circulation newspaper.

Let's consider the case of the newspaper in somewhat more detail. When modern conceptions of freedom of the press were congealing in the 1700s, it was relatively inexpensive to buy a printing press and launch a new paper. Journals representing a range of political and religious viewpoints flourished, within the limits of government tolerance. All that began to change with the emergence of capital-intensive, advertising-supported, mass circulation news-papers in the 1800s. Today, unless they have a few hundred million dollars to spare, dissatisfied consumers cannot simply start a news outlet that can com-pete with the media's big players.

True, it doesn't take much capital to launch an Internet web site, a mi-cro-radio transmitter, or a desk-top periodical. At this point, though, self-produced alternative news media created through the technologies noted above typically lack the production values, distribution muscle, brand name recog-nition, or cross-marketing potential needed to reach very large audiences on a regular basis. Even the Internet—the medium that holds the greatest possi-bilities for ensuring the diversity of news coverage and opinion—is increas-ingly influenced by major media corporations that now offer some of the jazzi-est web sites with the highest production values.

These passing comments do not exhaust the range of issues to consider in respect to the role of new communications technologies in the production of news, and we'll have more to say about such things a bit later. At this point we simply want to emphasize the extremely high entry costs necessary to participate in the dominant, agenda-setting media industries.

These high entry costs call into question the traditional libertarian idea that, left to itself, the market will produce a press that reflects society's diversity. The free marketplace of ideas is even more doubtful when we consider another factor that reduces consumer power and media accountability: the emergence during the 1990s of global media markets dominated by about ten huge conglomerates.

Integrating content production and distribution in a variety of media formats, global giants like Time Warner, Disney, Bertelsmann, Viacom, and Rupert Murdoch's News Corporation wield unprecedented cultural as well as economic power. There are also another 30 or 40 sizeable firms that fill regional or niche markets and that often depend on working arrangements with one or more of the top ten giants for their profitability.[4]

Such oligopoly—the economists' term for market domination by a handful of firms—is amplified within national markets. On this point, James Winter succinctly describes concentration in Canada's media industries in the mid-1990s:

> In Canadian television, five corporations reached 62% of viewers in 1993. In the cable industry, three companies now have 68% of the audience, up from 36% in 1983, even though the number of subscribers has increased by more than 40%. In radio, with 479 stations, just ten companies control 55% of the revenue share, up 50% in the past decade. In magazine publishing, the largest eight publishers controlled 52% of circulation in 1993-94. In book publishing and distribution...for 1991-92, just 21 out of 370 firms (6%) accounted for 51% of total sales.[5]

Compared to other media industries, and to the press in other Western countries, it is the newspaper industry where media concentration in Canada has reached truly impressive levels in the 1990s. This is especially important for journalism, because, with the exception of the CBC and a handful of the larger private-sector companies, few broadcasters devote many resources to original news gathering. Rather, newspapers remain "at the base of the information pyramid, providing much of the in-depth information that is then compressed and marketed by the electronic information purveyors."[6]

Newspapers also anchor Canadian Press, which is a crucial pipeline, almost a central nervous system, for national and international news in Canada. Owned by dozens of member newspapers as a non-profit cost-sharing cooperative, CP generates and exchanges news for other media as well, including radio and television.[7]

So the fact that a single company, by the end of 1998, owned 55 of Canada's 105 English- or French-language daily papers has important implications for the entire news system. That company is Hollinger, which has been acquiring not only individual papers, but entire "chains"—companies that publish two or more titles. Most notably, Hollinger has entirely swallowed Southam, once Canada's biggest and most venerable newspaper chain. By 1999, Hollinger accounted for 40.7% of Canadian dailies' aggregate weekly circulation as of June 1998.

The *Toronto Star*, previously Canada's largest "independent" (non-chain) daily, and long a critic of chain ownership, itself is now the flagship of a new chain. Its parent company, Torstar, already a conglomerate with other media interests, became a chain in 1998 when it acquired four more Ontario dailies.

Out of 100 copies of daily papers sold in Canada each week, only 3.5 are published by non-chain independents. Only six of these remain, the largest being the Halifax *Chronicle-Herald*. Four big companies (Hollinger, Quebecor, Torstar and Thomson) sell 93 out of every 100 copies of English-language dailies in Canada. Quebecor, Power and Hollinger account for almost 96% of French-language circulation.[8]

Press concentration is further magnified when we consider specific regions and provinces. In several provinces, all the English-language dailies are owned by a single company: Irving in New Brunswick, and Hollinger in Newfoundland, Saskatchewan, Prince Edward Island, and (except for two of the smallest dailies) British Columbia, Canada's third largest province.

Concentrated chain ownership of newspapers has arisen for understandable business reasons, as by-products of the commercial logic of the press, operating within an industrialized market system. One impetus for chains is the difficulty that the family-owned papers of yesteryear have sometimes had paying inheritance taxes. For the second or third-generation members of a family whose unity and commitment to newspaper publishing might be wavering, selling a paper to a large company that can deduct the purchase price from its taxable revenues may be the most attractive option.

Similarly, independent papers have sometimes found it difficult to raise the capital needed for technological renovations. Compared to independents, especially small ones, chains have more access to the managerial expertise, and can more easily borrow the capital (at lower rates of interest) required by the modern paper.

Chains also enjoy economies of scale, finding it easier to attract national advertising contracts, or to buy newsprint in bulk. Their deep pockets have enabled them to renovate and upgrade money-losing papers, to wait out work stoppages, or keep publishing a paper using managers and strike-breaking workers, and to outlast and undercut competing independent papers. Much of the growth of newspaper chains has been financed internally through profits that historically have been higher than the average for other industries, especially for papers without local competition.[9]

Similar pressures have brought other changes in patterns of press ownership. Since the 1970s and 1980s, more and more news outlets are owned by publicly traded firms dominated by investors with a much stronger commitment to the bottom line than to journalism. As non-media firms were attracted by high newspaper profits, and conversely as newspaper companies attempted to diversify their holdings, papers are increasingly owned by conglomerates—corporate empires with a range of holdings in different industries. The archetype is the Thomson family's corporate empire, which includes interests in wholesaling, retailing, real estate, oil and gas, insurance, and financial and management services. In New Brunswick, the Irving interests control not only all four English-language dailies, but also an oil refinery, a chain of gas stations, oil and gas distribution agencies, fleets of oil tankers and fishing vessels, a dry dock, a tugboat company, a bus line, pulp and saw mills, and two million acres of forest land.

In an effort to protect their market share or to use their resources optimally, some companies own media of different types. Such cross-media ownership has aroused particular concern when it is concentrated in the same geographical area. Some daily newspaper firms, such as Southam in Vancouver and Torstar in Toronto, have bought up suburban weeklies that might otherwise siphon ad revenue from their big city dailies. Some broadcasters, such as WIC in B.C., own television outlets and AM and FM radio stations in the same region, a situation subject to regulation by the CRTC. For a while during the mid-1990s, the cable giant Rogers had substantial print media holdings through the *Sun* chain of tabloids.

Another notable structural feature of Canada's newspaper industry is monopoly in most markets. As distinct from "concentration," which measures the extent to which one or a few companies dominate the industry regionally or nationally, "monopoly" refers to the lack of competition within a given market. For most dailies, the market is a particular city or metro region. Just as newspaper chains began to emerge nationally a century ago, competition in newspaper markets began to shrink locally. The days when a city of 200,000 might have had five or six competing papers soon went the way of the Model-T Ford.

The number of daily newspapers in Canada peaked at 138 in 1913. Nine years later, 40 of them had been swallowed up by rivals pursuing a larger market share. By the 1920s, the metropolitan daily had come to be regarded as a kind of franchise, a "privately-owned utility, free of any government control or regulation and enormously lucrative if managed correctly."[10]

Today most Canadian cities sustain only a single daily. In the several markets that still support two or more dailies, one is typically a Hollinger broadsheet, an "omnibus" paper trying to reach the broadest possible market, while the other is a tabloid (typically in the *Sun* Media chain) oriented towards lower to middlebrow readers and a generation of TV-oriented media consumers. At the other end of the market spectrum, *The Globe and Mail's* national edition with its strong international and business news reaches "upscale" readers.

The Globe and Mail is now facing competition from a new national Hollinger daily, *The National Post*. This new competitor at the national level may well contribute to Canada's press diversity in the end. But, for now, *The National Post* threatens to draw heavily on the resources of existing Southam papers across Canada, and it has already absorbed what was previously a separate business-oriented daily, the *Financial Post*.

On the whole, while newspapers do compete with other media for advertising dollars, there is much less direct competition within the industry for readers or editorial content by comparison with the early decades of the 20th century. Why? It has a lot to do with the rising costs of technology, distribution, and other expenses in newspaper publishing. Also, a growing emphasis on advertising revenue created a "jackal" or "bandwagon" effect: that is, an urban newspaper with a slight circulation lead over a competitor would (all other things being equal) attract more than its share of advertising revenue. Merchants who could afford ads in only one paper found the larger paper a more cost-effective way to maintain market share. The smaller paper would be caught in a downward spiral: revenues, quality and circulation would decline until it folded or was taken over.

Once a newspaper has killed off a competitor and acquired a monopoly, it is difficult to dislodge. Typically, monopoly papers have been quite profitable due to economies of scale: once the staff and printing press are in place, it doesn't cost much more to produce 50,000 instead of 30,000 copies of a newspaper. Thus, by taking over its former competitor's readership, the surviving paper can reach many more readers and charge much more for advertising space, without greatly increasing its production or distribution costs.

Furthermore, a monopoly paper is protected from new competition by high entry costs and the difficulty of luring readers and advertisers away from an established paper.

One of the key economic dynamics affecting the Canadian media system is its great dependence on advertising, which accounts for more than 70% of daily newspaper revenues, about 64% of magazine revenues, and much of the income for broadcasters, notwithstanding the importance of cable-TV subscription fees.

Even the CBC, with a mandate to provide a "public service" alternative to commercial broadcasting, depends on advertising for about one-fifth of its operating revenue, and relies in part on private/commercial affiliates to broadcast its programming across the country. In addition, CBC-TV feels compelled to compete for audiences with the commercial stations that fill the airwaves with popular American entertainment shows.[11]

Concentration, conglomeration, local monopolies, and advertising dependence are interlinked processes. We have already argued that, through the "jackal effect," the competition for advertising creates pressures that contribute to press monopoly. In turn, high profits earned in monopoly markets have fuelled the growths of chains. One of the most economically rational ways for a company to redeploy such profits is not to invest in better journalism where it already has a monopoly, but to start buying up other papers, thus extending and maximizing the skills, resources, and economies of scale that the large successful paper already enjoys. High profits also attract investment from conglomerates looking for "cash cows" to feed corporate growth.

Conversely, chain ownership has sometimes directly hastened the process of monopoly, as competing newspaper groups agree to exchange their shares of different local markets. Canadian journalism's infamous "Black Tuesday" on August 27, 1980, noted in the Introduction, provided a dramatic example of such a tradeoff. On that day, Southam closed its *Tribune* to grant the Thomson-owned *Free Press* a monopoly in Winnipeg, while on the same day Thomson closed the *Ottawa Journal*, leaving the Southam-owned *Citizen* alone to reap profits in the national capital. (Later, new tabloids emerged in both cities, but these don't compete head-on with the broadsheets for the same kind of readers and advertisers.)

WHY WORRY ABOUT CORPORATE MEDIA?

But, so what? Does it matter if most of Canada's news media are in business to earn profits attracting and competing for advertising revenues? What's wrong if more and more of Canada's news media are owned by a handful of companies with a wide range of corporate interests? Why should the average citizen care about who owns the news, or about the role of competitive business pressures in shaping the news product?

The most obvious—and the most widely-voiced—concern is that concentrated media ownership potentially puts too much political and cultural power into too few hands. This point is stated forcefully by the Pulitzer Prize-winning U.S. journalist and educator, Ben Bagdikian:

> In the last five years, a small number of the country's largest industrial corporations has acquired more public communications power— including ownership of the news—than any private businesses have ever before possessed in world history...Using both old and new technology, by owning each other's shares, engaging in joint ventures as partners, and other forms of cooperation, this handful of giants has created what is, in effect, a new communications cartel within the United States...At issue is the possession of power to surround almost every man, woman and child in the country with controlled images and words, to socialize each new generation of Americans, to alter the political agenda of the country...to exert influence that in many ways is greater than that of schools, religion, parents, and even government itself.[12]

Bagdikian's concern arguably has even greater register in the case of the Canadian press. In the United States, ten companies control 43.7% of total daily newspaper circulation. By contrast, in Canada since 1996, *one single company* controls a comparable share of the media pie. That company, as noted above, is Hollinger, led by the controversial Conrad Black.

Almost everybody, it seems, has an opinion about Conrad Black. It is hard not to, not only because Black has hardline right-wing views on a wide variety of subjects, but also because he is so committed to voicing his opinions. In the world according to Conrad Black, trade unions, human rights legislation, Aboriginal self-government, social democracy, public institutions, feminism, the poor, and accommodation with Quebec nationalism are typically viewed as signs of stupidity, vested interest, or social and moral weakness. By contrast, topics such as the free market, the value of wealth, highbrow intellectualism, the American way of life, Margaret Thatcher, and Israel's hardliners are on the side of the angels.[13]

On the one hand, Black's unique combination of uncompromising political views, arrogance, and bombastic style make him something of a caricature. He comes across as a man living in the wrong time—a hybrid between a hectoring 19th century schoolmaster and an early 20th century robber baron. That makes him ripe for parody. On the other hand, Black's critics maintain that there is a great deal about him that is not at all funny. It is worrying enough that he is the most powerful individual presence on the Canadian news media landscape, the argument runs, but, in addition, he seems fully willing to wield this power to promote his political agenda.

Black's critics note that he has often used his privileged access to Hollinger's news audience to publish his own editorial essays and book reviews. But, more importantly, the critics claim, Black and his senior associates can be accused of intervening actively in editorial decision-making.

Black has replied to critics of Hollinger—and to critics of newspaper chains in general—by arguing that fears about concentrated power are unfounded, and, indeed, that big companies can do good things for newspapers. Hollinger's official position on such matters is summarized by Black's comments to Hollinger's 1996 annual shareholders' meeting, and by Hollinger vice-president Peter Atkinson, in a May 1997 speech to the blue-ribbon Canadian Journalism Foundation:

1. Compared to independent papers, especially smaller ones, chains enjoy economic advantages "essential to the survival of quality Canadian newspapers," according to Atkinson. "Large newspaper chains are more attractive to advertisers," who are the lifeblood of the industry, but whose patronage cannot be taken for granted in "the highly competitive market for advertising." Chains "can achieve economies of scale through newsprint purchases, technology cost-sharing, and the more effective utilization of staff resources." Chains can enable smaller papers to face capital expansion, "labour issues," or "productivity problems."

2. Not only do chains have the resources, but they— Hollinger in particular—are willing to invest them to improve the editorial product. "In every metropolitan newspaper we own or influence...the editorial quality of newspapers has, by general consent, improved under our control," says Black. "No competent journalist or reasonable reader need have any fear of our impact on Southam." Atkinson selectively cites Senator Keith Davey's 1970 report on the mass media. Chain ownership "has rescued more than one newspaper from extinction...turned a number of weeklies into dailies...financially strengthened some newspapers," and does not necessarily reduce editorial quality. (Indeed, academic research in the U.S. suggests that chain ownership can in-

directly improve the independence of local journalism by helping to insulate journalists and managers from social conformity and élite pressure within a community.)[14] As evidence of Hollinger's own commitment to quality journalism, Atkinson noted the total revamping of the *Ottawa Citizen*.

3. Readers need not fear editorial bias in Hollinger papers, Black assured shareholders. The *Jerusalem Post* and (London) *Daily Telegraph*, the most renowned Hollinger-owned papers, published comment from both major parties. "The only way to build and maintain a great newspaper franchise is to earn and maintain a reputation for fairness, liveliness and insight." Here, Black echoes the "consumer sovereignty" theorists who say that we do not need to fear concentration and monopoly, because papers will cover the political and cultural spectrum in order to appeal to a wide range of readers.

4. Hollinger believes in local control of its papers, and is financially committed to the newspaper industry. "While this fact may scandalize some members of the working press, Hollinger is the greatest corporate friend Canadian working print journalists have," said Black in an oft-repeated quote. "We are...practically the only buyers in Canada of daily newspapers..." So try not to worry about cost-cutting and layoffs. Sometimes these are necessary to maintain financial viability, but "we have rarely sold and never closed a daily newspaper." Hollinger "did not make these very large investments with a view to shutting down newspapers or destroying their quality and thereby destroying our markets," adds Atkinson.

5. There is such "an enormous variety of media sources of information available to people throughout this country," assured Black, that press concentration constitutes no "threat to free or varied opinion formation in Canada." Southam/Hollinger's "grand total of newspaper copies sold is only 7.2% of the Canadian population" and, besides, "Public credulity cannot be abused without damaging the value of the newspaper franchise."

6. Critics of concentration ignore eroding circulations and escalating costs, according to Atkinson. They have an "anti-business bias" and an "unrealistic sentiment of another era, when multiple-owner newspapers were dominant and when newspapers were the primary source of news and commentary."

As we argue below, we don't believe that the critics' arguments can be dismissed quite as readily as Black and Atkinson suggest. Still, we do agree that, when critics of news media make exaggerated claims, focus on imagined conspiracies, or fail to make important conceptual distinctions—concentration is not the same thing as monopoly, for instance—they set themselves up for dismissal. Similarly, when critics pay more attention to issues of personality than to the broader structural dynamics of the news system, their arguments tend to be one-sided and incomplete.

This is not to say that an opinionated and aggressively partisan chain owner such as Conrad Black is nothing to worry about. Our point is simply that a thorough analysis of the effects of concentrated news ownership and editorial intervention on the production of news requires something more. We also need to pay attention to the largely impersonal, less dramatic structural features of corporate news production.

NEWS PRODUCTION AS A CORPORATE COMMERCIAL SYSTEM

Because commercial media are privately owned, profit-oriented corporations, it is no surprise that ownership ultimately determines key hiring and resource allocation decisions, and that management is accountable primarily to the dominant shareholders rather than to the audience or to working journalists. It also isn't surprising to find that media owners tend to be tied to the larger business community through shared social interests, background, and interaction, as well as through inter locking directorships. Because many members of its Board of Directors sat on other corporate boards, Southam, for example, was tied to several big companies in energy and resources, finance, and other media, even before its takeover by Hollinger.

In our view, there is no reason to revise the conclusion reached more than 20 years ago by Canadian sociologist Wallace Clement: members of the commercial media élite in Canada also tend to be part of a broader corporate élite.[15] Through exhaustive research, Clement also found evidence to suggest that corporate news media share a notable "elective affinity" with business values and business interests in general.

This argument was later reiterated by Paul Audley, after intenstive research into Canada's "cultural industries." Writing in the early 1980s, Audley argued that the corporate news media in Canada maintain a "basic commitment to the business community's views on public issues rather than to a wider range of interests."[16] Under such circumstances, information that casts business in a bad light is likely to be under-reported in the news.

Consider a further implication of profit-oriented media ownership. Competitive pressures, leading to a bottom-line perspective, pose significant challenges to any "public service" component that may be associated with editorial content. Editorials and columns can easily become viewed as business costs to be met as inexpensively as possible.

For example, it is cheaper to purchase syndicated columns that recover their costs over a national or continental market than it is to pay local writers.

That is why so much coverage of international events in Canadian media is still supplied by large multinational (usually American-based) news agencies: it is more economical to print or modify their copy or to televise their images than it is to send reporters overseas. Thus, overseas news reported from a Canadian perspective, seems likely to be a blind spot in the media.

The pursuit of profits at the expense of investment in journalism is especially pronounced in small-market monopoly papers. In monopoly markets, with little likelihood of a new competitor—the norm for most newspapers—there is usually little incentive to invest in improved journalism. To be sure, competition between media in small markets is certainly no guarantee of good journalism. It can lead to sensationalism or to mutual imitation between media rivals. But the absence of competition, combined with a cheapskate approach to news-gathering, makes it more likely that important local news may go unreported.

Interestingly, Black's and Atkinson's own arguments about investing in quality journalism apply only to "metropolitan" newspapers. Apparently, they prefer not to call attention to their far more numerous small-market papers, like the *Cambridge* (Ontario) *Reporter*, which Hollinger bought from Thomson in 1995. A reporter there told CBC's *Radio Noon* (on May 30, 1996) that Hollinger reduced the staff by 30% from its level under Thomson, already known as a penny-pinching company:

> Under Thomson, reporters were expected to write 40 stories each, per month. Under Hollinger, this has doubled to four stories a day, "plus editorials and taking pictures and writing opinion columns," she said. As for local news content, she said, "They have people there who are doing nothing but rewriting press releases and [they are] tossing these off as local news."[17]

A study of the impact of Hollinger takeovers at six Southam dailies, released by the Campaign for Press and Broadcasting Freedom in 1997, reinforces this picture. At large city papers, quality and diversity improved in some respects and declined in others; but the smaller market dailies displayed a consistent decline.[18] It is as if the smaller papers, their news staffs and resources strip-mined, are used to help finance investment in flagship papers like the *Ottawa Citizen* or the *National Post*.

Not only Hollinger, but other news organizations have imposed cutbacks on news departments in the past decade. Reporters are under greater pressure to do quick and easy stories—to forego investigative journalism and instead to reprint news releases and act as "stenographers with amnesia." One contributing factor was the recession of the early 1990s, when newspaper companies slashed newsroom staffs as one way to maintain or to regain their traditionally high profit levels.

Former *Chicago Sun-Tribune* editor James Squires points to another factor behind such cutbacks: the displacement of the old family-owned papers of yesteryear with multimedia conglomerates that often regard the media they own as cash cows to be milked for their short-run profit potential.[19]

In addition to their sometimes allegedly ruthless bottom-line approach to journalism, media-owning conglomerates pose other potential hazards for investigative or critical journalism. They introduce new risks of conflicts of interest, and of direct censorship or self-censorship of news stories. The key factor here is "synergy."

In business circles, "synergy" refers to two or more enterprises collaborating to achieve results—enhanced earnings or market shares—which they could not achieve acting on their own. The term is particularly appropriate to media and cultural industries. Disney may be the world's master of synergy, cross-marketing its key products through different branches of its own empire—movies, souvenirs, theme parks, television networks, a professional hockey team. Disney also achieves synergy by entering into marketing arrangements with other global corporate giants, such as McDonalds.

Synergy makes good sense from an investor's standpoint. But what about the integrity of journalism practised within news media owned by global conglomerates like Disney? Corporate integration on this kind of global scale has two worrying implications. First, news media may be obliged to carry promotional material, disguised as news or entertainment, on behalf of other portions of the corporate empire.[20] Thus, shortly after Disney's takeover of ABC, the network's *Good Morning America* presented an eight-minute celebration of the Disney Institute in Florida, the newest vacation spot developed by "our parent company."

Another example: *TV Guide* and the U.S. Fox television network are owned by Rupert Murdoch. A few years ago, *TV Guide* published a cover story, "The Best Show You're Not Watching," promoting the Fox network's (then) low-rated TV program, *Party of Five*.[21] When such promotion is disguised as the product of independent critical evaluation or news judgment, are the media keeping faith with the public? And what are the implications for cultural producers who do not enjoy such instant access to publicity? Could Southam newspapers, for instance, always give fair coverage to local cultural events when they were up against musical extravaganzas promoted by Livent—a company with Conrad Black on its board of directors and headed, until recently, by Southam director Garth Drabinsky?

Second, and more worrying, is the potential suppression of stories that reflect negatively on other interests of the parent company. A number of such cases have been documented in the U.S. For instance, the Center for the Study of Commercialism alleges that, in December 1989, NBC's *Today* show "removed from an investigative report an exclusive, documented statement to the effect that General Electric— the network's parent company—had been making dangerously substandard jet engine bolts for eight years."[22]

Many Canadian news media are also owned by large conglomerates, and this raises a number of similar concerns. Is it likely, for instance, that the Irving newspapers, with their corporate ties to the forest industry, would report vigorously on forest industry practices in New Brunswick?

Let's return now to consider more direct editorial interventions by owners. Most obviously, concentration multiplies the opportunities for a media owner to impose his (or, very occasionally, her) own agenda on news coverage. Ultimately, even if chains and conglomerates exist for wholly commercial reasons, questions about political slant and diversity cannot be avoided.

This is particularly true for Hollinger, because of its position in the news system as Canada's largest, and the world's third largest, English-language newspaper empire. Conrad Black's reputation for being an especially "hands-on" owner gives these questions an added relevance. Are Hollinger papers as editorially balanced and politically innocent as the company's leaders claim, or are they frequently conduits for free market evangelism and Black's own reactionary political views?

Overall, we believe that the historical record supports allegations made by Black's critics that he craves political influence as well as profits, and sometimes intervenes in editorial decision-making on political grounds. At Southam and some of Hollinger's flagship papers, Black's takeovers have often resulted in an exodus of directors, publishers and editors who didn't fit his mold.

Most dramatically, Black transformed the influential and leftish *Jerusalem Post* into a hard-right paper, steamrolling over its publisher and top editors, who resigned. At the same time, he also made what appear to be partisan political interventions at the *Daily Telegraph*—a paper, ironically, that had strong leanings toward the British Conservative Party. Trevor Grove, the former deputy editor, said that once he and senior editor Max Hastings had turned the *Telegraph* around financially, Black felt free to find other more ideologically compatible editors and they were fired. "I suspect that, in my case, he probably thought that I wasn't a sufficiently determined sort of conservative."[23]

Bringing that track record to Canada, Black's takeover of Southam in 1996 led in short order to the departure of editors at the *Montreal Gazette* (which Black felt was not sufficiently militant in its support of the anglophone minority) and the *Ottawa Citizen*. According to Hollinger spokespeople, these actions have been taken for nothing more than business reasons: streamlining, redundancy, the need to bring in new people to improve the quality of editing and reporting. But there is enough consistency in the mounting criticisms of former Hollinger/Southam employees to suggest other motives in at least some of the firings.

Columnist Chris Young, the former *Ottawa Citizen* editor whose verbal dustup with Black we noted earlier in Chapter One, is not alone when he asserts that Black:

...likes to say that he doesn't interfere with the editorial policy of his papers. He doesn't have to; policy can be changed by firing one editor and hiring another. On tours of Southam newspapers, he has disclaimed interference with editorial policy, but emphasized his belief in 'more balance.' This is taken to mean more right, less centre or left: Ignore it at your peril.[24]

Once again, a caveat is in order. The most important issues in question here go far beyond any one individual, even Conrad Black. Certainly, Black is only one of a long line of corporate media owners who have used their media properties to promote political interests when the stakes have been high enough. For example, Rupert Murdoch's track record indicates that he has used his extensive British media holdings on occasion to attempt to sway public opinion and to influence British parties and governments.[25] But let's conduct a small thought experiment. What if individual media moguls such as Murdoch or Black weren't at all concerned about politics and had absolutely no interest in editorial policy? Would that increase the chances of editorial diversity?

We think not. Because, even if media owners did not dictate editorial policy, or if they had no political motives, concentrated media ownership itself can still have profound consequences for the diversity of politically-relevant information available in the news media. For one thing, although newspaper chains do sometimes use their deep pockets to create new services for their news outlets, there is an offsetting tendency: big media companies also work to rationalize their resources. Chains may come to rely rather heavily on their own in-house syndicated columnists or news services, at the expense of local freelancers or independent news services. The Kent Commission called this process "editorial concentration."

A similar logic applies to political reporting. Once Southam/Hollinger acquired most of the dailies in Ontario outside of Toronto, only four of its papers retained bureaux at the Ontario legislature. "Eventually, there will be one Queen's Park reporter for Southam," says *Windsor Star* journalist Gail Robertson, a situation that already exists in the Thomson chain.[26] So we face a paradox: chains may sometimes improve the quality of individual papers—a syndicated book reviewer may actually be a better writer than a local scribe. But in the process, simply as a by-product of rational economic decisions, there may be less diversity in the news system as a whole.

Similar arguments apply to cross-media ownership, where one company owns media outlets of different types in the same market. Economically rational decisions to share editorial resources between the outlets would reduce the diversity available to local news consumers.

The generally impersonal homogenizing impact of chain ownership is aptly summarized by Michael Cobden, a former editor at the *Kingston Whig-Standard*, once an award-winning independent paper now owned by Southam. Commenting on Conrad Black and the impact of large newspaper chains, Cobden writes:

> It's not just a matter of Mr. Black having too much influence over people's view of public affairs (though that is a danger, even if he doesn't intend it). It's a matter of the head office of his chain influencing the journalism of all its newspapers, so that they all read the same, look the same, choose the same sorts of things to write about, and write about them in much the same way, in the same tone, at the same length, in the same story form, and using the same storytelling techniques. A newspaper chain tends to eliminate anything that doesn't conform to its way of doing journalism...It doesn't like essays or gossip columns or poetry in its newspapers. It frowns on columnists with politically incorrect views.[27]

Not surprisingly, Cobden's critique drew a vigorous response from the *Whig-Standard's* current managing editor, emphasizing the resources Southam has put into technology, community relations and journalism, "with no interference from anyone at head office."[28]

Still, this type of rebuttal has done little to silence the critics. For example, Jeffrey Simpson of *The Globe and Mail*—a man whose own views tend to be moderately conservative on most issues—also sees media concentration and cutbacks as threats to quality and diversity in the news. He describes single company ownership of all of a province's major papers as "a highly undesirable state of affairs against which our country's aenemic competition laws are apparently helpless."

Newspapers are "shrinking in size, personnel, ambition and, as a consequence, in their curiosity," Simpson adds. They had shed personnel, sometimes brutally, as in the case of the 170 employees summarily dismissed in 1996 after Hollinger bought the Saskatoon and Regina dailies. As some of the best independently-owned papers are swallowed by larger chains, he added, "I believe the result has been a diminution in quality." Moreover, Simpson concludes, "more commentators than ever are ideologues of the right."[29]

Similar views have also been expressed by columnist Dalton Camp, a former Conservative party insider. Camp argues that the "chaining" of Canadian newspapers "limits employment opportunities and career mobility" for journalists. More precisely, he suggests that "Someone who is sacked on one Black paper is likely banned from future employment at 57 others." The chilling effect on journalists is palpable, leading Camp to conclude that chain ownership is likely to produce "less dissent, fewer questions and more Velveeta," a measurable "lack of diversity of opinion in the Canadian print media."[30]

News — or Marketing?

This brings us back to audiences. Because, even if consumer power in an oligopolistic industry is limited, news corporations must still attract advertising, which provides most of their revenue. And that means that media managers are not necessarily completely free to treat their papers as vehicles for their personal opinions.

What are the implications of advertising for the news? When it comes up for discussion at all, advertising's defenders highlight its undoubted benefits. Advertising provides a financial basis for press independence from the government (which many people equate with press freedom). It ensures a reasonable degree of responsiveness to audience tastes (since commercial media need to attract audiences before their attention can be profitably sold to advertisers). And it enables media consumers to get the news for quite low direct costs—putting aside the indirect costs that may be buried in the prices of advertised products.

Still, there is obviously considerable pressure on the media not to bite the hand that feeds them. Indeed, the press independence created by advertising revenues comes with another kind of price to pay. Critics point to several ways in which advertising itself limits the diversity of the press and its independence from outside forces. For example, traditionally, many major news organizations tried to maintain a wall between their editorial and business functions. But, with growing competition for relatively stagnant advertising revenues, and with more and more media owners apparently focusing on the short-term bottom line, critics argue that this wall is breached with greater frequency.[31] According to professor C. Edwin Baker, advertising places pressure on media managers to tailor editorial content in the following ways:

> 1) to treat advertisers' products and their broader interests charitably, both in news reports and in editorials; 2) to create a buying mood that will induce readers or viewers to have more favorable reactions to advertisements; 3) to make content less partisan, often less controversial, in order to avoid offending advertisers' potential customers...[32]

In the first place, then, advertising encourages journalists to massage rather than to bite the hand that feed them. In allocating their advertising budgets, it is not unusual for advertisers to place preconditions, or even intervene directly, regarding news media coverage. Research undertaken at the Center for the Study of Commercialism in Washington, D.C., has documented dozens of cases in the U.S. where news stories have been spiked or journalists disciplined because of reportage that offended advertisers.[33]

Many of these cases involve car dealers, department stores, and real estate companies pressuring local media. To take just one example, an auto columnist with 23 years' experience in Birmingham, Alabama, was fired in 1991 by the *Birmingham News* after he publicly noted the influence of auto dealers on his paper. In a confidential survey of 42 real-estate editors, nearly half said publishers and senior editors had prohibited critical coverage of the industry for fear of offending advertisers.[34]

Similar Canadian examples are not hard to find. From his research at the *Windsor Star*, James Winter tells the story of a publisher, James Bruce, going "ballistic" (Bruce's own words) and reportedly screaming at his editors for running a February 5, 1996 CP wire copy story on a consumer association study that mildly criticized car dealers in Montreal. The next day, Bruce published a prominent apology to (Windsor area!) car dealers for this alleged departure from "balance, fairness, and factual accuracy." Without offering any factual evidence, Bruce's article asserted that Windsor auto dealers "adhere to the highest of ethical standards."[35]

Similarly, in May 1994, *the Sunshine Coast News*, a paper in Gibsons, B.C., published an editorial suggesting that local businesses were lazy and unidimensional. The advertising cancellations that followed were reversed only after an editor and reporter were fired and the paper apologized to the offended retailers for such "hate literature."

That incident was reported in the *Vancouver Sun* (May 27, 1994). The *Sun*, however, was silent about a much bigger blind spot: the symbiotic relationship between real estate advertisers and Vancouver's press. Later in this book (Chapter Seven) we'll discuss how the press failed to cover the widespread problem of leaky condominiums in Vancouver until it had become a billion-dollar disaster for average consumers.

Other advertising-related blind spots are more subtle. As advertisers seek a favourable "media context" or "editorial environment" for their marketing campaigns, commercial media are induced to favour consumerism over other social values. This arguably lends itself to increasing amounts of "lifestyle journalism," "infotainment," and celebrity-focused "junk-food news," at the expense of investigative and analytical journalism.

Of course, elements of these styles of popular journalism have always been an important part of the popular press, but now these styles threaten to overwhelm more traditional aspects of news in the interests of marketing. The more the press becomes a vehicle for celebrating consumer lifestyles, the greater the likelihood it will contain blind spots about alternative perspectives on consumer society.

If the press generally has a consumerist orientation, it is most evident in the fusion of "news" and advertising in the fashion, living, home, travel, sports, and leisure sections of Canadian dailies, or in lifestyle and entertainment segments on TV news. Arguably, even the hard-news reports subtly reinforce the ads. In selecting and telling news stories, it is as if middle-market commercial news media take the standpoint of the assumed "average" consumer.

Coverage of labour-management disputes, for instance, usually emphasizes inconvenience and disruption to consumers. The excluded alternative is news that addresses us as workers, as citizens, or as members of a fragile ecosystem, rather than primarily as consumers of products or as passive spectators of political scandals.[36]

Even more broadly and subtly, advertising acts (even if unintentionally) as a licensing system, a political filter, determining which media survive and flourish and which do not. As the financial basis of the press shifted from readership sales and political subsidies to advertising over a century ago, press content shifted as well. Advertisers were interested in two kinds of audiences: the affluent, who had sufficient disposable income to purchase luxury products; and the mass audience, whose lack of purchasing power as individuals was offset by its huge size.

Two kinds of media tended to succeed in this environment: general interest publications attracting a mass circulation through juicy scandals and non-political human interest stories, and "quality" publications appealing to the politically conservative sensibilities of the affluent élite.

Because advertisers have always been prepared to pay more for each affluent reader than for each mass reader, the affluent have had more choices, and more say, in determining which media survive.[37] The logic of the market is one dollar, one vote—not one person, one vote.˙ Media that promote the perspectives and interests of recent immigrants, or of the poor, or that consistently challenge consumerism and the business system, have had more difficulty surviving in an advertiser-driven business environment. Not surprisingly, as the Kent Commission on Newspapers admitted, "It was left-wing viewpoints that tended to be under-represented as commercialism increased its hold."[38]

If the need to attract advertising can be said to place constraints on media management, it is important to ask what those constraints are most likely to be. If media owners try to use their "franchises" to ride personal hobbyhorses, some of those horses will be more handicapped than others. If owners want to haul in advertising accounts for, say, luxury cars, they can't fill their pages with odes to environmentally friendly public transport, let alone intensely partisan support for the homeless or ringing denunciations of globalized capitalism. Mostly, owners don't feel this kind of advertising pressure as a constraint because they generally share (with a few "liberal" exceptions) their advertisers' commitment to the priorities and perspectives of the business world. To the extent that profit is the prime objective of news management, efficiently attracting advertising revenue is the best way to go.

These observations are by no means new. Widespread concerns about the consumerist and business orientations of the commercial media in North America go back decades. In the past 15 years, though, the accelerating processes of concentration, profit maximization, multimedia ownership, and the formation of conglomerates has arguably reinforced— and may well have deepened—the corporate media's structural biases and blind spots. These pressures appear to be "marketizing" the entire culture of journalism, reversing the traditional priorities described by former *St. Louis Post-Dispatch* editor William F. Woo—that the newspaper's first job is "to report and present issues, intelligently and clearly, and...if this job is done well, people will come into the paper."[39]

Other veterans of the craft share similar concerns about the growing trend since the 1980s for newsrooms to incorporate business strategies. For example, Doug Underwood draws attention to the influence of business-side executives in promoting a concept known as the "Total Newspaper." In this vision of the newspaper as a fully integrated business operation, "editorial, advertising, circulation, research, and promotion functions were all co-ordinated around the idea that newspapers must be more aggressive in finding new ways to make money."[40]

What are the implications of "total newspapering"? At the growing number of papers that have jumped on this marketing bandwagon, editors and news executives help promote the newspaper's marketing goals, including devising strategies for bringing in new advertisers. Conversely, business-side managers help devise or revamp editorial sections, most often on sports, en-tertainment, features, or special events. Even front-line reporters at some papers, like Knight-Ridder's *Kansas City Star*, have been asked by editors to participate in marketing efforts sponsored by the paper, such as public forums where advertisers set up exhibition space. Nor is such "hyper-commercial-ism" a uniquely American phenomenon; Underwood argues that some Cana-dian papers, such as the *London Free Press*, have also been leading the charge.

Hyper-commercialism comes with a cost for journalism. At dailies that have eliminated the barriers between the news and business departments, Underwood points out, journalists say they "feel intimidated when they write about issues of importance to advertisers. So they often engage in self-cen-sorship, and they don't suggest stories that risk offending important custom-ers." According to former *Arizona Republic* reporter Kim Sue Lia Perkes, "What happens in that climate—when marketing and advertising become more important than the copy—is that you begin to find you can't do anything con-troversial and count on management to stick by you."[41]

In the "Total Newspaper," Underwood concludes, there is less space for nonconformity. When MBAs take over newsrooms, news outlets in the future "will be less tolerant of oddballs and erratic visionaries—brilliant though they may be...The emphasis will be on collaboration, on building compatible teams, on taking fewer risks."[42] This is not just an internal organizational matter. It affects the mind-set of journalists, who are saying that it is increasingly diffi-cult "to question authority out in the world when they themselves are being pressured to become loyal corporate soldiers inside their organizations."[43]

This kind of conformity in the interests of marketing and managerial efficiency seems especially likely in large newspaper chains, where manage-ment is typically centralized and corporate owners have an ever watchful eye on share prices. The former managing editor of Southam's *Calgary Herald*,

Gillian Steward, comments on this point specifically in a poignant discussion of the changes that led to her departure from the paper in 1990:

> I have never been opposed to business making reasonable profits...But what I found most disappointing was that whenever I, as a new manager, had a chance to attend meetings with executives and other managers in the chain, all they ever talked about was the bottom line, the newspaper as a cash cow whose only value was the milk that could be squeezed out of her.
>
> I was still somewhat idealistic then...but I was truly disappointed that none of these people saw the newspaper as a service to the community. In fact, they appeared not to see the newspaper at all; they saw only the balance sheets that told them how much money it was making, or losing...And not only did the head office types look at it that way, they now expected editors, newsroom managers, reporters, and photographers to regard it that way too.
>
> Everyone was expected to do their part to push up the stock price.[44]

So, Steward concludes, the new business climate had consequences for the *Herald*'s journalism: more power for the advertising department vis-a-vis the editorial department, more and more market surveys, yielding "easy-to-digest, uncomplicated information," a focus on personalities, and "fast-paced, emotional news and current affairs"—and fewer resources for news gathering (for example, earlier deadlines for daily news, thus reducing coverage of evening events, to avoid overtime for press workers).

You don't find many journalists who express much enthusiasm for these changes. That's easy to understand, because when the marketers increasingly call the shots, there is a concomitant erosion of the status of journalism as a profession. The actual craft of working journalism is influenced, too; news work is subject to a kind of "de-skilling" process.

There is more than a little irony in this. At the very moment when journalism schools are producing more highly-educated people for the profession than ever before, the practice of news writing for many journalists threatens to become less intellectually free-ranging and demanding. And, in a market dominated by oligopoly, there isn't much room for opposition to the "total newspaper." In 1997, *Los Angeles Times* publisher and Times-Mirror CEO Mark Willes, a guru of hyper-commercialism, made clear that resistance to his vision would be dealt with sharply. Editors who "repeatedly got in the way of ideas" would have to change, he said, or "we'd be delighted to have them go get in the way of the ideas of one of our competitors." The relevant question for print journalists in Canada is: What competitors?

FREE EXPRESSION AND THE TECHNOLOGICAL FIX

Social commentators with strong libertarian inclinations—including many of today's self-styled "conservatives"—argue that the market offers the best defense of free expression in the face of potential government censorship. But they don't have many solutions to constraints that arise as a result of market transactions.

A commercial press, the libertarian argument runs, is a free press by definition, because it is not bound by anything other than the need to appeal to its readers. If owners try to force unpalatable ideas down the throats of their readers, the self-regulating, competitive mechanism of the market ensures that some competitor will arise that is more geared to public wants and needs. The partisan owner will either have to modify his or her position or face losing readers to a more competitive rival.

In this kind of analysis, commentators sometimes make a contrast between the goals of freedom in public expression and those of diversity. Freedom of expression—that is, freedom from direct government censorship—is something that can be constitutionally guaranteed by governments, but diversity, they argue, is not something that can be either mandated or guaranteed. The market will ensure at least some level of diverse expression, the argument runs, but if it fails to represent every view, there isn't really much that can be done about it. Most importantly, the argument continues, when governments try to legislate conditions to increase the diversity of opinion, the provisions they introduce always end up causing more damage to free expression than they resolve.

Viewed historically, this "theory" of market-based press freedom is not without a vague semblance of truth. The advent and subsequent expansion of a commercial printing industry in Europe between the 15th and 19th centuries played a significant role in opening up the range of political discourse. Suddenly, books with new—and sometimes radical—ideas became available on an unprecedented scale, printed in an array of languages. Even more notably, though, there was an explosion of periodicals and newspapers available in the marketplace for the literate public.

German sociologist Jürgen Habermas has argued that these numerous and diverse periodicals and papers were instrumental in the creation of a new bourgeois "public sphere" of free discussion and argumentation. Flourishing in the growing numbers of coffee houses and salons in Northern European cities, this new sphere of independent public activity played a decisive role in the emergence of Western liberal democracy.[45]

So it is easy to see the historical precedent for the argument that commerce and free expression can go hand in hand. There is a danger, though, in abstracting from this historically-specific set of circumstances in 18th and 19th century Europe, to assume that the market in general will *always* be the most effective provider of socially-necessary information or free socio-political commentary and opinion. This is one of Habermas's key ideas, for, in the end, he believed that the creation of a vital public sphere of comparatively free and diverse political opinion in Europe was relatively short-lived: it wasn't long, for example, before the commercial press became a more conservative force in social life than a liberating one.

Critics have accused Habermas of romanticizing the political diversity and democratic energies associated with the bourgeois public sphere, and of exaggerating the collapse of free public discussion in Europe in the 19th and 20th centuries. Still, his emphasis on the importance of historical context challenges the blind faith of today's free market evangelists. In the late 18th and early 19th centuries, the market provided a necessary vehicle for the critique of political absolutism and the dominance of conservative religious doctrines.

In this context, commercial book and periodical markets, along with markets for a diversity of partisan newspapers, emerged as powerful vehicles for the articulation and dissemination of new and diverse political ideas and viewpoints. But that was then and this is now. Does it still make sense to think of the market as the only, or even the best, provider of free expression in today's world of transnational media conglomerates, chain newspapers, and advertising imperatives?

We say No. The immense differences between past and present simply do not support the knee-jerk belief that the market, without either regulation or the existence of subsidized public competitors, will really provide sufficient "freedom" of expression in news media.

But what about technology? It has sometimes been argued in recent years that new communications technologies— again, in conjunction with the market—hold the promise of opening up political discussion, very much like the printing press and commercial printing industry seemed to do in Europe after the 15th century. The communication technologies that are most frequently cited in this connection are the new digital media, particularly the Internet and the World Wide Web.

During the Bill Clinton/Monica Lewinsky media frenzy in 1998, populist Internet news providers such as Matt Drudge became household names. And phone lines were jammed when people rushed to get online to read U.S.

special prosecutor Ken Starr's report on Clinton's behaviour. Commentators in the conventional news media were drawn to comment extensively on the striking new influence of "the Net" as a factor in the news production process.

At one level, management in conventional news media worry about fragmenting media markets and still more competition for their readers' attentions. But, at another level, the management of large media firms have quickly moved into the digital age to develop a strong presence on the Net, and they occasionally appear so enthusiastic about its possibilities that they sound like editors of *Wired* magazine.

It is particularly ironic to see defenders of corporate media concentration gush publicly about the Net as a guarantor of free and diverse political expression. For example, speaking at a Rideau Club luncheon, as reported in the *Montreal Gazette* (a Southam daily), Peter White, former editor of *Saturday Night* magazine and now a Hollinger director, argued that the Net's rising popularity contradicts critics who worry about Hollinger's domination of Canadian newspapers. The Net is the "ultimate bulwark and safeguard of freedom of information," White claimed, because it is nearly impossible to censor and because it is accessible to anybody with a telephone and a computer.

"Our society is far too fluid and open, and our media far too fragmented and competitive for any one media person and company to have a preponderant influence on the designing or the determination of the national identity of Canadians," he declared.

The presence of the Net, in the context of specialty news magazines, cable channels, and other media, White added, makes it a "physical impossibility" for someone like Conrad Black to "control" the minds of all Canadians[46]—a ridiculous caricature of the views of Black's critics.

The reality, though, may be less black and white than White and Black would have it. To be sure, digital technologies may well be transforming how journalism is produced, processed, transmitted and consumed. The Net is a medium with an almost unparalleled potential for interactive, horizontal communication (from the many to the many), distinct from the top down model of the conventional news media. Indeed, a vast range of information and opinion absent in the pages of the daily press is available on the Net.

Sometimes stories seething through the Net—such as the Clinton/ Lewinsky scandal, or CIA complicity in cocaine trafficking—come bubbling up into the conventional media. Still, the argument that the Net guarantees a diverse public agenda doesn't give adequate weight to the continued gatekeeping role of the dominant media—particularly the daily press at the base of the information pyramid. There may be thousands of Web sites published by grassroots groups—and we do not mean to trivialize their importance—but the handful of media organizations with mass audiences continue to set the terms of public debate.

Then, too, there is the question of access. The number of Canadians connected to the Net is still not a majority. Moreover, to highlight a point made earlier, it is likely that, in the absence of public policy to shape a different future, the digital media of the future will be dominated by the same handful of giants that dominate broadcasting and the press.

It is easy, in the current climate of techno-hype, to forget that the development of technology is influenced by economic and political forces. Since 1994 in the U.S., the Internet has been commercialized "at an exponential rate," according to Wisconsin professor Robert McChesney, and the Telecommunications Act of 1996 ensures that the market, not public policy, will direct the evolution of the information highway. If the technology's anti-monopoly biases are strong enough to foil the profit-seeking ambitions of the corporate giants, he argues, the Internet will likely languish on the margins of media culture; the huge investment needed to upgrade it and to make it popularly accessible and affordable will not be forthcoming.

But if it proves to be profitable, new "nodes" on the net will be owned and operated by private interests operating on a profit motive.[47] Either of these situations will minimize the potential of cyberspace to counterbalance the blind spots of a media system arguably dominated by the corporate pursuit of profit.[48]

ENDNOTES

1. For useful critiques of the consumer sovereignty thesis, see James Curran, "Mass Media and Democracy Revisited," in *Mass Media and Society*, eds. James Curran and Michael Gurevitch, 2nd ed. (London: Arnold, 1996), pp. 81-119; Robert W. McChesney, *Corporate Media and the Threat to Democracy* (New York: Seven Stories Press, 1997), esp. pp. 44-54.

2. A useful discussion of this point can be found in Roger Bird, *The End of News* (Toronto: Irwin Publishing, 1997), pp. 2-4.

3. Doug Underwood, *When MBAs Rule the Newsroom* (New York: Columbia University Press, 1995), pp. 176-177.

4. See Edward Herman and Robert McChesney, *The Global Media: The New Visionaries of Corporate Capitalism* (London and Washington: Cassell, 1997), p. 70.

5. James Winter, *Democracy's Oxygen* (Montreal: Black Rose Books, 1997), p. 3.

6. Underwood, *When MBAs Rule*, p.160.

7. Arthur Siegel, *Politics and the Media in Canada*, 2nd ed. (Toronto: McGraw-Hill Ryerson, 1996), p. 193.

8. The 1998 circulation figures were compiled by Tim Creery, research director of the 1980 Royal Commission on Newspapers, in an unpublished paper, "The More They Get Together—Fifty Years of Chains," presented at Simon Fraser University, April 15, 1999. Creery's figures, supplied by the Canadian Newspaper Association, do not take into account Hollinger's increased circulation resulting from the transformation of the *Financial Post* into the *National Post*.

9. The discussion here and elsewhere in this chapter draws upon Robert Hackett and Yuezhi Zhao, *Sustaining Democracy?*, pp. 61-71. Also see Peter J.S. Dunnett, *The World Newspaper Industry* (London: Croom Helm, 1988), esp. pp. 42-51 and 188-200; and Robert G. Picard and Jeffrey H. Brody, *The Newspaper Publishing Industry* (Boston: Allyn and Bacon, 1997), pp. 49-58.

10. Douglas Fetherling, *The Rise of the Canadian Newspaper* (Toronto: Oxford University Press Canada, 1990), pp. 102, 112.

11. Robert Hackett, Richard Pinet and Myles Ruggles, "News For Whom? Hegemony and Monopoly Versus Democracy in Canadian Media," in Helen Holmes and David Taras (eds.), *Seeing Ourselves*, 2nd ed. (Toronto: Harcourt Brace, 1996), p.264.

12. Ben Bagdikian, *The Media Monopoly*, 5th ed. (Boston: Beacon Press, 1997), p. ix.

13. For more on Black's world view (and the comparable views of his wife, columnist Barbara Amiel), see Maude Barlow and James Winter, *The Big Black Book: The Essential Views of Conrad Black and Barbara Amiel Black* (Toronto: Stoddart, 1997).

14. Picard and Brody, *The Newspaper Publishing Industry*, p. 58.

15. Wallace Clement, *The Canadian Corporate Elite* (Toronto: McClelland and Stewart, 1975).

16. Paul Audley, *Canada's Cultural Industries* (Toronto: James Lorimer/CIEP, 1983), p. 27.

17. Cited in Winter, *Democracy's Oxygen*, p.95

18. The Campaign for Press and Broadcasting Freedom, *Diversity and Quality in the Monopoly Press: a Content Analysis of Hollinger Newspapers* (Ottawa: The Council of Canadians, 1997).

19. "Plundering the Newsroom", *Washington Journalism Review* (December, 1992).

20. For a very useful discussion of how advertising can substitute for news on television see Robin Andersen, *Consumer Culture and TV Programming* (Boulder, Col.: Westview Press, 1995).

21. Institute for Alternative Journalism, *Bottom Line vs. Top story: The Synergy Report* (San Francisco: IAJ, 1997).

22. Ronald Collins, *Dictating Content: How Advertising Pressure Can Corrupt a Free Press,* p.28. (The Center for the Study of Commercialism's address is 1875 Connecticut Ave., Suite 300, Washington, D.C. 20009-5728. Phone 202/332-9110.)

23. "The Paper King," *The National Magazine*, CBC-TV, Oct. 22, 1996, Part 2.

24. Chris Young, "Too Much Power, Too Few Scruples," *Halifax Daily News* (May 31, 1996), p. 22.

25. See Hackett and Zhao, *Sustaining Democracy*, p. 179.

26. Cited in winter, *Democracy's Oxygen*, p. 97.

27. Michael Cobden, "Worried About the Heavy Hand of Hollinger," *The Globe and Mail* (May 6, 1997), p. A17.

28. Lynn Haddrall, "The Kingston Whig-Standard is at the Top of Its Form," *The Globe and Mail* (May 15, 1997), p. A29.

29. Jeffrey Simpson, "Our Industry is Chasing its Tail," *The Globe and Mail* (April 18, 1996), p. A17.

30. Dalton Camp, "Our Democracy's Quiet Crisis," *The Toronto Star* (March 12, 1997), p. A23.

31. See, for example, a description of this breach from a former editor of the *Chicago Sun-Tribune*, James D. Squires, "Plundering the Newsroom," *Washington Journalism Review* (December, 1992).

32. Cited in Ronald K. L. Collins, *Dictating Content: How Advertising Pressure Can Corrupt a Free Press,* p. 10. (The Center for the Study of Commercialism's address is 1875 Connecticut Ave., Suite 300, Washington, D.C. 20009-5728. Phone 202/332-9110.)

33. Ronald Collins, *Dictating Content*.

34. Collins, *Dictating Content*, pp. 24-25.

35. James Winter, *Democracy's Oxygen*, pp. 90-91.

36. Hackett and Zhao, *Sustaining Democracy*, p. 68.

37. See the discussion of advertising in Ben Bagdikian, *The Media Monopoly*, especially ch. 5.

38. Kent, *Report*, p. 15.

39. William Woo, "Why Whiles is Wrong," *Columbia Journalism Review* (January/February, 1998), p. 27.

40. Doug Underwood, "It's Not Just in L.A.," *Columbia Journalism Review* (January/February, 1998), p. 24

41. Underwood, "Its Not Just in L.A.," p. 24.

42. Ellis Close, *The Press* (New York, 1989), p. 21; cited in Underwood, *When MBAs Rule*, p. 13.

43. Underwood, *When MBAs Rule*, p. 37.

44. Gillian Steward, "The Decline of the Daily Newspaper," in Holmes and Taras, eds. *Seeing Ourselves*, p.279.

45. Jürgen Habermas, *The Structural Transformation of the Public Sphere: An Inquiry Into a Category of Bourgeois Society*, trans. Thomas Burger with the assistance of Frederick Lawrence (Cambridge, Polity Press, 1989).

46. Norman Greenaway, "Internet Called Guarantor Against Press Monopoly," *The Gazette* (Feb. 5, 1998). p. D8.

47. Robert W. McChesney, "The Internet and U.S. Communication Policy-Making in Historical and Critical Perspective," *Journal of Communication*, vol. 46, no. 1 (Winter, 1996).

48. For a more extended discussion, see Hackett and Zhao, *Sustaining Democracy?*, pp. 189-200.

Chapter Three

Journalists' Views of the Media

In recent years Canadians have witnessed one media feeding frenzy after another. The O.J. Simpson trial, the trials of Karla Homolka and Paul
Bernardo, the death of Princess Diana, and the Bill Clinton\Monica Lewinsky
scandal are notable examples. At some point, usually well into the coverage,
journalistic commentaries about the media's handling of events have emerged
as mini-stories in their own right.

Anxious self-examination about the practice of journalism is an almost
predictable component of any story that develops a seemingly unstoppable
momentum. At such times, viewers and readers of news media may get a
passing and partial glimpse of some of the factors that drive news production.
We say partial, because the very issues that journalists feel compelled to talk
about may arguably be involved in limiting the breadth and depth of their own
self-analysis.

Still, journalists occupy the front lines of news production and have a
unique vantage point from which to assess the pressures and limits involved
in the production of news. In the course of Newswatch Canada's research on
under-reported stories, we began to wonder what journalists might have to
say about the current state of their profession and what their response might
be to some of our own developing ideas about filters and blind spots in the
news.

We wanted to give journalists a chance to voice their opinions infor-
mally, and in greater detail than in a news column or a short television spot.
What do reporters and editors see as key issues in their chosen trade? Do
reporters and editors themselves perceive any systemic filters or blind spots
in Canada's news system? If so, what—or who—do journalists blame for
these gaps and lapses?

In an effort to answer these questions, Newswatch co-director Robert
Hackett conducted interviews in 1996 with approximately two dozen journalists and editors working for a variety of Canadian media outlets based in Toronto.[1] Later, we supplemented these interviews with a survey of journalists
and editors working for media outlets across the nation.

NewsWatch developed a questionnaire designed to examine journalists' perceptions of media filters and blind spots, and distributed it to Canadian journalists in three ways. First, we published the survey in the Spring 1997 issue of *Media magazine*. Second, we distributed it to delegates of the 1997 Canadian Association of Journalists' convention in Edmonton, Alberta. We also distributed the survey through the Vancouver newsroom local of the Communications, Energy, and Paperworkers (CEP) union. In addition, we posted a copy of the survey on NewsWatch Canada's web-site, allowing respondents to e-mail their responses directly to our researchers.

In the end, a total of 57 responses were received within the time frame that we set for the research. As usual in these matters, participants in the survey were guaranteed anonymity, and respondents were invited to submit personal comments on the questions and issues addressed.[2]

This small convenience survey of journalists is not statistically representative in any way. At best, we view the survey findings as preliminary and suggestive. Still, when taken together, the survey and interview respondents do offer a useful cross-section of the news profession in anglophone Canada.

With regard to their personal profiles, the journalists we surveyed and interviewed were a fairly diverse bunch. For example, while most of the journalists we personally interviewed were men, our survey respondents were more evenly split along gender lines (44% women). And, while many of the journalists we interviewed were grizzled veterans of the news business, a significant number of our survey respondents (47%) had logged less than ten years in the profession.

The survey and interviews also captured a diversity of work and professional experiences. For example, while most of our survey respondents worked in commercial 'for profit' media (79%), and in print journalism (75% worked for daily or weekly newspapers), the journalists we interviewed were more evenly split between for-profit and public media, and between print and broadcast media.

Finally, while two-thirds of our survey respondents worked as reporters, our interviews contained a healthy sprinkling of senior editors, producers, and columnists.

Overall, then, our two sources of information—the survey and the interviews—complement each other nicely. To the survey group of print journalists working in many of Canada's daily and weekly newspapers, the face-to-face interviews add the voices of experienced editors, producers, and columnists (many of whom work in public broadcasting).

We didn't find unanimous agreement among this diverse group about filters in the news, or about the constraints or forms of self-censorship that might lead to systematic patterns of under-reporting in Canadian news media. But most of the journalists we surveyed and interviewed acknowledged the existence of certain filters and blind spots in news media and a number of common themes emerged from the research. These themes were generally consistent with arguments found in the existing academic literature on the economic, social and organizational factors that influence news production and the practice of journalism.

JOURNALISTS' PERCEPTIONS OF NEWS FILTERS

LACK OF INSTITUTIONAL RESOURCES

What factors do journalists think are most important in shaping and filtering the news? Survey responses bearing on this question are listed in Table 3.1. Some clear themes are immediately evident. First, and not surprisingly, journalists tend to see a lack of institutional resources as the notable limiting condition on news. Approximately 84% of journalists surveyed said that a lack of resources (including time, money and news space) "occasionally" or "often" leads to the omission of significant news.

In one sense, there is nothing remarkable about this. Complaining about a lack of resources has become a common refrain in times of economic cutbacks and restructuring, one repeated increasingly by teachers, nurses, doctors, university professors, and other professionals: "If only we had more money, more time, and more resources," the complaint usually runs, "we could do a better job." But in another sense—and this was reinforced by the journalists we interviewed—the fact that most journalists in the survey saw the absence of resources as a major filter in news production revealed something more than simple frustration with the need to work on ever-tightening budgets.

In interviews, and in comments written on the survey, many journalists suggested that they increasingly have the feeling that their profession is under siege. It's not simply a matter of necessary belt-tightening, they believe, it is also a question of changing priorities, for example, from "serious" news to less expensive "features" that are tailor-made for advertising.[3]

One newspaper reporter summarized his perception of the problem as follows:

> The lack of resources is the most important filter. [There have been] staff reductions in almost every major newsroom in the country in the last seven to eight years, plus a shift in the allocation of resources.

TABLE 3.1: JOURNALISTS' PERCEPTIONS OF FILTERS

Filters (By Category)	Average Score*	% of Respondents			
		Rarely or Never	Occasionally	Often or Very Often	n**
Lack of Institutional Resources	average=3.26				
Lack of Resources	3.75	16.1	23.2	60.7	56
Insufficient Air-time/Column Space	3.21	28.6	26.8	44.6	56
Deadline Pressure	3.09	22.8	50.9	26.3	57
Lack of Access to Information	3.05	34.6	26.9	38.5	52
Work Routines	average=3.06				
Too Narrow Range of Sources	3.25	21.2	46.2	32.7	52
Journalist Ignorance/Laziness	3.07	31.6	38.6	29.8	57
Work Routines	2.96	37.7	28.3	34.0	53
Pack Journalism	2.94	38.8	24.5	36.7	49
External Pressures	average=2.69				
Court Reporting Restrictions	2.98	33.3	33.3	33.3	48
Need to Attract Particular Audience	2.84	45.5	25.5	29.1	55
Direct Pressure: Ownership	2.71	48.1	25.0	26.9	52
Direct Pressure: Advertisers	2.50	57.4	22.2	20.4	54
Interest Group Pressures	2.44	57.7	25.0	17.3	52
Internalized Pressures	average=2.55				
Fear of Antagonizing Sources	2.82	41.8	34.5	23.6	55
Sensitivity to Social Groups	2.63	51.9	31.5	16.7	54
Libel/Legal Concerns	2.52	53.7	29.6	16.7	54
Self-Censorship: Fear of Owners	2.50	55.4	25.0	19.6	56
Self-Censorship: Fear of Advertisers	2.27	67.3	20.0	12.7	55
Internal Biases	average=2.48				
Decency Standards	2.69	51.9	27.8	20.4	54
Cynicism	2.64	47.2	30.2	22.6	53
Ethnocentrism/Cultural Bias	2.57	49.0	25.5	25.5	51
Respect for People's Privacy	2.50	53.7	33.3	13.0	54
Right-Wing Bias of Journalists	2.28	60.0	28.0	12.0	50
Left-Wing Bias of Journalists	2.25	59.6	25.0	15.4	52
Other Filters					
Technical Foul-ups/Limitations	2.56	47.3	36.4	16.4	55
Overly Aggressive Reporting	2.12	76.0	14.0	10.0	50

* Scores were based on a five-point scale, from 1(never) to 5 (very often).
** n = the number of respondents for each question

So you might take the same number of staff, but allocate them to different things, like advertising recruitment...[as well as]...travel, fashion, and business writing.

In addition, our respondents often complained that resources for reporting local news are squeezed to a point where the ability to do good journalistic work on complex issues is substantially compromised. It is not hard to imagine how a lack of time and money can result in decreased coverage of important and complex issues. As operating budgets are slashed or reallocated, and reporters laid off, newspapers and broadcast media expect the remaining journalists to do "more with less" (the mantra of the 1990s). This downsizing of news reporting staffs means there are too few bodies to cover the basics, let alone any stories that stray outside the daily grind of party politics, crime, and sports.

One result of all this is a tendency for non-routine or complex stories to get ignored or be covered inadequately. Limited organizational resources particularly hamper investigative journalism, which requires the allocation of reporters to follow a story over a long period of time. One journalist in the survey noted: "[The] drive for financial profits has led to 'cheap stories' [i.e., stories that require] little investigative effort, serious research or travel."

Another reporter mentioned that his paper is moving:

"away from investigative journalism...There is a narrowing of the journalistic agenda [that] is shocking. The range of material deemed newsworthy has declined. The willingness of the Canadian news media, particularly print, to critically examine or investigate has virtually disappeared, largely under the guise of budget constraints and the shrinking editorial staff, blamed on a lack of resources."

The issue of diminishing resources was also referenced in several of our interviews with journalists. In one especially notable instance, a journalist commented on NewsWatch Canada's mandate to report on "under-covered" stories, and to analyze what appear to be systemic blind spots in the news media. The one thing common to all the potential blind spots in media identified by NewsWatch, this journalist argued, is "that they would require quite a bit of resources to pursue them properly." But increasingly, today "there's no capacity to investigate stuff. No real funding."

Sustained coverage of international news is especially affected in this context. Another journalist emphasized this point strongly: "From a newspaper's point of view, [international news] is all very nice, but who gives a shit? We got a fire down the street we've got to deal with."

In the written survey comments, and in the interviews, journalists often emphasized how recent cutbacks have put news workers under enormous pressure. This lends support to our argument in the last chapter about the "de-skilling" tendencies often associated with news work in the age of the "total" newspaper.

Journalists have long engaged in highly repetitive work routines that tend to make journalists dependent upon "official" sources. Events that fall outside the scope of established news "beats"—at police headquarters or places of government, for example—have generally failed to get sufficient coverage, except what can be pulled from wire services.[4] But now, in the face of de-creasing and reallocated resources, and the pressures of new marketing im-peratives, many journalists believe that the prospects for improving this situ-ation are more bleak than ever. Even well-established news beats have been affected by downsizing: there are simply too few bodies to do the job. The result is a reduction of in-depth coverage and a marshalling of resources into some beats at the expense of others. For example, the *Toronto Star*, one of the few papers in recent years that still retained labour reporters, no longer has them. Consequently, in the words of one interviewed journalist, "there is no one available to track down all sides" of labour-related stories.

Several of our respondents noted that some stories get filtered out of the news because they are simply "too complicated" for reporters to follow. Faced with a lack of resources for research, complex stories requiring intensive re-search tend to be ignored or reported in a superficial manner. It is typically much easier for journalists to rely on information supplied by easily available sources, especially large bureaucratically structured organizations such as government agencies, private corporations, and think tanks, usually conserva-tive in orientation.

This is an example of what Mark Fishman, in *Manufacturing the News*, calls the principle of "bureaucratic affinity": other bureaucracies are best po-sitioned to satisfy the information needs of the news bureaucracy.[5]

Some journalists also noted that they rely heavily on institutional sources to shield themselves from accusations of bias or, in extreme cases, from libel suits. This adds to journalists' dependence upon official sources. U.S. media scholar Leon Sigal summarizes the problem as follows: In a world of compet-ing interest groups and differing political voices, there is no "foolproof crite-rion for choosing sources who are likely to provide valid information," and journalists are often "uncertain about who to believe."

This creates additional pressure for journalists to seek out institutionally "authoritative" sources, such as senior officials, managers, and public rela-tions personnel in the police, government or business, or self-professed "experts" in universities or think tanks.[6] For example, a reporter suggested to us that corporate press releases are often reported uncritically because this is easier than "stepping back and asking hard questions" about the source's slant or bias. When this occurs, the reporter continued, journalists are too often "more lap dogs than watchdogs."

In another instance, a news editor summarized the problem as follows:

A fair rap is that the news media is an establishmentarian institution...Rather than an ideological issue, it's just comfortable to get news from the courts, and so on...from people who bring you the news. It's more convenient. It's easily digestible. Our view is skewed to institutional coverage [of] the established order.

WORK ROUTINES

In contrast to the tendencies described above, many of the journalists we surveyed and interviewed claimed they wanted the challenge of undertaking more complex stories requiring detailed investigation and a broader range of sources. However, they also said that established practices and constraints in their profession further increase the difficulty of doing this.

In this context, it is significant that "work routines" were listed by the journalists in our survey as the second most important "filter" influencing the production of news. Most notably, approximately 80% of survey respondents cited "Too Narrow Range of Sources" as a factor that "often" or "occasionally" leads to the omission of news, while 62% identified "Work Routines in General" as a significant filter in news-gathering.

Interestingly—in a candid recognition of how journalists sometimes adapt negatively to work pressures—more than two- thirds of respondents (68%) claimed that "Journalist Ignorance/Laziness" leads to news omissions "occasionally" or "often." A number of interviewed journalists also mentioned that journalists sometimes fall into a routine and stick to readily available sources of information (such as government officials and interest groups) simply out of habit. Thus, one columnist we talked to argued: "[The news media are]...so stuck in our hidebound ways of doing things" that there is a failure to use reduced resources creatively. Conceptualizing and researching alternative or more obscure perspectives, we were told, takes too much effort and time.

A respondent in the survey reinforced this point by noting that, while journalists should "go into [the] community to ask questions," they often end up "staying in [the] office and calling [their] buddy to find out what the story's all about."

This criticism certainly doesn't apply to all working journalists, perhaps not even to the majority. Even so, it is notable that a majority of the journalists we interviewed and surveyed were willing to admit that work pressures, established work routines and habits, and "pack journalism" can lead to less-than-thorough investigations of news stories.

Several journalists elaborated how such factors may lead to news stories that offer distorted and simplistic pictures of the world. To illustrate the point, one veteran newspaper editor offered a contrast between media interest in violent crime, compared to white collar crime, corporate fraud, or breaches in business ethics. Big scandals, where large numbers of investors are openly bilked or where shady dealing leads to huge losses, certainly get their share of coverage in contemporary news media. Nonetheless, this editor argued, in-depth critical analysis of the business world is under-represented in the news: "White collar crime requires following paper trails," and is thus much more time-and resource-consuming to cover compared to the "quick hit" of stories such as violent crime.

Conventional crime news has a ready audience because it plays on people's fears and concerns about public safety. It is also thought to be "easier to do," hence the clichéd expression, "if it bleeds, it leads." As a result, dramatic "easily-covered" crime stories are likely to get more attention on a daily basis from news workers than less dramatic, more complex stories.

This has implications for how news is framed: "The world is a much easier place to operate in if everything is in black and white and there are good guys and bad guys."

EXTERNAL PRESSURES

What about external pressures brought to bear upon journalists in their effort to cover the news? Two-thirds of respondents to the survey felt that "Court Reporting Restrictions" often or occasionally limit news coverage, while roughly 55% of respondents felt that pressure to "Attract Particular Audiences" for their employers "occasionally" or "often" limits the kinds of issues which get covered.

It is also notable that a majority of journalists identified external pressures from owners, advertisers, and interest groups as significant news filters. For example, nearly 52% of our respondents cited "Direct Pressure: Owners" as a factor that "often" or "occasionally" has the effect of "filtering" the news. This was followed by a 43% rating for "Direct Pressure: Advertisers," and a 42% rating for "Interest Group Pressures."

While the survey suggests that many journalists may chafe at restrictions on "court" reporting, the more interesting finding, from our perspective, is the substantial percentage of respondents who acknowledged a newspaper's need to attract audiences as a filtering effect on the news. This corresponds to a dominant theme that emerged in interviews, where many journalists noted that some stories, while they may be important, are not covered because they are "not sexy." In other words, the primary criterion for determining a story's newsworthiness is seen to be its "news value"—the degree to which it will appeal to the paper's audience.

There has been considerable research on the content of "news values" in North American journalism, and a number of key themes have been identified.[7] As we noted in Chapter One, these reputed news values include the timeliness of an event, its perceived political importance, the involvement of individuals rather than abstract structures or institutions, the presence of conflict, the presence of powerful people or celebrities, the need for drama, the preference for "negative" events, the scope and potential impact of an event, geographical and cultural proximity, relevance to some deep-rooted cultural theme, novelty, violation of social order, and human interest.

While journalistic work routines and source relations may have the effect of limiting news coverage of dense and complex issues—such as government debts and deficits, trade agreements, or the global consequences of international lending policies— many journalists have suggested that the lack of coverage of such stories can more likely be traced to a lack of news value. For example, one reporter noted in the survey that "the average viewer does not want to get bogged down in policy debates...Entertainment sells papers to viewers. Dramatic and immediate." Another reporter summarized the issue simply by noting how "debt stories make my eyes glaze over."

Stories with low "news values," the argument runs, simply cannot attract and hold the attention of audiences. Without audiences, newspapers and other profit-making media outlets cannot attract advertisers. The result underlines a point made earlier about the tendency to avoid complexity in reporting. In interviews, we were frequently reminded that news media are "driven by the need to tell a good story" and thus tend to play up "hot-button issues" such as war, sexual scandal, or violent crime, while at the same time downplaying stories that may be analytically complex and short on dramatic appeal. A newspaper columnist in the survey summarized the issue this way:

"The mass media are driven by melodramatic news...There is a crisis, there is a response, and everything is wrapped up at the end of the story." Still, many journalists, both in the survey and in interviews, suggested to us that this age-old tendency in news media has intensified as more and more newspapers become intent on "entertaining with snappy stories and cute leads" instead of challenging audiences with stories charting the complexities and gray areas of social and political life.[8]

Beyond the issue of news values, we were struck by the fact that a slight majority of the journalists surveyed cited direct pressure from ownership as a significant filter in news production. Apparently, many journalists are not convinced by newspaper owners' denials about the role of ownership as a factor that can shape the production of news. This theme in the survey data was also evident in several interviews. One interviewed journalist noted, for example, that chain ownership was a problem because "the chain wants to promote like-minded people." Promotions into management positions—people well placed to influence what stories are covered and how—most often go to people "who are safe and won't rock the boat."

Another reporter argued that, because newspaper owners come from the ranks of the affluent, it is unlikely that they will be interested in adopting editorial stances that criticize business or challenge the privileged place of affluent Canadians in shaping public policy. For that reason, critical stories on, say, tax breaks for wealthy Canadians or corporations do not receive much coverage. This trickles down to editorial ranks: "You have a level of management in the middle of it that spends a lot of time guessing what it is that upper management wants and what will or won't piss them off, so those kinds of stories just never get done."

Most journalists suggest that this is rarely a matter of explicit policy: "There are no commandments," we were told. Rather, it is a process of socialization, something that reporters and editors learn and "internalize on the job."[9]

Journalists were somewhat less emphatic about pressures from advertisers as a potential filter in news production. In the last chapter, we noted some examples of "filtering" pressures from advertisers in news media, especially in a time of increasing cross-ownership and cross-marketing in the media industries. While a sizeable number of respondents indicated that such pressures "often" or "occasionally" act as a filter in the news, the majority (57%) felt that pressures from advertisers "rarely" or "never" have this effect.

More notably, the filtering effects of pressure from advertisers was not widely acknowledged in the interviews: only a few journalists intimated otherwise, suggesting that people in news media always have to be concerned about biting the hand that feeds them. One reporter went so far as to argue that "a mind- set" permeates newsrooms today, based on a widespread belief that business interests are likely to "go after" reporters, and their news organizations, for being too critical. But another reporter qualified this view, suggesting that there are important differences between smaller papers and large urban dailies:

> ...people talk about advertising pressure. I think this is a minor factor at large media organizations, but it is substantial at smaller ones...either burying stories to not offend them, or running them forward to massage potential advertisers. I used to pooh-pooh this, because it never happened at the [large urban daily]. But it's blatant at smaller papers.

What about other interest groups beyond advertisers? Despite the reservations of a minority, most of the journalists surveyed and interviewed did not believe that pressure from interest groups in general acted to filter news in substantial ways.

INTERNALIZED PRESSURES AND INTERNAL BIASES

Perhaps understandably, survey respondents were more reluctant to acknowledge that such things as self-censorship due to anticipated pressures (e.g., "Libel/Legal Concerns") or internal biases (e.g., "Ethnocentrism" or "Left-Wing Bias") had much influence on what news gets covered and what gets ignored. Even in this sensitive area, however, many journalists expressed concern. About 58% of respondents tagged "fear of antagonizing sources" as a frequent or occasional news filter.

Our respondents suggested that there are at least two persuasive reasons for treating key sources with kid gloves. First, if a journalist "burns" a key source by printing a damaging story, the source can retaliate by cutting off the journalist and refusing to give him or her easy access to information. In a context where money is tight and the pressure is on to fill news holes quickly, losing access to a key source can threaten a journalist's career. Consequently, there is a tendency, according to some journalists we interviewed, to "pull punches" by suppressing some elements of a story if it could cost the reporter a valuable source.

Second, according to one journalist, many reporters simply do not want to risk falling into disfavour with their more prestigious and glamourous sources. Thus, the fear of becoming an "outsider" in the eyes of their élite and powerful sources can be a strong deterrent on negative coverage:

> Reporters will deny it [but] we're part of the same élite. And even if we're not in the league of the Desmarais's, we sure want to be. And you don't want to piss your contacts off; you don't want to become a pariah.

Numerous critics have suggested that it was precisely this kind of self-identification and concern with self-interest among Canadian sports reporters that prevented them from breaking the story about Alan Eagleson's fraudulent business practices (the story was first broken by a U.S. reporter). For years Eagleson had been the most powerful man in hockey—the ultimate inside source—and many reporters were either heavily in his debt or continually compelled to vie for his favours.

One of the editors we interviewed offered a somewhat similar example from federal politics, noting the claim in Stevie Cameron's book, *On the Take*, that stories on corruption in Ottawa during the years of the Mulroney government may have been slow to break because of the closeness between Ottawa reporters and their sources.

In addition to the fear of antagonizing powerful sources, almost half (45%) of respondents indicated that the fear of reprisals from owners "occasionally" or "often" leads reporters to censor themselves, while almost a third of our respondents (33%) said "Self-Censorship: Fear of Advertisers" at least occasionally leads to news omissions. Note that here we are talking not about *direct* or *open* pressure from owners or advertisers, but something more insidious—journalists censoring themselves for *fear* of reprisals.

Viewed collectively, these results suggest—despite the profession's image of beholden-to-no-one autonomy—that many journalists do admit to feeling pressured to write and research their stories within certain constraints. The fear of alienating sources, owners, or advertisers can create a powerful "internal" self-censoring mechanism that can potentially influence which issues get covered and how such issues are framed.

Nearly half of the surveyed journalists also acknowledged that their own sense of decency was involved in filtering the news "occasionally" or "often," and a slight majority recognized cynicism and cultural biases as notable filters. Journalists were somewhat less willing, however, to acknowledge that "internal" right-wing or left-wing political biases play a significant role in news production. This is consistent with the overall trend of results listed in table 3.1.

Journalists generally indicated that external factors beyond their control (e.g., lack of institutional resources) are more likely to act as news filters than more personal "internal" factors. Furthermore, even when the journalists in the survey highlighted the importance of external factors as filters in the news, they tended to emphasize factors—such as work routines— that pose little challenge to the image of journalists as disinterested and unaffected truth-seekers.

There is an additional interesting dimension to journalists' responses to the idea of personal political bias as a filter in the news. Approximately 40% of surveyed journalists indicated they thought that journalist's right-wing biases "occasionally" or "often" act as filters in the news (with approximately 60% suggesting that this "rarely" or "never" occurs). But virtually the same percentage made the seemingly opposite argument: that journalists' left-wing biases "occasionally" or "often" act as news filters, as well!

It is conceivable, of course, that respondents' ratings in our survey are derived from their perceptions of a wide range of other reporters and editors who variously seem to represent both political positions. A disinterested observer might easily claim to see examples of both types of apparent "biases," depending on the story topic or who is covering it. Still, some of our interview and survey respondents emphasized one kind of bias more than the other, suggesting that journalists are no less divided in their assessments of biased reporting than political partisans and media critics in society at large.

One final set of issues emerged out of the interviews pertaining to journalists' personal characteristics as possible filters in the news: the issues of age, gender and race. Newsrooms are mostly staffed with people who have been in the business for a long time, and cutbacks have limited the numbers of journalists hired in the last five or ten years. In this context, according to several respondents, news coverage overall tends to reflect the interests and perspectives of middle-class, middle-aged people.

In recent years, there has been some attempt in certain sections of some newspapers to recover a more youthful, more hip kind of voice. This corresponds to advertisers' increasing interests in youth and young adults as a valuable market segment. Still, as one journalist suggested, there seems to be "a serious disconnection between the under-30 and 30-plus generations" in news coverage and—even more notably—in editorials.

The lack of young journalists, able to bring fresh perspectives to reporting, prompted one newspaper editor to complain that "no new blood is coming in." The result, another respondent said, "is an age group of journalists between 35 to 50. These people cover baby boomer stories," often to the exclusion of other perspectives.

Several journalists also commented on the problem of unequal gender and racial representation in newsrooms. One reporter stated her perception of the problem in uncompromising terms: "This is white male land. Take a look." Hiring women and visible minorities in any numbers in news media, we were told, has been a comparatively recent development at best—mostly in the last 10 to 15 years and, in the case of visible minorities, even more recently.

As a result, many of these journalists lack seniority, making them especially vulnerable in the "downsizing" of recent years. In other instances, these
journalists are channeled away from "hard news" and into "softer" features,
or they are assigned to specialty sections of newspapers.

An under-representation of women and visible minorities in the field of
journalism arguably limits the range of reportorial and editorial perspectives
found in Canadian news media.

JOURNALISTS' PERCEPTIONS OF BLIND SPOTS

In addition to asking journalists about various news filters, NewsWatch
also inquired how journalists from around the country would evaluate the

TABLE 3.2: JOURNALIST PERCEPTIONS OF BLIND SPOTS

Blind Spot	Average Score*	% of Respondents			n**
		Under-Covered	About Right	Over-Covered	
Investigative Reporting	1.70	83.3	16.7	0.0	54
Business: Critical Coverage	1.98	73.1	21.2	5.8	52
Social Policies: Implications	2.02	74.0	20.0	6.0	50
Anglo Coverage of Francophone Views	2.02	76.1	17.4	6.5	46
French Coverage of Anglophone Views	2.08	72.0	16.0	12.0	25
Crime: Social Causes	2.09	75.5	11.3	13.2	53
International Issues	2.14	66.7	25.5	7.8	51
Environment	2.15	66.0	24.5	9.4	53
Youth Issues	2.20	68.6	27.5	3.9	51
Labour	2.25	56.6	35.8	7.5	53
Human Rights, Social Justice	2.28	64.8	25.9	9.3	54
Religion, Ethics	2.29	60.0	36.0	4.0	50
Positive News	2.52	54.0	34.0	12.0	50
Features, In-depth	2.53	52.8	39.6	7.5	53
Ethnicity/Race Issues	2.55	50.9	35.8	13.2	53
Education	2.58	45.3	45.3	9.4	53
Defense and Security	2.68	36.2	48.9	14.9	47
Gender/Women's Issues	2.73	47.1	27.5	25.5	51
Left-Wing Perspectives	2.74	51.1	23.4	25.5	47
Science and Technology	2.77	35.8	50.9	13.2	53
Politicians: Critical Coverage	2.87	39.6	32.1	28.3	53
Health	3.01	20.4	57.4	22.2	54
Business and Investment	3.17	21.2	46.2	32.7	52
Arts and Entertainment	3.29	15.7	47.1	37.3	51
Right-Wing Perspectives	3.80	15.2	21.7	63.0	46
Sports	4.15	3.8	23.1	73.1	52

* Scores were derived from a 5-point scale, ranging from 1 (seriously under-covered) to 5 (seriously over-covered).
** n = number of respondents for each question

amount of coverage given to a variety of news categories. In essence, we wanted to ask journalists: what issues, if any, do you think are most under-reported in the daily news? What, in your view, are the most glaring "blind spots" in the Canadian news agenda?

To gain answers to these questions, we asked journalists to rate the amount of coverage extended to a wide range of categories of stories or information. The survey results are displayed in Table 3.2.

As the table shows, a substantial majority of journalists in our survey felt that the Canadian media should be doing a better job of covering a number of important issues. Sixteen of the 26 categories listed in the table were listed as "Under-Covered" by 50% or more of our respondents. Even more sugges-tive ideas can be gleaned from examining the table in closer detail.

PERCEIVED AREAS OF UNDER-REPORTING

First, consider the high percentage of respondents (83%) who felt that "Investigative Reporting" was under-covered in the Canadian media. This survey finding is consistent with information collected from our interviews, and also shows consistency with the high ranking that journalists gave (in Table 3.1) to a "lack of institutional resources" as a filter on the news. In addition, approximately 75% of respondents felt the "Social Causes of Crime" deserved more coverage. Respondents (74%) also strongly felt that the "Im-plications of Social Policies" needed more coverage.

Given our previous discussion of news filters, it is understandable that journalists would feel that these issues get short shrift. The issue here is so important that it bears repeating: investigating complex stories like the social causes of crime and the implications of social policies takes money and staff time that are, with some exceptions, in increasingly short supply in today's profit-obsessed, "downsized" newsroom.

In this context, there is a danger that such issues will eventually drop off the media agenda. By contrast, as one interviewed journalist put it, "easy stuff" is increasingly the order of the journalistic day.

This sentiment corresponds to arguments made by journalists in the U.S., cited by Peter Phillips and Project Censored. The media's increasing concern with the bottom line helps fuel a "growing plethora of junk-food news."[10] In addition to selling papers, "junk-food news is easy to produce...There is no digging for facts. You just grab a file photo and come up with a semi-clever phrase for the headline, such as "Mama Madonna or...Jacko Facing Custody Battle."[11]

Jean Otto of Denver's *Rocky Mountain News* argues that in such reports: "Nothing needs to be explained...These stories allow lots of lip-smacking and not much more."[12] One of the journalists we interviewed discussed the effects of a trend towards such stories in both the U.S. and Canada by noting the inadequate news coverage given to political scandals that require complex analysis: "The Whitewater or Iran-Contra scandals are examples of how not to run public life...[but] most of the mainstream media just bailed out of such stories because they are too complicated. They need a lot of background to be understandable."

By contrast, the Clinton/Lewinsky scandal was more easily convertible to junk-food news reporting styles and visual motifs.

Beyond stories about complex social and economic issues, approximately 73% of our respondents also felt that "Critical Coverage of Business" deserved more attention in Canadian newsrooms. We were struck by this finding in the survey, because it corresponds quite closely with findings from NewsWatch Canada's own research on blind spots in the Canadian media.

A substantial number of the Top Under-Reported Stories we've documented over the last five years (summarized in Chapter Five) have detailed unseemly aspects of the corporate world. While it was not unanimously recognized in our survey or interviews, many journalists are clearly aware of the constraints on this kind of reporting derived from working in an advertiser-dependent and generally pro-business corporate environment. Business is rarely approached as critically, for example, as government. In this sense, the "watch-dog" function of the press seems to be rather selective.

Our respondents suggest that most often the incentives to adopt a softer line with business than government are subtle. But in some instances, the pressures—legal, financial, or otherwise—that large corporations can exert on news organizations that dare to print damaging stories can be obvious and overt. This sort of pressure can range from a sternly worded letter of complaint to the threat of a multi-million-dollar lawsuit.

For example, one television journalist told us about a particularly nasty run-in with a major clothing manufacturer over a story detailing substandard working conditions in one of its Mexican sweatshops. When the manufacturer got wind that a news story was about to air on their practice of hiring underage workers and firing workers who became pregnant, they immediately threatened to sue for libel. Despite the threats, this news organization decided to run the story—partly because they had, according to a journalist close to the story, "the best legal advisors" in the business on staff.

Unfortunately, many other news organizations have cut their legal budgets in recent years and are accordingly loath to antagonize corporations that have the wherewithal to launch retaliatory lawsuits. A former newspaper editor in our survey made special mention of his "fear of those phone calls from PR people."

Finally, the responses of the journalists we surveyed tell an interesting and poignant story regarding the coverage extended to questions around national unity and the Quebec "Neverendum." Approximately 76% of our respondents agreed that the English language media consistently give short shrift to francophone perspectives on national unity. This tendency was also noted by a number of the journalists we interviewed.

One respondent summarized the problem by noting that "the Quebec referendum and the English-speaking media's complicity in the 'No' side" was a significant under-reported story in Canadian news media at the time: "Nobody raised questions about the English media having corporate support in chartering buses to ferry people to support the Montreal rally." By contrast, "in the interests of national unity...the Quebec media were being held to different standards."

At the same time, journalists in our survey were nearly as critical of the French-language media as the English-language media: 72% indicated that, in their view, the French language media do an equally poor job of covering anglophone perspectives on the national question. The journalists we surveyed thus agree with those political scientists who have been arguing for over 20 years that Canada's media have not done much to bridge the "two solitudes" in Canadian political and social life. By failing to extend coverage adequately across linguistic and cultural boundaries, the English and French language media arguably play a role in widening the gap.

We find it especially disquieting that fewer than half of our survey respondents (who overwhelmingly worked for English language media) claimed they felt informed enough about the media in Quebec (and by extension, Quebec society) to even venture an opinion on the amount of coverage it extends to anglophone views on national unity. If nothing else, the inability of a majority of our respondents to answer a question on the quality of French language media shows the extent to which linguistic isolationism continues to dominate the Canadian media today.

Perceived Areas of Over-Reporting

If our respondents felt that complex social issues, anglophone and francophone perspectives on national unity, and the dark side of big business were all under-covered, then which issues did they feel received entirely too much media attention? The clear winner, with about 73% claiming too much coverage, is "Sports.". In addition to sports, however, about one-third of our respondents felt that "Arts & Entertainment" and "Business & Investment" received too much coverage. This finding is interesting because it is precisely "feature" or "specialty" sections such as sports, entertainment and business that appear to be the most significant areas of newspaper growth.

One veteran reporter we interviewed emphasized a point that we've noted earlier in this chapter: the continued expansion of these specialty sections has drawn scarce resources away from "hard news." The popularity of features and specialty sections lies in their capacity to recruit advertising that is specifically targeted to a clearly-defined and economically desirable market segment. That is why the sports pages of many papers mix ads for baldness cures or strip clubs in with reportage—ads targeted at middle-aged male readers. It is also why ads for mutual fund investing, or inspirational marketing seminars, clutter the business pages. Thus, our veteran reporter concluded, "you have huge numbers of papers that have beefed these sections up, while few have beefed up the news section."

Finally, 63% of our respondents said that "Right-Wing Perspectives" (although it is harder nowadays to decide exactly what this means than it used to be) were over-covered in the Canadian media (second only to "Sports"), while over one-half (51%) felt that "Left-Wing Perspectives" were undercovered. How do we explain this? One possible interpretation might be that many of the journalists who responded to our survey are a left-leaning group. As such, they might be hypersensitive to the amount of coverage afforded to right-wing perspectives and see "bias" in patterns of under-reporting where others would not see it. The fact that our sample of journalists was self-selected may lend a degree of support to this interpretation.

Publicity around NewsWatch Canada's top-ten lists of under-reported stories in the mid-1990s, as well as discussion at Canadian Association of Journalists conferences, and the material posted on the NewsWatch web site, have made it clear to anyone interested that we share the progressive and reformist impulses of journalism's "watchdog" traditions. So it certainly is not inconceivable that our survey has attracted a disproportionate number of journalists with similar views.

An equally credible possibility, though, is that the journalists who responded to our survey are actually on to something: in short, that the media are indeed skewed toward right-wing perspectives in certain areas of coverage. One reporter we've discussed this with suggests that newspapers can actually accommodate a slight diversity of political viewpoints, but that these tend to be segregated into the paper's various sections. According to this reporter, it isn't completely unusual for left-leaning stories to find their way into weekend "review" or book review sections, and sometimes in coverage of culture, religion and family life. But, he added, such perspectives are almost never found in coverage of economic and social policy issues associated with provincial, federal and international politics.

Similarly, it is exceptionally rare to find left-leaning discussions or interpretations in the business or sports sections of any paper.

The suggestion here is that we need to think much more precisely about how and in what ways news media might manifest political or ideological biases. If it is simplistic to claim that "the media" in general are wholly skewed to the left or the right, we need to map out the different areas in media coverage where particular political perspectives are most likely to be clustered. NewsWatch Canada's own research into this question tends to reaffirm the complexity of the issue. We have found some suggestive evidence, for example (discussed in more detail in Chapter Six), that Canadian news media often do play up "liberal" perspectives on social and religious issues, such as abortion, while downplaying the views of cultural or religious conservatives.

At the same time, certain newspapers and periodicals—the *Toronto Sun* and *Alberta Report* come to mind—have made an effort to counter-balance such "liberal" coverage by self-consciously representing the views of the social and cultural right. On economic questions and related public policy issues, however, there appears to be a much narrower range of opinion in the mainstream news media.

In this respect, we believe that our own research at NewsWatch Canada lends a measure of support to the views of journalists reported in our survey. Three years of research on under-reported stories in Canadian media between 1993 and 1995 (discussed in greater detail in Chapter Five) lead us to conclude that left-leaning perspectives on economic issues, and critical analysis of Canadian business in general, really are under-represented in mainstream Canadian news media.

This conclusion is supported by other NewsWatch research, as well. For instance, one of the studies discussed in later chapters of this book found that the *Globe and Mail* published "right-wing" solutions to the problem of government debt far more than left-leaning solutions.

A colleague remarked that such findings are hardly surprising, given the *Globe and Mail's* up-market target readership. Still, the *Globe and Mail* does advertise itself as Canada's "national" newspaper and is well-positioned to play an influential role in national debates. So the paper arguably has important responsibilities in the provision of diverse perspectives on important issues. Furthermore, it doesn't seem very likely that the "liberal" or left-leaning perspectives on economic issues so rarely found in the *Globe and Mail* will be found in very many other mainstream newspapers, and especially in the *Globe and Mail's* new "national" market competitor, *The National Post*, owned by Conrad Black.

After all, Black is the publisher who has vowed to challenge what he (laughably, in our view) calls the "monolithically politically correct, left-wing, anti-U.S., socialist, feminist and envious" Canadian media. Given his control over nearly 60 percent of Canadian daily newspapers, Black's strongly felt political views don't augur well for counter-balancing the "right-wing" viewpoints that the journalists in our survey believe are over-represented in Canadian news media.

Even if media chain owners such as Mr. Black keep their distance from direct editorial intervention, the combined effects of institutional and market pressures on news management and journalistic work routines still act as notable filters in the production of news. The journalists we have surveyed and interviewed have acknowledged that these filters can lead to significant blind spots in the Canadian news agenda. Battered by cutbacks and layoffs, forced to do more with less in an environment where marketing demands have assumed increasing priority, Canadian journalists say they are less likely to cover complex issues, less likely to uncover corporate wrongdoing, and more likely to routinely reproduce the statements of politicians and bureaucrats, corporate officials, self-serving lobby groups, and professional spin doctors—the people best placed to turn out a regular supply of digestible news.

In this environment, those groups in society that can afford to invest substantially in "media relations" are able to command the media spotlight, get their voices heard, and have their interpretations of events popularized. The diverse and competing perspectives that we often see debated in news media typically involve tensions and disagreements between powerful interests— for example, between government and business. But the views of people in Canada who lack resources, or the views of groups that represent minority interests, are infrequently included in such debates.

One of the journalists we talked to put the matter succinctly: "It's tough for people who are unorganized to get coverage." And, if such people do get coverage, they often find that their story has already been filtered or framed by somebody else's spin doctor. The result is a system of news production in Canada that even journalists themselves agree is peppered with blind spots.

ENDNOTES

1. Journalists who agreed to be interviewed included:

Scott Anderson	Reporter, *Toronto Now*
David Bazay	CBC Ombudsman
Andrew Coyne	Columnist, *The Globe and Mail*
Alan Dever	Senior Producer, English Network TV's News Service
Jeffrey Dvorkin	Managing Editor and Chief Journalist, CBC National Radio News
Esther Enkin	Deputy Managing Editor, English Radio News
Jock Ferguson	Independent Reporter, formerly with Th*e Globe and Mail*
John Ferri	Weekend Editor, *The Toronto Star*
Pat Kellogg	Manager of Program Resources (Archive), Radio News
Bill Knott	Supervisor, CBC Radio News
Colin MacKenzie	Managing Editor, The *Globe and Mail*
Eric Malling	*W5,* CTV Television
Andrew Mitrovica	Investigative Field Producer, CTV Television
Rick Salutin	Columnist, Th*e Globe and Mail*
Philip Savage	Head of Radio/Audience Research, CBC Research Department
Shirley Sharzer	Retired, former Asst. Managing Editor, *The Globe and Mail*
Lorne Slotnick	Communications Guild Representative, Local 87
Sylvia Stead	National Editor, *The Globe and Mail*
David Studer	Executive Producer, "*The Fifth Estate,*" CBC
Dave Taylor	Producer, "A*nd Now the Details,*" CBC
Antonia Zerbisias	Columnist, *Toronto Star*

2. The survey was divided into three sections. The first part of the survey asked about journalists' personal and professional backgrounds (i.e. age, sex, media sector, media level, job type and years in the profession). The second set of questions asked about journalists' perceptions of media "filters." Newswatch researchers derived a list of 26 potential factors or filters based on reviews of academic literature and our own research on under-reported stories in the news (this research is discussed in Chapter Five). We asked journalists if they thought any of these filters led to the omission of significant news and invited them to categorize their responses on a fivepoint scale (Never, Rarely, Occasionally, Often, and Very Often). The third set of questions asked journalists to evaluate the amount of coverage given to 26 news categories (such as Significant Environmental Stories, Business and Investment, Youth Issues) using another fivepoint scale (e.g. Seriously UnderCovered, Somewhat UnderCovered, About Right, Somewhat OverCovered, Seriously OverCovered). Summaries and comments on this survey by Michele Green and Bob Hackett were published in *Media* (Summer 1998), pp. 21-22.

3 . This theme is echoed in the academic literature as well. See, as examples, Ben Bagdikian, *The Media Monopoly* (Boston, Beacon Press, 1997 ed.) Pp. 83-84; 163-168;, and Doug Underwood, "When MBA's Rule the Newsroom," *Columbia Journalism Review* (March/April, 1988), p. 26.

4. An excellent discussion of this issue in U.S. journalism can be found in Leon Sigal, "Sources Make the News," in R.K. Manoff and M. Schudson (eds.), *Reading the News* (New York: Pantheon, 1986), p. 25.

5. Mark Fishman, *Manufacturing the News* (Austin: University of Texas Press, 1980).

6. Leon Sigal, "Sources Make the News," p. 20.

7. For a useful entry into this literature, see the classic study of news values in U.S. journalism, by Herbert Gans, *Deciding What's News* (New York: Vintage Books, 1979).

8. On the role of drama as a guiding principle for news journalism see, e.g., Pamela Shoemaker and Stephen Reese, *Mediating the Message: Theories of Influences on Mass Media Content*, 2nd ed. (New York: Longman Press, 1996), pp. 114-15.

9. This point, noted frequently in our survey and interviews, is consistent with arguments made in other studies of news production. See, for example, Michael Parenti, *Inventing Reality: The Politics of the News Media* (New York: St. Martins Press, 1986), p. 44; and Danny Schecter, *The More You Watch the Less You Know* (New York: Seven Stories Press, 1997).

10. This quote comes from U.S. Project Censored founder, Carl Jensen, in Peter Phillips & Project Censored, *Censored 1997: The News that Didn't Make the News* (New York: Seven Stories Press, 1997), p. 134.

11. Phillips and Project Censored, *Censored 1997*, p. 134.

12. Cited in Phillips and Project Censored, *Censored 1997*, p. 134.

Chapter Four

The Views of Interest Groups

People involved with various interest groups and advocacy organizations are typically the most vocal critics of news media. This tension shouldn't be surprising. Interest groups often resent having to continually beg and cajole journalists for publicity and favourable coverage. As Lawrence Wallack, an American media professor and public health advocate, has argued, advocacy groups depend on the media to promote their agenda to the public, but at the same time are often deeply dissatisfied with how they are portrayed in the news.[1]

Anyone who has been interviewed by the media can relate to the advocate's typical complaint: "I gave a 30-minute interview. They used five seconds of it, and I looked like an idiot!" It doesn't take too many experiences like that to cultivate a negative impression of reporters. So it's no surprise that advocate groups have churned out tome after tome on "how to handle the media," all in the hope of attracting and shaping coverage.

Even more established organizations and government agencies tend to view the media with a mix of envy and suspicion. For example, Canadian sociologist Richard Ericson has noted how police attempt to use the media to present the criminal justice system in a positive light, as the "thin blue line between order and chaos." But, at the same time, the police constantly fear negative publicity. They regard most reporters (other than the most familiar "police beat" scribes) with great suspicion, and they resent the intrusion of the media spotlight into ongoing investigations.[2]

In this respect the police are typical of many established organizations and agencies for whom continual media coverage is a mixed blessing. When it's flattering, it can lend an image of effectiveness and legitimacy. But when it exposes corruption and inefficiency, media coverage can undermine public confidence and spark an institutional crisis.

By the same token, journalists often have a mixed view of the influence of interest groups. For example, in the survey we discussed in the last chapter, slightly less than half of the surveyed journalists suggested that interest groups were responsible for filtering the news in significant ways. But those journalists who did acknowledge interest group influence often made a compelling case for the argument that it is precisely interest group sources—especially powerful, established, institutionalized sources—that control what becomes news on a daily basis. This is an argument that we have noted earlier, one that comes up again and again in the scholarly literature on the production of news, especially in the United States.

"The first fact of American journalism," writes Walter Karp, a media critic and former editor of *Harper's* magazine, "is its overwhelming dependence on sources, mostly official, usually powerful."[3] Karp argues that what the U.S. public views as "the news" is really just a summary of reports emanating from a handful of "great venues of power and policy—Defense, State, Justice, Central Intelligence, FBI, and so on"—which "form the daily beats of small claques of Washington reporters."[4]

Within these institutions, according to *Barron*'s reporter Alan Abelson, the reporter's job mostly entails "collecting handouts from those informational soup kitchens."[5]

There is also evidence—some of which we touched on in the last chapter—that, when reporters do stray consistently or fundamentally from powerful sources' version of events, the repercussions can come fast and furious. This "flak," as Noam Chomsky and Edward Herman have termed it, can run the gamut from something as innocuous as a tersely worded letter from an unhappy advocacy group, to libel suits, and even more chilling examples of official intimidation and retribution.[6]

For instance, when former *New York Times* journalist David Halberstam's stories on the Vietnam War angered the Kennedy administration, White House hacks spread rumours that Halberstam "was a Saigon bar hopper who had never been to the front."[7]

A few years later, after *CBS Nightly News* ran a lengthy piece on the Watergate scandal, the Nixon administration put in a call to CBS president Bill Paley, telling him that, if the network did not kill a scheduled follow-up piece on the scandal, CBS would be stripped of its five lucrative TV stations.[8]

This being said, we shouldn't exaggerate the tensions between sources and reporters. Much of the time, sources and reporters work together and even develop lasting personal friendships. Still, even in the best of relationships, sources and reporters can find themselves at odds over a particular story or a particular ideological spin or angle.

On the one hand, journalists need stories that are *newsworthy*, but this often runs them afoul of groups representing particular ideological perspectives. Interest groups, on the other hand, scramble to obtain *favourable* publicity and try to manage the portrayal of their organizations in the media. In this way, much of the daily news is the result of a continual negotiation for control between reporters and their sources over what issues get covered and how the issues are framed.[9] Some hurt feelings are bound to pop up in such a politically charged and emotional relationship.

When we have asked about such things, journalists have often indicated that interest group complaints come with the job. Despite some notable exceptions, most of the journalists in the interviews and survey discussed earlier seemed quite unconcerned by the criticisms levelled at them by interest groups, usually dismissing them as emotional outbursts from self-serving organizations with a political axe to grind. A number of journalists expressed relief that they are criticized from "both sides" of the ideological spectrum. As one journalist told us, "The fact that no one is happy with us is a clear indication that we are doing a good job!"

But is this necessarily true? What, in fact, are the criticisms that different interest groups typically level at journalists? Does the fact that these criticisms come from groups with different political perspectives absolve journalists from allegations of bias? Do the criticisms, in effect, "cancel each other out?" In order to provide some preliminary answers to these questions we surveyed 300 interest groups and organizations in 1995. This survey had three broad objectives:[10]

1. To broaden our search for potential blind spots in the news agenda, as a basis for further research.

2. To enable a comparison of journalists' perceptions of the news agenda with those of some of their sources—specifically, the interest groups and institutions that frequently provide the media with information and analysis.

3. To see if different types of interest groups—for example, "advocacy" versus "establishment" groups—have differing perspectives on the media.

We wanted to survey relatively well-institutionalized groups representing conservative viewpoints or dominant political and economic interests (like government, business, and professional groups). But we also wanted to survey non-profit and non-governmental advocacy groups that arguably reflect subordinate and/or "progressive" positions (including labour, environmental, anti-poverty, and social welfare organizations). Our goal was to achieve an approximate balance between establishment and advocacy groups.[11] In the end, we identified and surveyed 145 groups from the establishment camp and 155 groups representing advocacy positions.

Once we derived our list of advocacy and establishment groups, we mailed each group a questionnaire that included some preliminary information about NewsWatch Canada and its search for "blind spots" in the media. Representatives of each group were then invited to answer a series of questions inquiring about their perceptions of important blind spots in the media, why the media may tend to ignore certain issues, and how well the media cover issues and perspectives relevant to their own organization. In addition, we asked interest groups to offer their views on the main purposes of news media in Canada and to assess how well the media perform in meeting these purposes.[12]

Ultimately, the survey yielded 89 responses (a 30% response rate) which were coded and categorized for summary purposes and for comparison with responses from the survey of journalists discussed in the last chapter. Again, like our survey of journalists, this sample of interest groups is not statistically representative, so the results should be regarded as exploratory. We suspected, for example, that groups that felt particularly marginalized or aggrieved— groups with an axe to grind—might be more likely to complete the questionnaire than more mainstream groups and organizations. This suspicion was borne out by the fact that we received nearly twice as many completed questionnaires from advocacy groups than establishment groups. Still, in the absence of more systematic research on the topic, the findings of the survey offer a useful preliminary understanding of interest group perceptions of media blind spots and news filters.

INTEREST GROUPS ON BLIND SPOTS IN THE CANADIAN MEDIA

What issues do interest group representatives think get routinely under-reported by the Canadian news industry? Unlike the questionnaire we used to survey journalists, our interest group survey employed "open-ended" questions that allowed for detailed and multiple responses.[13] For example, part of the first question in the survey asked respondents to list three issues or stories of significance that the media tend to ignore. The most frequently mentioned of these issues and stories are listed in Table 4.1.

First, 26% of our interest group respondents felt that "social implications of economic policies" deserved more coverage, making this the most frequently cited blind spot in the survey (along with "positive stories"). There was also a notable consistency on this category between the views of establishment and advocacy groups. On the advocacy side, one interest group respondent emphasized that the media should do a better job in covering "the ways tax policies and other mechanisms...that favour the corporate élite are

TABLE 4.1

INTEREST GROUP PERCEPTIONS OF BLIND SPOTS

(Percentage Response)

Blind Spot Category	Total (n = 89)	Estab. (n = 30)	Adv. (n = 59)
Social implications of economic policies	25.8	26.7	25.4
"Positive" stories	25.8	23.3	27.1
Challenges to dominant or official powers	19.1	13.3	22.0
International relations	14.6	16.7	13.6
Role of religion in Canadian life	13.5	0.0	20.3
Ethnic and race issues	12.4	6.7	15.3
Women's issues	6.7	3.3	8.5
Environmental issues	6.7	6.7	6.7
Justice/human rights issues	6.7	10.0	5.1
Health issues	5.6	0.0	8.5
Canadian nationalism	5.6	0.0	8.5
Education issues	4.5	3.3	5.1
Defense/security issues	4.5	10.0	1.7
Investigative reporting in general	3.4	0.0	5.1
Objective reporting in general	3.4	10.0	0.0
Decline of political institutions/processes	3.4	0.0	1.7
Ethical issues	3.4	0.0	5.1
Science and technology issues	3.4	6.7	1.7

Percentages total over 100, as multiple responses were permitted.

producing and maintaining a deeply divisive class structure in society." This was a perspective shared by many other respondents, some of whom encouraged the media to focus more attention on, for example, "human interest stories of how government cutbacks" affect "ordinary people." Representatives of more socially conservative groups also wanted the media to focus attention on the social implications of economic policies; however, these groups seemed more concerned with the "moral decay of society" and "the links between welfare policies...and crime" than with the unravelling of Canada's social safety net.

If our interest group respondents wanted to hear more about the social implications of social and economic policies, they claimed they wanted to hear more "good news" as well. And, once more, on this issue, establishment and advocacy organizations seemed to be in general agreement. Just over a quarter (26%) of all respondents pointed to the absence of positive news in the media, arguing that the lack of coverage afforded to social and political "success stories" reinforced a pervasive sense of negativity in Canadian public life.

In their critique of this negativity, some respondents focused on the lack of positive news in general, and argued that the media should do more to emphasize such general themes as "Canadian spirit, uniqueness, [and] achievements." However, most respondents seemed particularly (and perhaps not surprisingly) concerned about the lack of positive coverage afforded to their own issue or perspective. The list below, gleaned from the survey, illustrates the point nicely. What constitutes "good news" about Canada typically depends upon your particular point of view:

FROM TWO PRO-BUSINESS THINK TANKS

"...more coverage of business contributions of time and money to non-profit organizations;" and "...positive accomplishments of business as a result of restructuring, cost control, etc."

FROM A SENIOR CITIZENS GROUP

"...positive portrayals of seniors."

FROM TWO ANTI-RACISM GROUPS

"Stories of successful Aboriginal people"; and "[the] positive and significant contributions many Jamaican immigrants are making to Canadian society."

In addition to wanting more good news, our interest group respondents also frequently cited challenges to dominant or official powers as an important omission in the news agenda. This was particularly true for advocacy groups, where 22% listed the absence of stories challenging dominant or official powers as a media blind spot (compared with 13% from the more establishment groups). Thus, one respondent from a left-leaning advocacy group wrote that the media too often kowtow to big business and therefore intentionally conceal "the fact that we are not governed by democratically elected governments, but by banks and multinationals."

Other respondents talked darkly of "the conspiracy of capitalism" and wanted the media to focus more on "the growing disparity between the few rich and the increasing masses of the poor."

Conversely, a few interest groups turned their ire not toward big business, but toward the perceived misdeeds of the federal government. For example, one respondent complained about "the lack of objective coverage and critical scrutiny of the federal Liberal government." Another respondent stated his beliefs even more forcefully: "The taint of corruption and venality is common throughout the country at every level of government."

In a somewhat similar vein, the exploits of international associations also attracted attention by groups that felt the media should devote more coverage to "the role of international organizations (like the World Bank, World Trade Organization, and [the] International Monetary Fund) in governing the global economy."

Insufficient media coverage of international relations in general was the fourth ranked blind spot identified by interest groups and, on this point, there was a high level of agreement between advocacy and establishment groups.

Finally, a number of interest group representatives in the sample expressed dissatisfaction with the amount of coverage extended to social and cultural issues. For example, 22% of advocacy group representatives identified coverage of religious issues as a significant blind spot in Canadian media coverage, although this issue wasn't mentioned by any of the establishment groups in the sample. This is explainable by the fact that a number of the advocacy groups in our sample had strong ties to broader religious organizations, whereas the establishment groups in the sample tended to be more secular.

One advocacy group commentator captured the sentiment of several other groups by arguing that religion is "a great source of hope and strength" for millions of Canadians, yet the media "only cover religion if it involves sex and violence."

Other groups also picked up on this theme of sensationalism and negativity, and took the media to task for offering one-sided or slanted coverage of Canada's visible minorities. As one anti-racism representative wryly quipped, it would be nice for the media to cover "crimes not committed by ethnic peoples" every once in a while.

Advocacy groups took the lead in their identification of ethnicity/race issues (ranked 6th), and women's issues (ranked 7th) as media blind spots, as well as issues pertaining to health (ranked 10th) and national identity (11th). Surprisingly, environmental issues were fairly far down the list of interest groups' blind spots (ranked 8th), although the issue tended to be mentioned in equal proportion by both establishment and advocacy groups. By contrast, establishment groups showed a preference for justice and human rights issues (ranked 9th) and, further down the list, for defense and security, and problems of objective reporting.

In general, advocacy groups were more likely to identify challenges to dominant or official powers, equity, and "identity" issues as significant blind spots in the news, whereas establishment groups were somewhat more likely to believe that issues around justice, policing, victim's rights, defense and security deserved more coverage.

How do these interest group perceptions of blind spots in the Canadian news agenda compare to views expressed in the survey of Canadian journalists that was discussed in the previous chapter? Our research suggests some intriguing points of agreement between the views of journalists and those of the interest groups. For example, both the interest groups and the journalists that we studied rated the social implications of social and economic policies quite highly as an important yet undercovered topic in the news.

Interest groups—especially the advocacy groups in the sample—also cited "challenges to dominant or official powers" as one of the leading under-covered issues, a finding that may correspond loosely to the significant number of journalists who suggested that "critical coverage of business" was under-reported in the daily news.

Still, for the most part, journalists and their sources failed to see eye to eye regarding the most important blind spots in the Canadian news media. For instance, while over 80% of journalists we surveyed felt that "investigative reporting" deserved more play in the media, this blind spot barely registered a blip among our interest group respondents (logging in at under 4%!).

Journalists and interest groups also differed in their feelings about the amount of coverage extended to social and cultural issues. Religion, ethnicity, and women's issues all ranked in the top ten of under-covered stories in our interest group survey, yet journalists ranked these issues lower (13th, 16th and 19th respectively).

Finally, while the lack of "positive news" failed to upset many of our journalist respondents, interest groups pointed time and again to the pervasive negativity in the news and the lack of coverage afforded "success stories" and the "good works" evident in social and public life.

INTEREST GROUPS ON NEWS FILTERS

We also asked interest groups to speculate on *why* the media tend to ignore particular issues. In short, we wanted interest group representatives to list their perceptions of those factors in the news production process that act to filter the news. Table 4.2 displays responses to this question, grouped into broad categories derived from the survey coding.

TABLE 4.2

INTEREST GROUP PRCEPTIONS OF NEWS FILTERS

Filter Category	Totals (%) (n=89)	Establishment Groups (%) (n=30)	Advocacy Groups (%) (n=59)
Commercialism of the Media	61.8	63.3	61.0
News Values	60.7	63.3	59.3
News Workers and Work Routines	52.8	53.3	52.5
Dominant Powers and Beliefs	41.6	30.0	47.5
Bias	30.3	36.7	27.1

Percentages total over 100, as multiple responses were permitted.

We were struck by the fact that comparable percentages of both advocacy and establishment groups suggested that the *commercialism of the news industry*—that is, the corporate control of news outlets, and the accelerating thirst for audiences, advertisers, and profit—acted as an important filter on the news (61% and 63%, respectively). In noting the commercialism of news, comments from interest group representatives often echoed a concern common among contemporary media critics: the concern that corporations place the bottom line ahead of more intangible values such as "democracy" and "public service."

One respondent made the point forcefully: "Corporate control of major media decides what is news." Most other respondents were more cautious, but there was widespread agreement that, in today's media environment, "selling is more important than telling." As a result, important but less sensational issues—especially issues "which don't attract advertising revenue" are routinely downplayed or ignored.

Because the "media follow the money," and because attention to complicated social and economic issues" rarely generates profits," our respondents told us that the Canadian media seem more driven by the demands of marketing than by anything else. On this point, interest group representatives in our survey echo the views of U.S. media critic Doug Underwood, who argues that many corporate-controlled and profit-obsessed newspapers simply produce a "slick, pre-planned news product" that "gives the feel of a newspaper that doesn't really know what's going on in the community." Such papers brim with the light-hearted material advertisers flock to, including "food sections and special how-to sections—how to manage your personal finances, say, or how to repair your car."[14]

In addition, according to many of the respondents in our interest group survey, today's marketing imperatives seem directly related to the media's well-known penchant for "sensational" or "controversial" stories. Accordingly, the media's *news values*—that is, the media's predisposition to run stories long on style and drama but short on substance and significance—was also cited by a majority of interest groups as a "filter" on the Canadian news agenda (logging in at 61%).

This drive to maximize audiences and advertising dollars, according to many of our respondents, leads the news media into a frenetic "search for spectacular controversies" and stories that are "sexy and sensational enough to sell." As a result, important and complex political and social issues (which cannot be "easily grasped in the news bite style" of contemporary news outlets) are consistently eschewed in favor of "hot" and "entertaining" events such as the Paul Bernado trial and Bill Clinton's latest sex scandal.

Interestingly, many respondents also tied the media's slide into sensationalism to their inability to cover "positive" stories or "good news."

"The media," one respondent quipped, are "more interested in smut, problems, [and] destroying leaders than in reporting positive events." Why is this? Because, in the words of one respondent, "good news makes lousy copy [but] death sells papers."

This perception of an expanding obsession with "smut" in contemporary media strikes a chord with many media critics, who also decry the slide into "junk-food" news at the expense of ostensibly more serious local, national, and international coverage. Often, this complaint about "sensationalism" and "junk-food news" is overdone. We have already noted that "junk-food news" has a long history in North American journalism, and certainly the desire to attract large audiences with cheap and easy-to-produce rumour and sensation is nothing new. All the same, many thoughtful media critics, while recognizing that "junk-food" has always been a staple in the news diet, have nonetheless noticed a recent acceleration in the media's reliance on "hot button" stories, especially in the case of television news.

There was a time, not so long ago, when major television networks simply assumed that their news divisions would operate as a loss. News divisions were allowed to lose money primarily because a strong news division was a badge of prestige for media owners and, perhaps more importantly, because a commitment to "public service" (in the form of strong news divisions) kept national regulators like the FCC in the U.S. and the CRTC in Canada off owners' backs. But, over the past decade or so, television news divisions have increasingly fallen sway to the imperatives of marketing and direct profitability. For example, in their book *The Global Media*, Edward Herman and Robert McChesney note how media empires such as Disney and Time Warner have informed their news divisions (e.g., ABC News and CNN in the U.S.) that they, like any other part of the company, are expected to turn a profit.[15]

In the era of satellite television, cable TV, and online entertainment, this means that news divisions have been abruptly tossed into an already frenzied competition for media audiences. As a result, network news executives now routinely exhort reporters to play up the dramatic and emotional dimensions of their news stories.

Even in its formative years as a mass medium, network news sought to exploit television's capacity for dramatic narrative. "Every news story," counselled a memo sent to NBC news staffers in 1963, should "...display the attributes of fiction, of drama. It should have structure and conflict, problem and denouement, rising action and falling action, a beginning, a middle, and an end. These are not only the essentials of drama; they are the essentials of narrative."[16]

The problem is that some stories, especially stories long on numbers and analysis but short on "sex appeal," don't fit neatly into a dramatic narrative. As a result, these are the stories most likely to be left on the metaphorical cutting room floor.

More than half of the interest group representatives in our survey (53%) also argued that the individual character and professional routines of Canadian *news workers* influence what gets covered and what gets ignored. On this point there was also a general agreement between establishment and advocacy groups. We were struck here by the number of interest group representatives whose comments showed a significant lack of respect for the press. For example, several respondents argued that the "ignorance" and "laziness" of journalists and editors is a major factor that leads them to ignore important but undercovered issues. Others complained that the media are "collectively uninformed;" they "lack a broad base of integrated information," and "don't understand the issues."

Similarly, in a few instances, journalists were accused of being too "apathetic" to do the homework necessary to "acquire background [on] various issues." The result—from the perspective of many interest groups—is news coverage that either ignores complex stories completely or covers them in a superficial way.

In journalists' defense, it should be said that interest groups are nothing if not passionate about their particular social or political issue. Therefore, it is likely that some of this vitriolic criticism stems from the frustration many interest groups experience with the kind of coverage (or, even worse, the utter lack of coverage) the media extend to issues close to their hearts. Regardless, it is safe to say that many interest groups are not at all pleased with the professional practices and routines of many Canadian journalists.

Just over 40% of our interest group respondents also pointed to the influences that powerful social groups and dominant beliefs exert on the Canadian news agenda. This news filter was cited by just a third of the establishment groups (30%) and, not surprisingly, by nearly half of the advocacy groups (47%). On the advocacy side in particular, several respondents told us that they perceived a subtle "bias toward reporting on people with power." Most notably, there was a suggestion that the national media seem "too close to politicians" and often simply preach "on their behalf."

This perceived tendency for the media to stick closely to official or élite sources was identified by a number of interest groups as a reason why certain issues never receive the coverage they deserve. If "no prominent public figures" bring an issue to the media's attention, we were told, then that issue will drop off the media's radar screen. What also disturbed one group in particular was what it saw as many journalists' "reluctance to irritate 'key' or 'inside' sources" for fear of endangering "cozy 'inside' relationships." As a result, stories that might offend the powerful or the élite are more likely to fall through the cracks of the news agenda.

No less an authority on press manipulation than former U.S. president Lyndon Johnson would have agreed with many of our interest group respondents on this point. "Reporters are puppets," he once said. "They simply respond to the pull of the most powerful strings."[17]

In addition, interest group respondents also pointed to the subtle influence of pervasive cultural beliefs in determining what gets covered and what gets ignored. An example from the academic literature helps to clarify what we mean by "pervasive cultural beliefs." In his studies of the U.S. media over the years, Daniel Hallin has persuasively argued that "the journalist's role is to serve as an advocate or celebrant of consensual values," including the deeply held view that, if you work hard and play by the rules, anyone in America can "get ahead" in life. Stories that contradict this "common sense," stories that hint that equality of opportunity may be a myth we like to tell ourselves, are therefore much less likely to be covered; they seem too "ideological" or "out there" to merit serious attention.[18]

Many of our interest groups offered comparable arguments. For example, we received numerous claims that journalists are afraid of going out on a limb on an issue that contradicts received cultural wisdom about the social and political world. This fear of getting too far ahead of public opinion translates, for some respondents, into a widespread "distrust of 'unofficial' sources" or those advocacy organizations outside the media's comfort zone.

Many of our respondents argued that "fringe" issues or stories that "challenge conventional wisdom" are therefore ignored because journalists and editors are "afraid to tackle issues that are not already widely accepted."

Finally, less than one-third of the interest groups in our total sample (30%) identified *bias*—the conscious attempt to promote a particular political agenda—as a filter that limits news coverage of key issues and events. The majority of interest group respondents adopted a more complex perspective on the question of news filters. It is worth noting, however, that there was an approximately 10% difference in the identification of bias as a news filter between establishment and advocacy groups.

Interestingly, establishment groups were more inclined to see outright bias in reporting than advocacy groups. Indeed, several representatives of establishment groups articulated variations of the "left-liberal" media thesis that we have discussed in earlier chapters. One respondent stated graphically that the most significant filter in the news is the "left-of-centre slant" of media workers who, "as products of the 1960s cultural revolution," falsely project their leftist leanings as the "norm of Canadians."

Another respondent argued that journalists today are on balance "uninformed and vulnerable to trendy left-wing opinion."

By contrast, advocacy groups that identified "bias" as a problem typically took the opposite view, suggesting that the media are in fact biased to the political right rather than the left. Thus, one respondent claimed that important issues go uncovered by the media because "the media gravitate to the clear, simple message of the right" and thus frame "human rights" as having a "lower priority than the bond market."

Another advocacy group respondent argued that "corporate ownership... [of the press]...translates into like-minded staff" generally biased toward conservative views. In another instance, an advocacy group respondent suggested that pressures from advertisers, corporate owners, and like-minded editors create an environment where conservative world views take on the aura of journalistic "common sense."

For our part, we agree with the majority of interest group respondents who opted for a more complex understanding of bias in the media. It is simplistic merely to point one's finger and accuse reporters or media organizations of being unambiguously biased towards "a left-liberal" or "conservative" world view.

One final comment about interest group perception of filters. Once again, interest group perceptions of news filters pose an interesting contrast to those of the journalists we surveyed. For example, we noted earlier how journalists were most likely to identify a general lack of organizational resources as a significant news filter, implying that, if they were given more time, space, and money, they could cover some of the issues that otherwise fall into a blind spot.

Interest group respondents, however, barely mentioned such technical or organizational constraints, and for the most part seemed far less concerned about the ins and outs of the daily media grind. Instead, interest groups were most likely to identify systematic filters—such as commercialism and news values—that have more to do with entrenched and institutionalized practices and ideologies than with a mere lack of resources.

According to a majority of our interest group respondents, the news media's commercial imperative to attract audiences and advertisers—with an accompanying thirst for drama, sensation, and conflict—are the most significant filters that lead to blind spots in the news.

LEVELS OF INTEREST GROUP SATISFACTION WITH THE MEDIA

In addition to discovering interest groups' perceptions of news filters and blind spots, we also wanted to hear what they felt about the news media's coverage of particular issues, as well as interest groups' more general evaluation of the Canadian news media's performance as a whole. First, we asked interest groups, "In terms of both quantity and quality, how would you rate media coverage of the issues and perspectives of greatest concern to your own organization?" NewsWatch researchers then coded the responses according to a five-point "satisfaction" scale.[19] Responses to this question are presented in Table 4.3.

TABLE 4.3

SATISFACTION WITH MEDIA COVERAGE OF SPECIFIC ISSUES

Level of Satisfaction	Total (n = 89)	Estab. (n = 30)	Adv. (n = 59)
Unqualified Satisfaction	2.2	3.3	1.7
Qualified Satisfaction	18.0	26.7	13.6
Neutral/Mixed	12.4	13.3	11.9
Qualified Dissatisfaction	12.4	10.0	13.6
Unqualified Dissatisfaction	53.9	46.7	57.6
No Response	1.1	—	1.7
Total	100.0	100.0	100.1

Percentages may not total 100, due to rounding errors.

Criticizing the media is in vogue these days, so we weren't surprised to find that a large majority of our interest group respondents expressed a high level of dissatisfaction with the news media's coverage of their own particular issue or perspective. Next in frequency (but a long second to unqualified dissatisfaction) was qualified satisfaction, followed closely by qualified dissatisfaction and neutral/mixed responses. Overall, 67% of respondents expressed some level of dissatisfaction, while only a meager 20% expressed satisfaction of any sort with the media coverage extended to their issue.

While some respondents had praise for a few specific reporters or news outlets, for the most part interest group representatives agreed with one respondent who adamantly claimed that media coverage of specific issues was "poor on all accounts." Many respondents objected both to the rarity of coverage (e.g., "our concerns are rarely covered unless there is a scandal") and to the overall quality and detail of coverage if the media do take notice.

News coverage of interest groups' issues was said to be "generally unbalanced, often out of context, and superficial." One respondent singled out such television "news magazine" programs as *W5* and *The Fifth Estate* for particular criticism, claiming that these shows "begin with a premise and only use footage that supports that premise." The news, in short, always looks "for an 'angle,' but life is not about angles."

Our next question asked interest groups to set aside their concern for their own issue and rate the performance of the news media as a whole. We again coded their responses according to a five-point satisfaction scale. Once more, as Table 4.4 indicates, a large majority of respondents expressed unqualified dissatisfaction. Mixed or neutral responses were expressed with the next greatest frequency (but again logged in as a distant second), followed by qualified dissatisfaction and qualified satisfaction.

In the end, almost two-thirds of our interest group respondents expressed at least some amount of dissatisfaction with the media's performance as a whole, while only 18% partly or wholly approved of the status quo of the Canadian news media. Some of their written comments were scathing. One respondent summed up the media's general performance with one word: "terrible!" Other respondents were more specific. One group, for example, argued that "the emphasis is on sensationalism, entertaining, and money-making—to heck with the facts...even serious journalists arrive on your doorstep with the story already written in their minds."

Another group was so disgusted with the perceived commercialism of the media, the "sell papers at all costs" ethic, that, when asked to rate the general performance of the media, it simply wrote: "ask their accountants!"

Earlier, in Table 4.3 you can see a slight difference in levels of satisfaction about media coverage of specific issues between establishment and advocacy groups. Establishment groups were somewhat more likely to express "qualified satisfaction" with media coverage of their issues than advocacy groups. This pattern continues in the results displayed in Table 4.4. A majority of interest groups in the sample expressed dissatisfaction with media coverage in general, but advocacy groups were measurably more dissatisfied than their establishment counterparts. For example, 66% of advocacy groups ex-

TABLE 4.4
SATISFACTION WITH MEDIA'S OVERALL PERFORMANCE

Total Level of Satisfaction	Estab. (n = 89)	Adv. (n = 30)	(n = 59)
Unqualified Satisfaction	5.6	3.3	6.8
Qualified Satisfaction	12.4	20.0	8.5
Neutral/Mixed	16.9	23.3	13.6
Qualified Dissatisfaction	14.6	16.7	13.6
Unqualified Dissatisfaction	47.2	36.7	52.5
No Response	3.4	–	5.1
	100.1	100.0	100.1

Percentages may not total 100, due to rounding errors.

pressed "unqualified" or "qualified" dissatisfaction, while 53% of establishment groups registered such displeasure.

Why might this be the case? Within the general pattern of dissatisfaction with news media indicated by interest groups, why are advocacy groups apparently more dissatisfied than establishment groups? One reason for the lower level of discontent expressed by establishment groups may lie in their higher level of routine access to the media. As we argued in earlier chapters, deadline pressures and a scarcity of resources often force reporters to rely heavily on institutionalized and readily-available sources for information.

This is a role that establishment groups, especially well-funded think tanks and powerful government agencies, can play to perfection. With their large budgets, legions of PR staff, and the air of "authority" that comes with being a government agency or a respected institution, establishment groups can become an almost indispensable source of information for harried journalists.

Their ability to become an "indispensable source" for reporters works to the advantage of establishment groups in two ways. First, they gain regular access to reporters and are thus in a better position to shape the media's portrayal of their agency or issue. Second, they can exert more control over the journalists who depend on access to their organization for a steady supply of quotes and information. As New York Times columnist Tom Wicker once said, "establishment disapproval" in response to unfavourable coverage can lead to the dreaded "establishment lash," including lost access, complaints to editors and publishers, and leaks to competitors.[20]

Given this enhanced ability to both command coverage and shape the portrayal of their organization, it is perhaps not surprising that establishment groups express more satisfaction with the media's overall performance.

In contrast, advocacy groups can neither command coverage nor effectively shape the media's portrayal of their organization or issue. Year after year of begging reporters for attention—and then often being disappointed with the coverage that results from these efforts—can build up a lot of frustration and dissatisfaction. The advocacy groups we talked to, in fact, often seemed frustrated by their inability to become an "official" or "élite" source for information-starved reporters. They talked of editors "satisfied with the status quo" and of reporters who are unfairly "biased toward...people with power." They argued that the media were fearful of "new or 'alternative' ideas." And they spoke of the difficulty in attracting attention to "issues...on the fringe," especially when editors and reporters have an almost innate distrust of "unofficial sources." All in all, you would expect advocacy groups to express less satisfaction with what seems to be a somewhat distant and even hostile news industry. And, indeed, this is exactly what we found.

INTEREST GROUPS' RECOMMENDATIONS FOR THE CANADIAN NEWS MEDIA

Our last question in the survey asked interest groups to think more generally about what, in and ideal world, *ought* to be the main purpose of function of the news media in Canadian society? We gave our interest group respondents wide latitude to come up with their own recommendations, which we subsequently corralled into six broad categories. Response rates for each category are presented in Table 4.5.

TABLE 4.5
PRESCRIBED ROLE FOR NEWS MEDIA IN CANADIAN SOCIETY

Total Level of Satisfaction	Estab. (n = 89)	Adv. (n = 30)	(n = 59)
Mirror	62.9	73.3	57.6
Facilitate Public Sphere	36.0	36.7	36.0
Advocate	14.6	6.7	18.6
Educate	13.5	16.7	11.9
Analyze	10.1	16.7	6.8
Watchdog	5.6	13.3	1.7

Percentages total more than 100, as multiple responses were permitted.

The data presented in Table 4.5 suggest that interest groups most frequently commented that the media should serve ideally as *an objective mirror* to a wide range of social events and issues. Many respondents, for example, argued that the media should "dispassionately inform Canadians" and militantly "avoid any hint of...bias." Along these lines, one interest group told us that the news media should provide "objective, unbiased, and accurate information, rather than propagandizing or taking sides." The media's primary task is to provide people "with sufficient information so that they can make informed decisions."

Still, once again, different groups had their own opinion of what "being informed" was all about. For example, one group argued that the media should provide "accurate news to the people of Canada, [thereby] making them aware of how fortunate they are [to be] living in this great country." Other groups, however, felt that providing "accurate information" would instead inform the public about the failings of Canadian society, particularly regarding "the in-justices and inequities" in Canadian political and judicial institutions.

After "mirror" functions, our interest group respondents argued that the media should act as a *"public sphere"*—that is, the media should take a more active role in facilitating public dialogue, representing diverse opinions, and providing background for decision-making processes. Respondents whose comments were coded in this category expressed a desire for the media to provide "a public forum for policy debates," with the goal of cultivating an informed public discussion of political issues.

A number of respondents also argued that, in constructing this public forum, the media should take great pains to "represent the variety of political life in Canada" by giving "a voice to...marginalized segments of our society." In the end, these respondents hoped that this reorganization of the media's role in society would provide for "communication and dialogue involving people affected by societal conditions" and would allow citizens to hear "a wide range of opinions, information, and critiques."

A few interest group respondents (15%) also felt that the media should fulfill an *advocacy* function (such as promoting social justice and examining social and moral values), and a similar percentage (14%) emphasized an *educational* function (i.e., raising public awareness and encouraging critical thinking). Interestingly, only a small minority of interest groups (10%) argued that the media ought to fulfill an *analytical* purpose (i.e., interpreting events) or the traditional investigative *watchdog* function (6%) so celebrated by many of our journalist respondents.

We were struck by the fact that a majority of both establishment and advocacy groups recommended that the media perform the function of a dis-passionate mirror to society, although establishment groups were measurably more enthusiastic about this ideal of objectivity than their advocacy counter-parts (73% as compared to 58%). In addition, a nearly identical minority in both camps (37% and 36%) argued that the media should take on a more positive or active "public forum" role within Canadian society.

The strength of this minority position indicates an intriguing contradiction or split within both establishment and advocacy groups. The view that media should play an active role as a "public forum" (as embodied in the recent "public journalism" movement) implicitly challenges traditional understandings of detachment and objectivity in the media—the very ideals embodied by the "mirror" function. So it would seem that, while the majority of interest groups want the media to perform its traditional "objective" role in

Canadian society (though clearly they want the media to perform this role more effectively), a substantial number of respondents from both the establishment and advocacy groups would like to challenge the media to take on a more self-consciously active "public" role in Canadian public life.

Finally, Table 4.5 also provides another potential hint regarding why advocacy groups are, on the whole, somewhat more dissatisfied with the media than their establishment counterparts. Advocacy groups were almost three times as likely as establishment groups to call on the media to adopt a proactive role as advocates of social change (19% to 7%). In other words, nearly a fifth of advocacy groups in the survey wanted journalists to be more like the crusading Superman and less like the mousy Clark Kent. They wanted Woodward and Bernstein, not Strunk and White. In doing so, they may be asking the impossible from reporters schooled in the journalistic ethos of neutrality and objectivity.

By contrast, establishment groups were more likely than advocacy groups to feel that journalists should merely live up to their own ethos of balance and neutrality—a more passive approach that works against the notion of the crusading, muckraking journalist, and that arguably perpetuates (or at least fails to challenge) prevailing values, beliefs, and power relations in society. With their expectations of reporters more in line with the professional ethics of journalism, establishment groups are much less likely to be disappointed.

DO THE COMPLAINTS OF INTEREST GROUPS "CANCEL EACH OTHER OUT"?

What can we conclude from interest group critical perceptions of blind spots, news filters, and the media's overall performance? As we discovered earlier, journalists are prone to wear interest group criticisms as a badge of honour. For many journalists, "getting it from both sides"—that is, from "establishment" and "advocacy" groups—is not cause for concern but rather proof that you're "doing a good job."

In this concluding section, we use the results from our interest group survey to subject this claim to critical examination—to find out, in short, whether or not the criticisms of establishment and advocacy groups indeed "cancel each other out."

At first blush, the findings appear to support journalist claims that interest group criticisms do indeed cancel each other out. For instance, a strong majority in both the advocacy and establishment interest groups expressed support for journalism's own traditional ideal of objectivity and independence (i.e., the "mirror" function), but an equally large majority of respondents were at least somewhat dissatisfied with the media's actual performance. Such dissatisfaction, many journalists would argue, is inherent in the tensions between highly partisan interest groups and reporters who seek to report all interest groups in an independent and often adversarial manner.

The "mutual cancellation" theory is also supported by the interest-specific manner in which our respondents identified news blind spots. Establishment organizations, for instance, were more likely to identify such issues as defense and security (a classic conservative touchstone), while advocacy groups disproportionately mentioned challenges to dominant or official powers, the role of religion, Canadian nationalism, and ethnic, women's and ethical issues.

Furthermore, there was a somewhat self-serving flavour to most interest groups' call for more "positive" coverage. In short, both camps seemed much more interested in securing positive coverage for their own specific interests or issues than in the benefits that positive or inspirational coverage might bring to society in general.

Finally, both advocacy and establishment groups expressed somewhat more dissatisfaction with the media's coverage of their specific issue than with the media's performance in general. This difference, though slight, is still consistent with the notion that an interest group's emotional attachment to its own issue makes it hypersensitive to negative or even neutral coverage. As a result, interest groups would be more likely to object to the media's coverage of their own issues than to the media's general performance.

Still, while this study provides at least superficial support for the "mutual cancellation" theory, a more detailed analysis suggests that the criticisms of advocacy and establishment groups cannot be dismissed so easily. First, the two types of groups offered similar criticisms of, and recommendations for, the news media—criticisms and recommendations that do not "cancel each other out." For instance, both establishment and advocacy groups felt the media insufficiently covered positive stories and the social implications of economic policies. More importantly, both types of groups identified commercial pressures and audience-attracting news values as the most important filters within the Canadian news agenda.

And finally, a significant minority of respondents in both camps also agreed that the media should perform a more active "public forum" role in Canadian society.

Leaving aside for a moment the validity of these criticisms and recommendations, the crucial point here is the surprising amount of agreement between advocacy and establishment groups. In their perceptions of blind spots and filters, in their overall dissatisfaction, and in their recommendations for the media in general, our establishment and advocacy respondents often spoke in a single voice. This amount of agreement between the two ideologically opposed camps thus seems to contradict the idea that all interest group criticisms stem from an emotional and self-serving perception of media "bias."

A final finding from our survey also casts doubt on the idea that the criticisms of advocacy and establishment groups "cancel each other out." If this idea were indeed accurate, you would expect that both groups would be equally dissatisfied with the media, thereby supporting the journalists' claim that they succeed in "playing it down the middle." And indeed, when we asked the two camps to evaluate the media's coverage of their specific issue, as well as the media's overall performance, both groups expressed a lot of dissatisfaction. However, within this broad pattern of discontent with the news media, advocacy groups were, for a variety of understandable reasons, measurably more dissatisfied with the media than were their establishment counterparts.

In conclusion, although the findings of our survey are more suggestive than definitive, the results raise questions about many journalists' easy dismissal of interest group criticisms as self-serving and offsetting. To argue that the criticisms of advocacy and establishment groups simply "cancel each other out" would be to ignore both the overlap in their critiques as well as the different levels of dissatisfaction with the media's performance. It would also ignore the very real possibility—a possibility supported by other branches of NewsWatch's long-term research into the Canadian news media—that when different political groups attack the media, one side may well have a more valid case than the other(s).

In short, the mutual cancellation theory arguably ignores the mounting evidence that, just because the media are criticized from "both sides," this by no means should suggest that the media indeed succeed in playing it down the middle. Quite the opposite. As later chapters will demonstrate, the bulk of NewsWatch Canada's research points to the opposite conclusion: that the structure of the Canadian news media does in fact give disproportionate access and weight to conservative and establishment opinions and analysis on key economic and political issues.

ENDNOTES

1. Lawrence Wallack et al., *Media Advocacy and Public Health: Power for Prevention*. (Newbury Park: Sage, 1993), pp. 127.

2. Richard Ericson, "Patrolling the facts: Secrecy and Publicity in Police Work," *British Journal of Sociology*, 40 (1989), pp. 205226.

3. Walter Karp, "All the Congressmen's Men: How Capitol Hill Controls the Press," in David Shimkin, Harold Stolerman, & Helene O'Connor, *State of the Art: Issues in Contemporary Mass Communication* (New York: St. Martins Press, 1992).

4. Karp, "All the Congressmen's Men," p. 109.

5. Cited in Karp, "All the Congressmen's Men," p. 109.

6. Noam Chomsky and Edward Herman, *Manufacturing Consent* (New York: Pantheon, 1988).

7. Cited in Karp, "All the Congressmen's Men," p. 112.

8. Karp, "All the Congressmen's Men," p. 113.

9. On this point see Richard Ericson, Patricia Baranek, & Janet Chan, *Negotiating control: A Study of News Sources*, (Milton Keynes, UK: Open University Press, 1989).

10. An earlier version of this chapter was first published as Michael Karlberg & Robert A. Hackett, "Canceling Each Other Out? Interest Group Perceptions of the News Media," *Canadian Journal of Communication*, 21 (1996), pp. 461-472. Karlberg coded and summarized the interview data; NewsWatch researchers Katherine Manson and Cheryl Linstead provided much appreciated assistance as well.

11. This distinction between "establishment" and "advocacy" groups conflated two dichotomies: first, conservative versus progressive political orientations; and second, institutionalized interests (for which media relations constitute merely marginal costs) versus issue-oriented advocacy groups (for which political communication work represents their primary costs). In the few cases for whom the first and second distinctions did not coincide (e.g. a women's advocacy group with conservative views), the conservative/progressive distinction took precedence in our organization of research data.

12. More specific information on the structure and wording of the questionnaire in this study is available in Karlberg and Hackett, "Cancelling Each Other Out?"

13. Because the survey allowed multiple responses, the percentages listed in Table 4.1 are not cumulative.

14. Douglas Underwood, "When MBA's Rule the Newsroom," *Columbia Journalism Review,* March/April (1988), pp. 26.

15. Edward Herman and Robert McChesney, *The Global Media: The New Missionaries of Corporate Capitalism* (London: Cassell, 1997).

16. Edward Jay Epstein, *News from Nowhere: Television and the News* (New York: Vintage Books, 1974), pp 4-5.

17. Cited in Karp, "All the Congressmen's Men," pp. 109.

18. See, for example, Daniel Hallin, *The 'Uncensored' War: The Media and Vietnam*, 2nd edition (New York: Oxford University Press, 1989); and "We Keep America on Top of the World." in Todd Gitlin (ed.), *Watching Television* (New York: Pantheon, 1987).
19. Our five point "satisfaction scale" was constructed as follows: unqualified satisfaction, qualified satisfaction, neutral response, qualified dissatisfaction, and unqualified dissatisfaction.
20. Quoted in Karp, "All the Congressmen's Men," pp. 112.

Chapter Five

Searching for Canada's Under-Reported Stories

Project Censored Canada—the precursor to NewsWatch—was formed initially to identify and publicize significant under-reported stories in Canadian news media. Our first task was to come up with a consistent set of criteria for defining "significant under-reported" stories. Borrowing from the work of Carl Jensen and Project Censored in the U.S., we adopted a seven- point selection system:

1. The story must be one that deserves to be known by a large proportion of Canadians, but

2. Rreceived minimal coverage in the major news media. While the story might not be "censored" in the traditional sense of the word, it may have been overlooked, downplayed, or ignored. Even stories published in major dailies could be considered, if they were buried in the back pages.

3. The story must be of major significance. It must have the potential of affecting a large number of people (or a small number of people very profoundly, and with broader implications).

4. The story should present a clear, easily understandable concept backed by solid documentation and reliable sources, as opposed to a tangled web of undocumented claims from questionable sources.

5. The story must be national or international in scope, rather than simply local or regional.

6. The story should be timely, contemporary and ongoing.

7. The exposure of the story through our project should potentially stimulate journalists to further explore and publicize it, and encourage the general public to seek out more information about it.

Secondly, we needed a research strategy designed to find stories that the mainstream media might have overlooked or underplayed. In the end, we adopted a two-pronged approach. To begin, we publicized our project through conferences, libraries, e-mail, and the news media, and we invited individuals from across the country to nominate documented undercovered stories. We also wrote to all federal MPs, almost 300 of them, eliciting just one or two substantive responses.

In addition, we asked for story nominations in surveys of journalists and interest groups. At the same time, our researchers set out to do their own digging for likely stories that the media may have either missed or underplayed. In doing this, we made a conscious effort to cast a wide net. Regional and national "alternative" magazines with a progressive focus, such as *Canadian Forum* or *This Magazine*, were the obvious choice to begin the search, because they often strive to cover issues and viewpoints excluded from the dominant media.

But, recognizing the need to look farther afield, we broadened our search well beyond the alternative press, especially in the second and third years of the project. To do this, we turned to nationally recognized publications linked to major religious groups and to more conservative perspectives, including *Alberta Report*, *Fraser Forum*, *Canadian Banker*, and *Canadian Business*.

Our research team compiled lists of nominated stories for three years, 1993, 1994 and 1995, and in each year, used the best data bases available in public and university libraries to determine whether a story was under-reported according to our criteria. These data bases have improved almost annually, as major media companies repackage news stories for distribution in new technological forms.[1] Given the limitations of these databases—they primarily cover the English-language press in Canada—our search for mainstream media coverage of under-reported stories focused more on print than broadcast media.

In this regard, we followed the long-standing approach of Project Censored in the U.S., which argues that the broadcast media's news agenda tends to parallel that of the print media, so that gaps in the latter can be extrapolated to gaps in the former. In addition, given our focus on the English language press in Canada, we make no claim that our research necessarily applies to the French-language media system in Quebec or to other French-language media across the country.

In an annual project seminar, university students assembled the relevant data and debated the merits of all the nominated stories—111 in 1993, about 150 for 1994, 181 for 1995. In these discussions, the seven selection criteria noted above provided the basis for a 20-point scoring system, through which students winnowed our initial lists of nominated stories down to a "short list" of approximately 20 in each year.

In this exercise, we found the diversity of experiences, backgrounds and perspectives among our student researchers to be a good counterbalance to the assumptions and preferred interpretations of the senior investigators. Once the short lists of nominated stories were available, we submitted them to a national panel of judges—31 distinguished Canadians in the fields of public service, academe and journalism, selected with an eye to regional, gender and political diversity. Each of these judges studied our short lists of nominated stories and ranked them in importance. A summary tally of the judges' rankings allowed us to determine a top ten list of under-reported stories for each year.[2]

This chapter offers selected highlights from our judges' ranked short-lists of under-reported stories between 1993 and 1995, including follow-up comments about subsequent coverage, updated to March of 1997.[3] In some instances, we have also added additional brief commentaries by the authors of the original stories.

We only offer highlights here because there simply isn't space to summarize all of the ranked short-listed stories for each year. Interested readers can find detailed summaries of the complete list of short-listed stories on NewsWatch Canada's web-site. Because a number of the original short-listed stories were later covered more adequately by mainstream media—for example, stories related to the North American Free Trade Agreement (NAFTA)—it seemed more important here to focus on significant stories that the mainstream media have generally continued to downplay.

The selection of under-reported stories that follows includes the leading four stories from the top ten lists of 1993 through 1995, in addition to eight other stories picked through an informal poll of NewsWatch Canada's principal investigators. The original rank order of each story, based on results from our panels of judges, is listed in brackets at the end of each subheading, and the original authors and media sources for these stories are listed in the chapter's Endnotes.

Under-Reported Stories From 1993

Did Oil Prospects Fuel The Humanitarian Effort In Somalia? (#1)

When Canadian peacekeeping troops joined the United Nations relief effort in Somalia, their role was to protect aid for starving Somalis. However, the revelation that U.S. oil interests had been active in this war-torn country before the intervention has led some oil experts to believe that the potential presence of oil in commercial quantities was a decisive factor in the U.S. decision to send in its troops.

In 1986, four U.S. oil companies—Conoco, Chevron, Amoco and Philips—obtained exclusive land concessions and exploration rights covering more than half of Somalia from then-dictator Mohammed Siad Barre. A 1991

World Bank study listed Somalia as one of the world's top prospective commercial oil producers. The outbreak of civil war that year forced three of the four oil companies to halt their operations. But, citing the opinions of geologists and industry sources, *Los Angeles Times* reporter Mark Fineman wrote that Somalia could yield significant amounts of oil and natural gas if the military mission restored peace.

Even as the war continues, the American companies are "well-positioned to pursue Somalia's most promising potential reserves the moment the nation is pacified," Fineman reported in a story picked up by the *Toronto Star*.

The U.S. State Department and some military officials have acknowledged that one oil company "has done more than sit back and hope for peace." Conoco Inc. was "directly involved in the U.S. government's role in U.N.-sponsored humanitarian military efforts." The U.S. government "rented" Conoco's corporate compound and "transformed it into a *de facto* American embassy" and temporary headquarters for George Bush's special envoy. As well, the president of Conoco's Somali subsidiary acted as the U.S. volunteer "facilitator" during the intervention.

Although Conoco has described the arrangement as just "business" and part of being a "good corporate citizen and neighbour," its close relationship with the U.S. intervention force has raised questions about the boundary between the public authority of the U.S. government and the private power of a large oil company.

In the view of some Somalis, such as journalist Mohammed Urdoh, U.N. interventions in Africa have been characterized by a history of "kowtowing to a big power, enforcing unrealistic solutions for complex issues, and ignoring the wishes of peoples whose interests are at stake." Whether or not that interpretation is valid, it seems reasonable to ask why Canadian forces were sent to Somalia and not to other equally desperate, war-ravaged and impoverished African nations, given that the combined U.N. forces, including the Canadian peacekeepers, have been under the *de facto* leadership of the U.S., which may have less than altruistic motives.[4]

TRACKING THE COVERAGE

This story first broke in the *Toronto Star* in January of 1993. It was picked up shortly after in the *Globe and Mail*, and then seemed simply to disappear from the mainstream press. NewsWatch researchers tracked the story for three more years and the only references to it we could find were limited to four articles in 1994, all reporting on the release of the Project Censored Canada top ten list. These appeared in the *Vancouver Sun* and the

Toronto Star (both April 8, 1994), and in *Media* magazine, and *Canadian Dimension.*

*   *   *

TORIES "REVAMP" 21-YEAR RULE AND FORGIVE THE WEALTHY MILLIONS IN TAXES (#2)

January 1, 1993 was a typical New Year's Day for most Canadians recovering from the excesses of the previous night's festivities, but for a few Canadians, the richest families, it was a day for continued celebration. Had it not been for the Mulroney government's decision to revamp Canada's 21-year rule regarding the capital gains tax, some wealthy Canadians would have owed the federal treasury hundreds of millions of dollars on that day.

The story goes back to 1972 when the Trudeau government brought forth a sweeping tax reform package that removed Canada's inheritance tax and substituted a tax on capital gains. The tax on capital gains became the focus of concern for the well-to-do. The law required capital gains to be taxed only when an asset was sold. This allowed for the possibility that owners could hold on to their property and not sell it, thus avoiding the tax.

To prevent this from happening, the government required that all property would be assessed for tax at the time of the owner's death, just as if it had been sold. But wealthy families could still avoid the tax by putting their holdings into private trusts. Because trusts never die, taxes would never be collected. The Trudeau government decided to allow this tax-avoidance scheme, but required that, after 21 years, holdings stored in trusts would be subject to taxation. The 21st anniversary of this law was Jan. 1, 1993.

It was probably no surprise to the powerful and influential group of private trust owners when an "information" notice released on Feb. 11, 1991, by the Finance Department announced amendments to the 21-year law. The notice read: "The amendments provide that a trust may elect to defer the application of the 21-year rule until the interests of exempt beneficiaries under the trust have terminated."

Translated, this meant that, instead of collecting the tax at the end of 21 years, the government would allow the tax to be deferred until the last child of the owner of the trust had died. The "information" notice never made it clear that a huge tax deferral was at stake. And, according to tax experts, tax deferred is tax saved.

The government's decision to forgive the country's wealthiest citizens hundreds of millions of dollars in taxes came during the midst of its crusade for fiscal restraint. The same month the draft legislation was introduced, Finance Minister Michael Wilson cut social spending and lectured Canadians about the need to reduce the deficit. Jan. 1, 1993, could have been a day when the federal treasury received much-needed, and much owed, money from Canada's richest families. The Mulroney government ensured this would not happen.[5]

TRACKING THE COVERAGE

The Tories' deferral of the capital gain tax was subsequently covered by one Canadian Press Newswire story (July 3, 1994), and received mention in *Media* magazine's coverage of the 1994 PCC list. However, when Liberal Finance Minister Paul Martin reinstated the tax in 1995, this was reported in a dozen articles carried by most of Canada's news media.[6] The Liberals have given Canada's wealthy families until 1999 to pay up. As we write this, there is no word about possible further extensions.

*   *   *

CANADA'S COZY RELATIONSHIP WITH INDONESIA'S AUTHORITARIAN REGIME (#3)

Canada has enjoyed a healthy economic relationship with Indonesia over the years. In 1993, Indonesia was the second largest recipient of Canadian bilateral aid, receiving approximately $40 million. It is also an important Canadian trading partner, with two-way trade approximating $500 million annually. Many Canadian companies have moved to trade with Indonesia and exploit its significant natural resources. However, Indonesia's horrendous human rights record in East Timor has raised serious concerns about Canada's relationship with this country.

In 1975, Indonesia invaded East Timor, killing over 60,000 civilians in three months. Since then, many international bodies, including the United Nations, have urged the Indonesian government to withdraw from East Timor, citing severe human rights abuses and social injustices. Canada's relationship with Indonesia has nevertheless continued to be supportive. For instance, Canada:

• abstained from U.N. votes calling for East Timor's right to sovereignty and demanding withdrawal of Indonesian troops in 1975 and 1976;

• increased aid to Indonesia by $200 million six months after the invasion of East Timor; and

• voted against U.N. General Assembly resolutions calling for Indonesian withdrawal from East Timor in both 1980 and 1982.

As the death toll of the East Timorese rose above 250,000 in the early 1990s, Canada continued to support the Indonesian government, and Canadian businesses continued to invest in the region. In 1993, Canada was the third largest investor in the Indonesian economy, and more than 300 Canadian-based companies were doing business there. An example is the pulp mill engineering consultant, H. A. Simons Ltd. of Vancouver, which stands to earn as much as $200 million for the design and development of an Indonesian pulp mill.

Not only government and business supported the authoritarian regime led by Indonesian President Suharto. Some Canadian universities—Simon Fraser University, for example—established ties with the Indonesian government; S.F.U. was involved in upgrading three universities through the CIDA-funded Eastern Indonesian University Development Project.

Peter Monet, a member of the East Timor Alert Network, argues that Canada has helped to legitimize the Indonesian occupation through aid and trade policies such as these, and by allowing Canadian weapons manufacturers to sell arms to Indonesia.

Amnesty International estimates that by 1993 over one-third of the East Timor population had been killed since the Indonesian invasion. Canadians might well ask why their government and business leaders continue to support such an oppressive regime.[7]

TRACKING THE COVERAGE

When this story first ran in 1993, there was a notable silence in the mainstream Canadian media about Indonesian repression in East Timor and Canada's relationships with the Indonesian government. Since then, the occupation of East Timor has been well-publicized. For example, we found more than 30 stories in the mainstream media between 1993 and 1997 that pointed to Canada's close trading relationship with Indonesia and our government's silence on the ongoing oppression in East Timor. The issue received even greater media attention in the late 1990s because of the controversy that surrounded the RCMP's handling of protests over Suharto's presence at the Vancouver APEC summit.

*   *   *

BUSINESS-ORIENTED PR FIRMS GRAB THE ENVIRONMENTAL AGENDA (#4)

Facing growing concern about environmental degradation, multinational corporations and their public relations advisers moved quickly in the early 1990s to blunt the criticisms by establishing a variety of seemingly moderate front groups. Examples include:

1) The Business Council on Sustainable Development. To ensure that the agenda for the 1992 Earth Summit in Rio De Janeiro suited

business interests, 48 top world business leaders set up the Business Council on Sustainable Development headed by Swiss billionaire industrialist Stephan Schmidheiny, a key adviser to Summit head Maurice Strong. Schmidheiny is worth about $3 billion and heads a family construction materials empire. Other Council members represent resource exploitation and development companies, such as Mitsubishi Corp., which has been charged with destroying Asian rain forests.

The Council was able to ensure its voice was heard early, at the policy planning stage, before other non-governmental organizations (NGOs) had a chance to participate. The result, claims writer Joyce Nelson, is that business was seemingly able to place front and centre the view that economic growth is essential to achieve sustainability, with little interference from NGOs and government leaders.

2) The Share movement. At the local level, this corporate strategy pits workers in the resource communities against environmentalists. Share is the Canadian version of the American Wise Use movement, which advocates multiple use of government lands and was brought to Canada by Ron Arnold of the Centre for the Defense of Free Enterprise. Key to Share is the view that environmental challenges should be faced, not by the corporate entity, but by the local community.

Arnold's advice to the forest companies: "Give your money to grassroots organizations. Let them defend you; ...citizen groups have credibility and industries don't." Share the Forest, Share the Stein, Share the Clayoquot and, in Ontario, Share the Temagami, are some of the organizations of loggers, their families and townspeople in resource-based communities that stand up to environmentalists and oppose initiatives to protect land from logging.

Another corporate strategy is the SLAPP—Strategic Lawsuit Against Public Participation—usually comprising flimsy evidence and astronomical damage claims, which is designed to intimidate activists into silence or force them to spend their time and scarce funds on concocted legal battles.

Tying many of these corporate initiatives together, Nelson argues, is global public relations giant Burson-Marsteller (BM), which helped create the Business Council on Sustainable Development for its corporate clientele. BM offers unique services such as coalition-design experts and a 25-member grassroots lobbying unit. Its contribution to British Columbia's forest companies was the B.C. Forest Alliance, which it promoted as a coalition of citizen representatives but which had a BM employee as executive director, funding from 13 forest companies and the loggers' union, and included such citizen-directors as MacMillan Bloedel chairman Ray Smith.[8]

TRACKING THE COVERAGE

While the B.C. Forest Alliance and the Share B.C. movement have en-joyed media exposure throughout the 1990s, their origins as part of a forest industry-funded public relations campaign remains under-reported. SLAPP suits, however, have drawn greater coverage. For example, tracking this story into 1997, we found two notable discussions of SLAPP suits in the main-stream media, one in the *Globe & Mail* (July 2, 1995) and the other in *Maclean's* magazine (Aug. 26, 1996). In addition, we also found articles on SLAPP suits in *Alternatives* and *Catholic New Times*. In our view, this story raises a broader issue: the presence of public relations firms as successful media definers in more and more areas of political debate.

CORPORATE, MEDIA TIES TO POLITICAL POWER (#7)

Links between large media corporations and Canada's major political parties have raised concern about the ability of citizens to receive credible information about their political system from the mainstream news media. Though political parties have been associated with large corporations for years, it is the relationship between government and those who supply Canadians with news that is most troubling. University of Windsor communication pro-fessor James Winter asks: if the men who own our media also "own" the politicians, then whom can we turn to for accurate information?

In Canada, some senior members of the major political parties are inte-grated into an intricate corporate web dominated by Paul Desmarais, owner of Power Corporation, Power Financial, Investors Group, Power Broadcasting, and dozens of other companies. In the early 1990s, Desmarais acquired a substantial interest in Southam Inc., making him an important player in Cana-da's largest daily newspaper chain, along with his ownership of three televi-sion stations and 18 radio stations in Ontario, Quebec and New Brunswick, as well as several newspapers in Quebec. Though such high concentration of media ownership is an issue in itself, the fact that Desmarais has close ties with both former Prime Minister Brian Mulroney and Prime Minister Jean Chrétien is cause for further concern.

In 1972, Desmarais hired Mulroney as a negotiator during a labour dis-pute at his paper *La Presse*. In apparent appreciation for Mulroney's work, Desmarais became Mulroney's biggest financial backer, starting with his lead-ership bid in 1976. Mulroney confirmed the relationship after becoming Prime

Minister. In September 1990, Mulroney appointed John Sylvain, Desmarais's brother-in-law, to the Senate, one of eight controversial appointments that ensured the passage of the Goods and Services Tax.

In June 1993, Mulroney appointed Desmarais's brother, Jean Noel Desmarais, to the Senate as part of a final flurry of patronage appointments. Now Mulroney has returned to work for Power Corporation's long-time law firm, Ogilvy Renault.

Jean Chrétien was on the board of directors of Power Corporation until he ran for the leadership of the federal Liberal Party in 1990. Chrétien's daughter, France, is married to Desmarais's son. The national coordinator of the 1993 federal Liberal election campaign, John Rae, is also a vice-president at Power Corporation (and the brother of Ontario premier Bob Rae). Paul Martin, who designed the Liberal Party's policy book for the 1993 election campaign and was appointed minister of finance, worked for Paul Desmarais as president of Canada Steamship Lines until he purchased the company from Desmarais in 1981.

According to Winter, Desmarais's power comes mainly from the extreme concentration of corporate ownership in Canada. A small élite of corporate owners has close political connections, and these connections are important when tax reform and government aid issues are on the agenda. The 1976 Royal Commission on Corporate Concentration stated that Desmarais was well aware that "political power exceeds the power of capital." Today Paul Desmarais has it all: the power of capital, the power of media, and the power of politics.[9]

TRACKING THE COVERAGE

Although this item was under-reported in 1993, we found that Paul Desmarais's links to Jean Chrétien and Brian Mulroney were documented in ten stories by 1997, published in the *Calgary Herald*, *Vancouver Sun*, *Toronto Star*, *Toronto Sun*, *Financial Post*, and *Saturday Night* magazine. In addition, we found eight articles addressing concerns that the Liberal government showed favouritism to Desmarais's Power Corporation in April 1995, when the federal cabinet ordered the CRTC to allow Power's direct-to-home DirecTV channel to apply for a broadcasting license.

*   *   *

IS MILITARY POLLUTION AN OVERLOOKED CRISIS? (#11)

While many major polluters in the world are known for their activities, the world's No. 1 polluter—the military—has gone largely unnoticed. In 1993, Science for Peace, at the University of Toronto, published a report entitled *Taking Stock*, which attributes 10-to-30% of global environmental degradation to military activities. Two-thirds of the world's ozone-depleting CFC-113 comes from military sources, according to this report, while the Worldwatch Institute says the military produces 10% of all carbon dioxide emissions and consumes 9% of the world's petroleum products.

An estimated 6-to-10% of global air pollution may arise from the military, while a 1989 report estimated that at least 50 nuclear warheads and 11 nuclear reactors lie on the ocean floor. Worldwatch Institute also reports that the Pentagon's 500,000-ton annual toxic output exceeds that of the top five U.S. chemical companies combined.

Canada produces substantial volumes of uranium, tritium and nuclear waste, while toxic chemical dumps on 35 military bases across the country place soil and ground water at risk. No inventory is kept of the Canadian military's ozone-depleting emissions. In the North, estimates range from $250 million to $350 million to clean up the obsolete Distant Early Warning (DEW) radar stations. Contaminants from the DEW Line include PCBs, copper, zinc, lead, and untreated sewage. Early cleanup practices included dragging sledfuls of waste onto the ice and waiting for the spring thaw.

Environmentalists attempted to place the military's environmental impact on the agenda of the 1992 Rio Earth Summit, but this issue received minimal attention—perhaps due to a fear of disrupting the highly lucrative arms trade that so many governments depend upon. The summit refused to declare stockpiling or using nuclear weapons to be a "crime against the planet."

Arguably, some of the military's lack of environmental accountability may be justifiable in the name of national security. But when security from supposed foreign aggressors is purchased at the cost of the ecological security of the planet, the practices of the military need to be scrutinized.[10]

*   *   *

Tracking the Coverage

Tracking this story through 1997, we found no further articles pointing the finger at the military as the world's No. 1 polluter. Still, individual examples of military pollution have been reported sporadically in the press since 1993. Between 1994 and 1997, we found over 20 stories on environmental transgressions by the military around the world.

These included stories on buried toxic waste, hazardous abandoned military bases, and the environmental impact of nuclear testing. More recently, the issue of military pollution received brief coverage in stories about the high cost of cleaning up former DEW line sites, and the disagreement between Canada and the U.S. over who should assume the major share of costs.

*   *   *

CAMECO AND ITS WEAPONS CONNECTIONS (#12)

Exporting uranium for military purposes has been strictly forbidden in Canada since 1965. However, the Inter-Church Uranium Committee has released documents indicating a link between Canada's Cameco Corporation and the depleted uranium armour-piercing shells used by U.S. forces in the Gulf War. Even two years after the war, the used radioactive casings for these shells continued to present a significant health hazard to the citizens of Iraq and Kuwait. Government investigations into possible Canadian origins of this uranium have yielded contradictory findings.

Formed in 1988 by the merger of federal and Saskatchewan Crown corporations, Cameco is the world's largest uranium producer. It has shipped a significant amount of uranium yellow-cake (mined in Saskatchewan) to the Sequoyah Fuels Uranium Conversion Facility in Oklahoma. Sequoyah Fuels converted the yellow-cake into uranium hexafluoride for use in reactor fuel, a process that creates depleted uranium tetrafluoride (UF4) as a radioactive byproduct.

Sequoyah Fuels had a contract to supply Aerojet Ordinance Tennessee (AOT) with this substance; AOT, in turn, had contracts with the U.S. Department of Defense to manufacture depleted uranium shells out of it.

Before AOT could manufacture these shells, its UF-4 from Sequoyah Fuels needed to be further refined and turned into depleted uranium metal, which makes up the actual shell core. To do this, AOT obtained a license from the U.S. Nuclear Regulatory Commission to ship "up to 1,000,000 pounds of uranium tetrafluoride" to Eldorado Resources, Cameco's uranium refinery in Port Hope, Ontario.

The license, which covered the period between early 1988 and the end of 1990, further specified that: "AOT will supply the UF-4 to Eldorado Resources, who will use it to manufacture Depleted Uranium metal for AOT's use in manufacturing uranium penetrators [armour-piercing shells] on the U.S. Department of Defense contracts," according to Phillip Penna writing in *Briarpatch.*

During the Gulf War, U.N. forces fired at least 10,000 penetrators, littering the Iraqi and Kuwaiti countryside with 40 tons of used radioactive uranium shell-casings. No effort has been made to clean up the debris, or to assess the extent of radioactive contamination of soil, air, and drinking water. Increased cancer rates and stomach ailments in Iraq may be linked to uranium exposure. As many as 500,000 civilians may be affected over the next 10 years, resulting in "tens of thousands of potential deaths," according to the United Kingdom Atomic Energy Authority.

Canadian uranium may have been used in these shells. Once Cameco's uranium was processed by Sequoyah Fuels, it could be classified as "U.S. material," becoming uranium of "U.S. origin," even though it was mined in Saskatchewan. Thus, in the years preceding the Gulf War, Cameco was technically able to "legally" export and to refine uranium for the American military without violating official government policy. What makes the situation even more ironic is that 39% of Cameco's shares are owned by the Saskatchewan government, and 12% by the federal government.

Both Saskatchewan's Ministry of the Environment and the federal Department of External Affairs launched investigations, leading to contradictory results. Saskatchewan's Report of the Joint Federal-Provincial Panel on Uranium Mining Developments in Northern Saskatchewan confirmed the uranium exports, while the federal investigation denied them.

The Pentagon has insisted that the shells are only "very mildly radioactive," but this issue still calls into question the effectiveness of Canada's policies toward uranium exports and the public accountability of the uranium industry.[11]

TRACKING THE COVERAGE

CAMECO's alleged contributions to radioactive shell casings in the Gulf War received no further coverage that we could find between 1993 and 1997, with one partial exception. The company's weapons connections were the centre of controversy in April, 1995, as Greenpeace held protest demonstrations at Cameco's Port Hope facility, claiming that Cameco has supplied uranium for French nuclear weapons. This received five stories in the *Hamilton Spectator*, the *Toronto Sun*, the *Toronto Star*, the *Calgary Herald*, and CTV News.

In March and April of 1999, the issue of radioactive weaponry by NATO forces in the war in Kosovo—particularly the use of depleted uranium in anti-tank shells—was again raised by peace and environmental groups, although without specific reference to possible involvement by Canadian companies. The issue continues to receive little play in the mainstream media.

* * *

SNAPSHOTS OF OTHER STORIES FROM THE 1993 SHORT LIST

In 1993, our judges' fifth-ranked under-reported story, based partly on the work of Frances Russell of the *Winnipeg Free Press*, concerned the undemocratic implications of NAFTA for Canada. In a letter to our project, Russell paid our "top ten" list a high compliment, saying it was "worth more to me than any number of nominations for a National Newspaper Award."

For years, Russell wrote, she had experienced "the pressure to become silent created by watching the topic be shunned and avoided by my fellow journalists," but, finally, "other journalists have validated that what I see happening around me is, in fact, news."

Other ranked stories for 1993 described the secrecy with which the NAFTA agreement was forged (#6); subsidies to forest companies and other complex issues behind the well-publicized confrontations over logging practices in B.C. (#8); the role of Canadian mismanagement in the collapse of the Northern Atlantic cod fishery, usually blamed on foreign over-fishing (#9); and Canada's heavy involvement in foreign arms sales and its relatively small expenditure on international peacekeeping, contrary to Canada's self-image (#10).

Other stories on the 1993 short list called attention to the location of the Pickering nuclear power plant in a potential earthquake zone (#13); the squandering of taxpayers' money through the federal Western Economic Diversification Fund, according to critics such as the Fraser Institute (#14); the controversy over the health risks of mercury in dental fillings (#15); municipal governments' avoidance of effective alternative technologies for treating sewage (#16); the conflict between Aboriginal people and the Canadian Forces over low-level training flights in Labrador and Quebec (#17); the problematically close relationship between automotive journalists and car companies (#18); the scope and depth of homophobia in professional sports (#19); and the secrecy surrounding taxpayer-funded vivisection of animals in medical and scientific research (#20).

UNDER-REPORTED STORIES OF 1994

CLEANING UP AFTER AECL (#1)

While ordinary citizens were asked to accept cuts in social spending, Atomic Energy Canada Ltd. (AECL), the money-losing Crown corporation, required an estimated $200 million to $300 million bailout from the federal Treasury for the cleanup of potentially toxic hazards at old nuclear facilities.

AECL was sharply criticized by Auditor General Denis Desautels following publication of the corporation's 1993-94 annual report because AECL's financial statements did not properly account for the cost of cleaning up its decommissioned nuclear plants. He stressed that this oversight violates established accounting procedures, which require companies to include foreseeable future expenses in their annual reports. This was the third time the Auditor General had chastised AECL management for distorting the organization's true financial picture. Desautels insisted that the corporation should immediately begin setting aside an annual fund for the cleanup of abandoned reactor sites, rather than receiving unconditional assistance from the federal government.

In a November 1994 press release entitled "Nuclear Nightmare in the Ottawa Valley," the Oshawa-based environmental organization "Nuclear Awareness Project" used the 50-year-old Chalk River site to illustrate the hazards associated with radioactive contamination. It contended that toxic materials from this site have entered the nearby Ottawa River through surface and groundwater networks. It also claimed that "radioactive emissions from reactor operations are causing contamination of drinking water, precipitation, air and food." As of 1994, AECL had no cleanup plans in place at Chalk River.

AECL management acknowledged the need to address problems posed by aging atomic reactors, and that their cleanup will be extremely costly. However, it contended that uncertainty regarding the exact amount involved disallowed the inclusion of these expenses in current annual reports. The corporation's financial officers supported this assertion by emphasizing that such liabilities have traditionally been covered by the federal treasury, and they expected this practice to continue. AECL recorded a $155.5 million consolidated deficit for the 1993/94 fiscal year, a figure that does not include cleanup costs.

Politicians from all levels of government vigorously campaigned in the early 1990s to convince Canadians that reducing the national debt is imperative to ensure continued economic stability. In this political climate of economic restraint and deficit reduction, Canadian taxpayers may wonder why this clearly unprofitable Crown Corporation merited any fiscal generosity from the federal government and why the potential "nuclear nightmare" at Chalk River has been resolutely ignored by the federal regulatory agency.[12]

TRACKING THE COVERAGE

Between 1994 and 1997 there was little mention in the mainstream media of AECL's accounting practices when planning ahead for its cleanup operations. We could find only two relevant references: AECL's reliance on government subsidies was covered by a Canadian Press Newswire article (Feb. 14, 1996), and a Parliamentary committee report calling for cuts to subsidies for the nuclear industry was also reported by CP on Dec. 14, 1995.

*   *   *

CANADA'S OWN FREE TRADE DEAL (#2)
Opponents of the 1994 Interprovincial Trade Agreement (ITA) expressed

fear that provincial governments have relinquished powers to enforce standards that help local workers and protect the environment. After a year of closed-door negotiations, ITA was finalized at the end of June 1994, despite appeals from labour and environmental groups for public consultations.

Some journalists and business groups did see the draft agreement, but for most interested Canadians it remained inaccessible. Responding to the charge that the negotiations were too secretive, Steven Van Houten of the Canadian Manufacturers' Association (CMA) said that "we and others had the opportunity to read the draft and that's the way it should be." However, critics were unable to respond until they received a leaked copy shortly before the June deadline.

The Ottawa-based Canadian Centre for Policy Alternatives (CCPA) concluded that the ITA would curb the ability of provincial governments to set higher environmental standards and would restrict expenditures meant to encourage regional development and local employment. The ITA went beyond NAFTA, the CCPA charged, in allowing companies to participate in the dispute settlement process. It also placed the burden of proof upon the provinces to defend their policies, unlike NAFTA.

The B.C. magazine *Pacific Current* called the ITA a "bill of rights for the private sector." The ITA would transfer matters controlled by provincial legislatures to a new bureaucracy and disputes would be handled in a closed-court system under a process that would grant corporations access to panels while excluding virtually everyone else.

In addition, Ken Georgetti, president of the B.C. Federation of Labour, claimed that companies could challenge the tough environmental rules in the B.C. Forest Practices Act as a trade barrier. Even health care standards could be attacked. "Provincial standards requiring that a specific minimum of time be spent on a lab test, for example, could be challenged by private labs as a trade barrier," he said.

The ITA was meant to reduce costly interprovincial trade barriers, based on estimates provided by the CMA that such barriers cost the Canadian economy $6.5 billion a year. This figure was challenged by the CCPA and by a separate study by University of British Columbia economist Brian Copeland. They concluded that the CMA figures were "seriously flawed" and that the real costs were closer to $750 million a year. But, if the ITA won't save much money, it will, in the view of its critics, give corporations the "ability to challenge in court" the rights of legislatures to decide how the people in a province go about their affairs.[13]

Tracking the Coverage

As we tracked this story into 1997, we could find no further coverage of the anticipated impact of the Interprovincial Trade Agreement upon local workers and environmental standards. Much better documented, however, has been the squabbling between various provinces over job poaching (notably B.C. and New Brunswick) and the ITA's ineffective provisions for dispute resolution in such conflicts. Between 1994 and 1997, we found over a dozen stories that dealt with this issue in most of Canada's major media, and, in August 1996, the General Accountants' Association of Canada called for a round of renegotiations to try and make the deal work.

*   *   *

Third World Battles GATT Over Plant Patenting (#3)

The intellectual property of indigenous peoples and the livelihood of vast numbers of agricultural workers is being put at risk by the General Agreement on Tariffs and Trade (GATT).

GATT allows genetically altered plants and plant extracts to be patented. This has led multinational corporations to take out patents on a variety of valuable food and medicinal crops.

The broad scope of this plant patenting prohibits farmers from saving seeds of genetically engineered plants. Also, it will not permit private and public researchers to experiment with these "engineered" plants unless they pay royalties to the company owning the patent. Thus, patenting will limit scientific research and stifle instead of stimulate the economy for farmers. In Canada, a policy research organization called Rural Advancement Foundation International (RAFI) expressed particular concern about the European soybean patent. The organization was assessing the possibility of revoking the patent held by W. R. Grace & Co., with the help of the Canadian Environmental Law Association. With the patent, W. R. Grace & Co. has had an exclusive monopoly over all types of genetically altered soybeans, "regardless of the technique employed or the germplasm involved," wrote Mary Pickering, associate editor of *Alternatives* magazine. Some countries do not allow life-forms to be patented because it conflicts with their moral or religious ethics.

In India, where patenting of life-forms is prohibited, an evergreen called the neem tree is hailed as "the curer of all ailments," and is held up as a symbol of Indian indigenous knowledge, Vandana Shiva and Radha HollaBhar wrote in *The Ecologist*. Indian farmers and doctors use the neem tree to treat a wide range of diseases, for contraception, as a mouthwash, and even as a natural insecticide. Access to its products has been free or cheap.

In the past few years, over a dozen neem tree patents have been taken out by American and Japanese multinational corporations. These companies were able to obtain patents on natural products because they claimed their chemical extraction processes are innovative and distinguishable from the indigenous people's methodology, and the nature of "synthetic" copies of neem tree chemical compounds are patentable. However, to the indigenous people who have used neem products for centuries, this amounts to intellectual piracy.

Furthermore, GATT requires all countries, in particular Third World nations, to adopt patent laws similar to those of First World nations for plants and microorganisms that are similar to those in First World nations. Under the agreement, countries with species patent laws could block imports of products derived from "pirated" technology, Pickering wrote. That could include things like cotton clothing, soybean paste, or neem soap.

GATT has sparked Third World nations to develop their own notion of intellectual property called Collective Intellectual Property Rights. Under this law, knowledge concerning the properties of indigenous plants would be a social product defined as a local common right, rather than a right through the marketplace. And any intellectual piracy disputes between Third World nations and any other country would be resolved through village organizations, not by GATT panels. But it remains to be seen if this initiative will overcome the pressure to conform to GATT.[14]

TRACKING THE COVERAGE

This story was covered in three further articles between 1994 and 1997, in the *Ottawa Citizen* (Jan. 20, 1996), the *Calgary Herald* (Dec. 6, 1995), and the *Edmonton Journal* (Oct. 29, 1995). In addition, the story's appearance on the PCC "top ten" list in 1995 was mentioned in the *Vancouver Sun*, the *Edmonton Journal*, *Canadian Dimension* and *Media magazine*, and the issue was also mentioned in a piece about the career of Vandana Shiva in the *Toronto Star* (July 16, 1995). One article also appeared in the periodical *Edges: New Planetary Patterns*.

Stories about such issues as Third World farming, plant biology, and their relationships to property law do not have high news value to the mainstream press. Still, as bio-technologies continue to advance, the issues surrounding the assignment of property rights to living organisms will likely become increasingly difficult to ignore. The key question is whether the exploration of these issues will spill over from specialist and alternative publications into the mainstream press.

*   *   *

White-Collar And Corporate Crime Overlooked (#4)

Non-violent crimes committed by white-collar workers and corporations have been overlooked due to a "public and political preoccupation with violent offences," says a leading corporate fraud investigator. From its inception, Justice Minister Allan Rock's crime prevention strategy focused primarily on violent crime. But Don Holmes, a fraud investigator with Ernst & Young, believes that the "social ramifications" of white-collar crime may in fact be more serious. The initial responsibility for investigating white-collar crimes, such as employee theft and fraud, falls on forensic accountants like Holmes.

Aaron Freeman and Craig Forcese, founding directors of the Ottawa-based Democracy Watch, argue that the Liberal government's "war on crime" largely ignores not only such white-collar employee crime, but also violations committed by corporations. These include tax evasion, bribery, fraudulent advertising, illegal mergers, and monopoly pricing.

While individual cases are reported, the media rarely convey the scope of corporate and white-collar crime. The impact of such crimes is illustrated by the following:

- Federal statistics show an annual increase of 7% in the incidence of white-collar crimes.
- A Statistics Canada report in the early 1980s found the number of workplace deaths attributed to unsafe or illegal working conditions to be equivalent to the number of street homicides. This does not include "lingering deaths" resulting from exposure to "hazardous workplace pollutants."
- According to Holmes, Canadians pay increased taxes and prices for consumer goods amounting to as much as $20 billion a year as a result of white-collar crime. American statistics show that white-collar and corporate crime accounts for $10 for every $1 lost to robbery, burglary, larceny and auto theft combined. If this 10-to-1 ratio applies to Canada, Freeman and Forcese estimate that corporate crime costs Canadians about $30 billion a year.
- While over one million charges were laid against street criminals in 1988, only 23 were laid against corporations in the first two years of the 1986 Competition Act.

According to Holmes, the lenient treatment of non-violent crime has led to the growth of a "get-something-for-nothing attitude." Similarly, many corporations view the penalties for corporate crime as a "mere cost of doing business." Freeman and Forcese claim Exxon spent less money cleaning up the Valdez oil spill than it spent on spin doctors and positive publicity for its cleanup efforts. Through stronger legislation, enforcement and penalties for white-collar and corporate crime, argue Freeman and Forcese, the government could "begin to correct the biases of our two-tiered system of justice."[15]

TRACKING THE COVERAGE

Corporate and white-collar crime received a considerable amount of media attention in 1995-1997: at least 62 stories have appeared on the subject since this issue appeared on the PCC top ten list. Fraud, employee theft, bribery, and other crimes appear to have been on the rise through the 1990s, and special investigative units of forensic accountants and ex-police officers have been hired by many firms to combat the annual losses (estimated by accounting firm KPMG to be over $39 million in 1996).

Still, we found that coverage of crimes by employees against employers was more extensive than coverage of crime committed by corporations: of the 62 stories, only six dealt with the latter form of crime. However, coverage of both these forms of crime remains a small fraction of the coverage devoted to violent offences in the media.

*   *   *

TOBACCO MANUFACTURERS AND CIGARETTE SMUGGLING: THE UNTOLD STORY (#5)

The extent to which Canada's tobacco companies have lobbied the federal government to reduce cigarette taxes was one of the top news stories of 1994. But an important under-reported aspect was the manufacturers' own complicity in the smuggling of cigarettes. For example, according to Dr. Jack Micay of Physicians For a Smoke-Free Canada, several companies set up distribution plants, either on their own or in partnership with U.S. manufacturers, right in the heart of areas where smuggling was taking place. Packaging was designed to be virtually identical to cigarettes sold legally in Canada.

The companies insist they are not directly involved with the smuggling. But a Canadian Cancer Society study suggested they may be making $100 million more on cartons smuggled back into Canada than they would by selling here directly.

Another under-reported aspect is that the tobacco companies fudged the numbers that were the source of much of the information used by the Liberal government to reach a decision, according to writer Scott Anderson. Contraband cigarettes were estimated to be a one-billion-dollar market by the tobacco companies. But David Sweanor, counsel for the Non-Smokers' Rights Association, has stated that the manufacturers exaggerated the size of the illegal cigarette market "every step of the way."

The Canadian Cancer Society issued a report saying that the tobacco manufacturers had been providing stock analysts with annual sales figures that were several billion units lower than those it gave Statistics Canada. The inflated StatsCan numbers formed the basis of the industry's other estimates that the federal government relied upon, including government revenue losses and consumption rates.

Also suspect are the contraband estimates included in a series of reports compiled on behalf of the tobacco manufacturers by the accounting firm of Lindquist, Avey, MacDonald, Baskerville Inc. Anti-smoking groups argued that the reports contained a number of serious errors in methodology. For example, the firm's 1992 estimate of contraband cigarettes was based on subtracting from total exports the amount of tobacco products sold in the U.S. or legally returned to Canada. But that didn't account for products that were sent to the U.S. for distribution to other countries.

Revenue Canada reported that in 1992 seizures of illegal cigarettes had a total retail value of $35 million. The accounting firm counted these as consumed. Even after an allegation of supplying misleading information to the government, the accounting firm failed to correct any of the smuggling estimates. But an estimate that only 10% of Canadian-blend contraband smuggled here was produced elsewhere was quickly revised upwards to 34% by the accounting firm. This made it appear pointless for the government to reimpose the Conservatives' 1992 export tax on Canadian-produced cigarettes.

Cutting the taxes on cigarettes initially cost the government between $2.2 and $3.2 billion annually in revenue, which raises the question of why it didn't put up more of a fight to control smuggling through other means. While it may or may not be relevant, the tobacco industry donated a total of $269,000 to the Liberals between 1988 and 1992. In the 1980s, Finance Minister Paul Martin sat on the board of Imasco, the parent company of Imperial Tobacco and the largest cigarette manufacturer in Canada. Because liquor companies have also complained about high taxes on their products causing smuggling, Anderson suggests that critics examine their figures very closely if the government ever decides to reduce liquor taxes.[16]

TRACKING THE COVERAGE

While tobacco companies were much in the news through the mid-1990s, we could only find one additional story by 1997 alleging a tobacco company's role in the smuggling business; it was in the *Toronto Sun*, March 26, 1996 ("Weed firm staff called smugglers"). Most of the coverage of tobacco companies in recent years has focused on issues and revelations made public through the (increasingly successful) legal suits brought against the tobacco industry by U.S. state governments and other organizations. (We note that CBC-TV, at least, did a follow-up on this story in 1999.)

*   *   *

THE CANADIAN WILDLIFE FEDERATION: HIDING ITS HUNTING CONNECTION (#7)

The Canadian Wildlife Federation (CWF), which claims to be Canada's largest protector of wildlife, is run mostly by people who kill animals for sport. But, from the way it publicizes itself, few of its supporters are likely to know this. The CWF encompasses 650,000 members and supporters, or about one out of every 43 Canadians. Most of these are people who donate money to the organization or buy its merchandise. The CWF itself is made up of 12 provincial and territorial federations of rod and gun clubs and individual hunters and anglers. All of the federations, including the largest, the 74,000-member Ontario Federation of Anglers and Hunters (OFAH), promote hunting and fishing interests.

Members of the affiliate federations comprise less than one-third of CWF supporters, yet they hold 34 of the board's 40 seats. They also hold all of the executive positions. The executive vice-president is a former minister of natural resources in Saskatchewan under Grant Devine. In contrast, people who join CWF because they love animals are considered associate members and have no vote. These non-voting supporters get their information about the organization mainly from its glossy magazines and catalogues, which avoid any mention of the CWF's connection with hunting. The material features pictures of live bears and wolves, but fails to state that federation affiliates support bear-baiting and the wolf kill. In fact, in the mid-1980s the CWF sued celebrated Canadian author and wildlife advocate Farley Mowat for statements about the kill in his book *Sea of Slaughter.*

No policies that conflict with hunting appear in the CWF policy manual, and the organization maintains silence on hunting issues. Meanwhile, its affiliates actively oppose gun control and promote practices such as "harvesting" black bears, which often means shooting unsuspecting females with cubs who have emerged "hungry from hibernation, follow the smell of bait and [are] shot from close range with a crossbow or a high-powered rifle," explains author Helen Forsey.

The CWF publicly supports its affiliates when it can conceal its status as their umbrella organization. For example, echoing an OFAH stand, the CWF wrote a position paper opposing Aboriginal land claims, saying wildlife rights should "be applied equally to all Canadians." The OFAH opposes land claims because they infringe on hunting areas. The CWF supports only neutral causes, such as research projects on non-game species such as bald eagles, or causes that both hunters and environmentalists can support. For example, the CWF opposes game farming, which hunters and non-hunters dislike for its health risks to wildlife.

Although the CWF purports to promote conservation, only 12% of its expenditures are devoted to research, education and advocacy. Most of the CWF's money goes into merchandising, administration and fund-raising. The merchandising rakes in $5 million a year. Most of it comes through the CWF catalogue, which states "every purchase helps wildlife." Thousands of animal lovers who help fund the organization would probably disagree with that statement if only they knew the CWF's real priorities.[17]

Tracking the Coverage

We were unable to find any subsequent references in mainstream media to the Canadian Wildlife Federation's link to hunting interests. However, the story was mentioned in both *Media magazine* and *Canadian Dimension* in 1995 in conjunction with their coverage of the 1995 PCC top ten list.

*   *   *

Snapshots of Other Stories From the 1994 Short List

Other top ten stories for 1994 were an alternative option for reducing public debt—lower interest rates rather than social program cutbacks and higher taxes (#6); the forced resettlement and often impoverishment of two million people in developing countries, due to dam projects funded by the World Bank (#8); the biological hazards of salmon farming on Canada's west coast (#9); and the low-profile but largely successful "damage control" exercise by supporters of NAFTA to misleadingly portray the Mexican Zapatista rebellion and the trade deal as two separate issues, obscuring NAFTA's serious threat to Mexico's indigenous farmers (#10).

Additional 1994 stories included the federal government's cutbacks and growing indifference to national standards for income assistance to the poor (#11); the implications of growing corporate concentration in media industries (#12); the vulnerability to contamination of vaccines produced through bio-technology (#13); the economic, environmental and social costs of excessive dependence on the automobile (#14); an advertising campaign which claimed that overnight use of tampons was safe for women, notwithstanding independent experts' warnings of toxic shock syndrome (#15); growing user fees for access to government information, potentially creating an "information underclass" (#16); and the toll of military life on the wives of armed forces personnel (#17).

UNDER-REPORTED STORIES OF 1995

PROPOSED U.S. ENVIRONMENTAL POLICY COULD HARM CANADA'S AIR AND WATER (#1)

The United States and Canada share the world's longest undefended border and one of the world's biggest fresh-water basins, but pollution doesn't respect borders. That's why Canadians should be concerned about moves in the U.S. to weaken key federal environmental laws. For example, proposed changes to U.S. environmental law to weaken the Clean Water Act and declare southeast Michigan an "ozone attainment area" will have an alarming and immediate impact on the Great Lakes and Canada's environment overall.

In May 1995, the U.S. House of Representatives passed a bill amending the Clean Water Act of 1972. In essence, the amendments lift protection for many wetlands, make regulators give greater consideration to costs before requiring water quality improvements from cities and industry, and allow states to opt out of environmental water regulations deemed too expensive or unenforceable. The Great Lakes, home of 20% of the world's fresh water supply, is particularly susceptible to these changes in several ways: The Great Lakes Initiative, requiring all eight U.S. states bordering the lakes to meet consistent water-quality standards, would become more voluntary and harder to enforce; discharges of toxic chemicals could now be measured downstream rather than at their point of discharge; industries could "trade" reductions in some emissions for increases in others; the mandate to treat storm water before it runs into waterways would be removed; and restrictions on city and farm runoff into water-ways would be relaxed.

In 1995 the bill went before the U.S. Senate (where it quickly became mired in committees), and Canadians are speaking out against it. While still environment minister, Sheila Copps called on the U.S. government to continue working with Canada to protect the environment and maintain strong environmental laws, because these changes "...will have a devastating effect on our collective environment." Copps also commented that the bill may be vetoed. U.S. President Bill Clinton opposed efforts to weaken environmental protection and called this bill the "dirty water act."

Environmental groups were also strongly opposed to this bill. Brett Hulsey, director of the Sierra Club's Great Lakes program, said amending the Clean Water Act "basically puts the 25 million people who drink from the Great Lakes at risk. There's an increased chance of animal manure and deadly parasites in their water. There's an increased chance of PCBs and dioxins and other deadly pollutants in their fish, and an increased chance of human waste fouling their beaches."

Another proposed change in the U.S.'s environmental policies is the declaration of southeast Michigan as an "ozone attainment area," meaning that Detroit is no longer considered to have excessive levels of ground-level ozone. This designation would relax programs to control ozone-producing emissions, while maintaining voluntary controls of that lung-damaging pollutant. The already polluted air of Windsor would be directly affected by this decision. The Windsor Air Quality Study found that Michigan was the source of two-thirds of Windsor's airborne toxins. Similarly, a study done by Queens College in New York, and released in May 1995, found incinerators as far away from Canada as Texas, Florida and Utah are to blame for as much as 50% of 17 kinds of cancer-causing dioxins that fell on the Great Lakes. At press time these changes were mired in the Senate; if they go through and become policy, Canada and the U.S.'s history of environmental cooperation will be tarnished.[18]

TRACKING THE COVERAGE

Three stories relating to U.S. pollution policies were carried in *The Globe and Mail* in 1995; one in March and two in May (but all far back in the news section). Regional media coverage was similarly buried deep in the papers and focused on then federal Environment Minister Sheila Copps's reaction to the proposed changes. Locally, *The Windsor Star* carried three stories directly referring to The Windsor Air Quality Study and the potential environmental impacts of a new incinerator in Michigan.

CBC-Radio national coverage included discussion of U.S. President Clinton's battle with the Republican-dominated Congress on the changes to the Bill (*World at 6*); *World This Weekend* coverage referred to the changes and their implications to the Great Lakes cleanup. CBC-Radio Regional (Toronto) covered the environmental study and the concern over possible U.S. deregulation. Locally, CBC-Windsor covered the impact that the proposed changes would have on Windsor. But we only found two more stories on the effects of American environmental legislation on Canada in the mainstream media between 1995 and 1997: one in the *Ottawa Citizen* (Jan. 25, 1996) and one in the *Montreal Gazette* (June 27, 1996).

AMERICAN-STYLE HEALTH CARE COMING TO CANADA (#2)

In 1966, the Government of Canada created a national Medicare plan, one of this country's most cherished social programs. The original document stated that all in-patient diagnostic services and hospital prescriptions were to be free. In 1995, however, Prime Minister Jean Chrétien argued that the original intention of Medicare was only to cover catastrophic illness, and that federal funding was only intended to help provincial programs become established.

With falling federal transfer payments for Medicare, some provincial governments turned to private insurers and health care organizations to help restructure provincial health care. Many of these organizations are largely American for-profit companies. For example, Ontario, Manitoba, Alberta and British Columbia have all opened their doors to American consultants and companies. In that sense, the Liberal government's actions can be seen as facilitating the entry of U.S.-style health care delivery into Canada.

During the mid-1990s, Canada's health-care market was estimated to be worth $72 billion per year. Federal cutbacks provided opportunities for private companies to take up the slack. Thus, in 1994, Liberty Mutual Insurance Group of Boston entered the Canadian market when its Canadian subsidiary, Liberty Canada, opened a number of for-profit acute-care clinics in Toronto called International Managed Health Care (IMHC). Liberty Mutual also bought Ontario Blue Cross, a private non-profit supplemental health insurance provider formerly owned by the Ontario Hospital Association. That move gave Liberty access to two million Ontario customers, 200 hospitals, 2,500 pharmacies, and 2,500 dentists. Liberty is also lobbying the Ontario government to introduce possible American-style private workers' compensation plans.

While Liberty is delivering actual services, several American health-care management companies have already established themselves in Canadian hospitals. In 1993, Chilliwack General Hospital in B.C. instituted a program by American Practices Management Inc. (APM) called Patient-Focused Care (PFC). It guarantees to reduce operating costs by 5-to-10%, operating space by 15-to-20%, and staff by 10%, while supposedly providing better care for patients. The PFC approach uses "multi-skilled health practitioners," some of whom have had as little as 11 days' training, to perform nursing tasks.

Ivory Warner, spokeswoman for the British Columbia Nurses Union, states, "It's all about replacing highly skilled workers with unlicensed, unregulated and underpaid workers." A Hospital Employees Union study of the Chilliwack facility claimed 75% of the employees felt the system compromised patient safety, 89% reported greater stress, and only 20% said their work had become more interesting.

Manitoba hired APM consultants to overhaul health-care programs there. The resulting PFC program eliminated 403 positions at St. Boniface General Hospital and the Winnipeg Health Sciences Centre. The University of Alberta Hospital has hired the same consultants. The Ontario government is looking at another system called Comprehensive Health Organizations (CHO), which provide and purchase services for their members. CHOs "shop around" for the best services, and CHO clients are expected to shop around for the best CHO provider. While purportedly community-based and non-profit, that's how American Health Maintenance Organizations (HMOs) started in the 1970s before funding cuts forced them to convert into for-profit organizations.

The Ontario government is considering a proposal by Magna International to set up a CHO for its employees. If such a CHO were put in place, American HMOs could not be denied access to the Canadian market under the NAFTA agreement. As Maude Barlow and Bruce Campbell, authors of *Straight Through the Heart*, a book about the Liberal government, state: "If our health care system goes, it will likely disappear in small little-noticed steps. Then, one day we will realize it has vanished..."[19]

TRACKING THE COVERAGE

Through 1995, coverage of the Americanization of Canadian health care was limited to reporting specific incidents (such as the change of policy at a Winnipeg hospital) rather than the implications of the overall trend, which was the focus of our nominated stories. For example, we found stories in *The Winnipeg Free Press* concerning the new profit orientation of the Sports Medicine Clinic and a story in *The Globe and Mail* referring to the resignation of the president of the Ontario Hospital Association soon after he was involved in the sale of the non-profit Blue Cross to the profit-oriented American insurance firm, Liberty Mutual Insurance.

We also found a CP Newswire story and a *Toronto Star* story. All other coverage appeared in media outlets serving a particular occupational community (such as the *Canadian Medical Association Journal, Canadian Lawyer, Canadian Underwriter*) or the alternative press (*Our Times, The Georgia Straight* and *Canadian Forum*, where our nominated story was initially found). National CBC-Radio only reported briefly on the "Americanization of Canadian health care," but specific incidents of U.S. for-profit corporations' involvement in Canadian health care were reported regionally: a Fort Frances CHO plan (Thunder Bay); and a comparison of U.S. and Canadian health care systems, with a focus on the economics (Edmonton).

Locally, there were reports on the sale of Blue Cross (Ottawa, Calgary); U.S. Medicare offered to Ontarians (Toronto); mergers and acquisitions of Canadian health care organisations by U.S. companies (Fredericton). CBC-TV (*Prime Time Magazine*) aired a documentary called "Health Care, American Style," and reported on various regional decisions vis-a-vis private clinics and the public health system.

For a story of such ongoing national importance and clear interest to Canadians, this level of coverage seems barely adequate. Tracking the story through 1996, we found that *The Globe and Mail, Financial Post, Montreal Gazette, Toronto Star, Ottawa Citizen,* and the *Edmonton Journal* ran one article each on the restructuring of Medicare and the introduction of CHOs and HMOs into several provinces. Further coverage up to 1997 was limited to specialist periodicals such as the *Medical Post,* the *Ontario Medical Review,* and the *Canadian Medical Association Journal.*

*   *   *

HAARP: THE U.S. MILITARY'S PLANS TO ALTER THE NORTHERN IONOSPHERE (#3)

The U.S. government is constructing a military radio physics research facility in a remote part of Alaska. The High Frequency Active Auroral Research Program (HAARP) will enhance the U.S. military's long-range radio communications and surveillance by injecting high-frequency radio energy into the fluctuating ionosphere, 50 to 800 kilometres above the earth. Although HAARP's use of high-frequency radio energy or "heat" into the ionosphere could have serious global repercussions, no concrete knowledge exists about the impact of these enormous amounts of energy being injected into the upper atmosphere. Rather, HAARP is an ongoing experiment designed to modify and manage the ionosphere to suit military purposes, with no serious consideration about the consequences.

The high-frequency radio waves will create enormous extremely low-frequency (ELF) virtual antennas. ELF radio waves will enable the U.S. Air Force and Navy to communicate with submerged submarines and to distinguish nuclear warheads from decoys. In addition, the HAARP facility, when complete, will contain a large array of sensing and analysis systems, clustered around an ionospheric research instrument (IRI). The IRI will be able to temporarily modify portions of the upper atmosphere by heating the atmosphere's electrons with beams of powerful high-frequency radio energy. Heating regions of the lower and upper ionosphere forms virtual "lenses" and "mirrors" that can reflect a broad range of radio frequencies for detecting stealth missiles and aircraft.

One environmental study by the U.S. Air Force has found that IRI transmissions can raise the internal body temperature of nearby people, ignite road flares in the trunks of cars, detonate aerial munitions, and scramble aircraft communications and flight-control systems (this explains the high fences designed to keep visitors away from the low-angle beams). It would also have the potential to disrupt human mental processes, interfere with wildlife migration patterns, and negatively affect the Earth's upper atmosphere.

HAARP also has weather manipulation capability. For instance, differential heating of specific areas of the atmosphere could cause local adverse weather conditions such as floods, droughts or sea squalls, all of which could offer a military tactical advantage. In addition, in the spring of 1993, the Federal Aviation Administration (FAA) began to advise commercial pilots on how to avoid the large amount of intentional (and some unintentional) radiation that HAARP would generate.

The HAARP Research Program remains an extremely low-profile project in the U.S. and Canada. Alaskan state officials have not even been briefed about the project. HAARP officials are satisfied with the military capability of their "weapon," yet seem unaware and uninformed of the potentially devastating effects of their research. Professor Alfred Wong, a HAARP researcher and professor of physics at the University of California at Los Angeles, said, "I don't see any problems, only surprises; that's why we do research." One surprise might occur if anyone investigates HAARP and finds it violates the 1977 Environmental Modification Convention, which bans "any hostile use of environmental modification."[20]

TRACKING THE COVERAGE

Other than the original nominated story on our list, and a synopsis compiled by Project Censored (USA), we found no media coverage of HAARP in 1995. In the following year there were two small stories referring to the project on a 1996 edition of CBC-TV's *Undercurrents*. We found no CBC-Radio coverage of this project and only the *Undercurrents* (1996) coverage on CBC-TV. Mainstream press coverage of HAARP has consisted of only two stories appearing in the *Toronto Star* (April 20, 1996) and the *Halifax Daily News* (April 26, 1996), both covering the story as part of their coverage of PCC's 1995 top ten list. *Media* magazine (Summer 1996) also reviewed the PCC list, mentioning HAARP, and *Peace Magazine* ran an article about HAARP in its Sept/Oct 1996 issue.

Our source story's author, Mark Farmer, has gone on to produce a major piece on HAARP for Paramount Pictures' television program *Sightings*, which aired in October 1995. He has also written stories on HAARP for *Defence Weekly*. In addition, Farmer notes coverage in the *Anchorage Daily News* and on Alaskan Public Radio.

When asked about the amount of press coverage, Farmer has argued that: "High-energy radio physics and the ionosphere are not the stuff of dinner conversation...Even some scientists refer to the ionosphere as the 'ignorosphere.'" This makes it difficult to convince media outlets to publish or air secret—or even previously unreported—military projects. "It took me two years to get *Popular Science* to let me do the story [on HAARP]." Still, due in part to his stories and television appearances, Farmer suggests that public involvement and legislative interest in HAARP has risen dramatically. Not only are "the counter-proliferation people keenly interested" in the technology, but "The Alaska State legislature held hearings on HAARP, at which I testified." Meanwhile, the program seems to be going forward. "U.S. Senator Ted Stevens (R-Alaska) made sure HAARP received $15 million this year," said Farmer.

*   *   *

THINGS THE RIGHT WING DOESN'T WANT YOU TO KNOW (#4)

A 1991 Statistics Canada report challenged what neo-conservatives were saying at the time about the impact of social spending on government debt. Those same neo-conservatives furiously attacked the report in 1995. The report, published in *The Canadian Economic Observer*, argued that social spending is not a major contributor to the debt and deficit problem. It blames high real interest rates and a gradual decline in tax revenues from high income-earning individuals and corporations.

Throughout the 1990s, neo-conservatives in Canada argued that social programs must be reduced. For example, *Globe and Mail* columnist Andrew Coyne, one of the right's most forceful voices on debt and deficit issues, suggested that social spending in Canada should be scaled down to the U.S. level of 14% of GDP. According to Bruce Campbell in *Canadian Dimension*, this is the lowest level in the industrialized world.

In the same vein as Coyne, economist William Watson, writing in *The Financial Post*, argued that, regardless of whether social program spending growth caused the current debt problem, it must be reduced to tame today's deficit. Others, such as *Western Report's* Lorne Gunter, attacked the left's argument that corporations are not paying their fair share of the tax burden, claiming corporations in 1995 were paying three times more than in 1961 in "hidden taxes" such as occupational safety regulations and employment equity.

The StatsCan report suggests that a major contributor to the debt has been the cost of servicing it. Between 1975 and 1989, high real interest rates mean that payments added 44% to the debt. In an article on "Reforming the Bank of Canada," George H. Crowell argued that the real reasons that social programs were targeted by governments while interest rates were maintained was "not to cope with the debt, but rather to cater to the interests of wealthy bondholders..." Similarly, Mary Rowles, in *Our Times* magazine, points out that Canada only rates in the middle of the industrialized pack in social spending, according to the Organization for Economic Cooperation and Development (OECD). In addition, during the period covered by the StatsCan report, the federal government received 50% less tax revenues due to the implementation of tax breaks for higher-income individuals and corporations. In 1961, corporations provided 20% of total federal revenues. By 1994, this had dropped to 7.5%.

Finally, a disturbing allegation made by Campbell was that political pressure was brought to bear by the federal Finance Department on StatsCan to modify its findings. There was a difference between the final draft and the published version, which was toned down: "It is a chilling example of how vulnerable, as a line department, Statistics Canada is to political meddling." Campbell recommended making the agency directly responsible to Parliament, much like the Auditor General, to protect its autonomy.[21]

TRACKING THE COVERAGE

Mainstream media coverage of the findings of the 1991 Statistics Canada report, and of alternative ways to reduce Canada's public debt, was scarce in 1995, although we found some references to the relative cost of social programs in articles published in *The Financial Post*, *Western Report*, *This Magazine*, and *Canadian Dimension*. Very little coverage was found on alternative debt reduction approaches; for example, one *Globe and Mail* article in June 1995. In the broadcast media, CBC-Radio (National) reported on protests to the proposed budget cuts by various advocacy organizations (including the National Action Committee on the Status of Women, the National Anti-Poverty Organization, and the Canadian Union of Public Employees). Regionally (Vancouver, Edmonton, Regina), CBC-Radio noon programs included interviews with Linda McQuaig, author of *Shooting the Hippo*, a book critical of neo-conservative fiscal policy. We couldn't find any reference to the Statistics Canada report on CBC-Radio.

The 1991 Statistics Canada report received no further mention in Canada's anglophone media as we tracked this story into 1997. Still, the argument that social spending is not fully responsible for the national debt, and that high interest rates are more to blame, did receive passing coverage. We found seven articles that discussed this issue, appearing in the *Ottawa Citizen* (Feb. 19, March 9 & Oct. 19, 1996), the *Halifax Daily News* (Jan. 13 & Oct. 11, 1996), the *Calgary Herald* (March 9, 1996), and Canadian Press (Jan. 12, 1996).

Responding to this story, Lorne Gunter, of *Western Report*, claims the "revelations" in Linda McQuaig's *Shooting the Hippo* typify the kind of "alternative" analysis of government debt offered in the story discussed here. Rather than being under-reported, though, Gunter argues that McQuaig's revelations were "one of the most over-reported stories of last year, in large part because they weren't revelations at all and weren't true, to boot." In his view, the attention paid to McQuaig and her book "went way beyond the ordinary...the majority of reporters called on to cover her book wanted to believe what she had to say. They wanted there to be 'proof' that social spending cuts weren't necessary."

Gunter argues, contrary to McQuaig's thesis, that "Spending causes deficits and debts, not revenue shortfalls. A government can always make up for a revenue shortfall by reducing its spending. The converse is not so easily accomplished, except by taking on debt...Instead of calling this entry on your top 10 list 'Things the right wing doesn't want you to know,' I'd entitle it 'Things the left wing fervently wishes were true, but aren't.'"

By contrast, George Crowell—an author of one of the stories that led to the appearance of this item on our list—told us that his story didn't get more play when it first appeared, largely because: "It is about the last thing the powerful banking and other financial institutions want people to know... ignoring opposing views is the best strategy for them." As for further developments to his story, Crowell noted that "there has been a little positive response to my article, judging by letters to the editor. I have seen no negative reaction to the article or to an earlier article on the issue in the *Canadian Association of University Teachers' Bulletin* (April 1995), or to an op/ed piece I did for the *Windsor Star* (March 25, 1996)."

Another nominated story author, trade union leader Buzz Hargrove, likewise points to corporate interests as being one of the main reasons alternative approaches to paying down the federal debt received little media attention. "The mass media has close corporate connections (indeed, is a corporate interest in its own right), and hence doesn't want Canadians to know of any possible solutions to our deficit problems other than social cutbacks."

* * *

CANADIAN MEDIA MUM ON HUMAN RIGHTS ABUSES IN MEXICO (#7)

Two years after the signing of the North American Free Trade Agreement (NAFTA), Mexican human rights abuses continued to be ignored in the Canadian mainstream news media. Sparse coverage of Mexican human rights abuses prompted *Globe and Mail* columnist Rick Salutin to write: "Now that we are in NAFTA along with Mexico, they matter so much (to us) that our government pledged $1.5 billion we thought we didn't have so U.S. bond-holders wouldn't get upset...over their Mexican investments. Surely we need to know what's going on there."

Examples of troubling events in Mexico include the mysterious deaths of babies at a hospital in Durango. Suspicions were raised, and never cleared, of organ-trafficking or other illegal activity. The hospital is the only one in the area for uninsured poor people. Victor Janoff of *Xtra West* reported that Mexican homosexuals in particular are demoralized by rampant police brutality, including extortion, beatings and rape. Similarly, Linda Diebel of *The Toronto Star* reported that an army intelligence blacklist of "presumed Zapatistas" led to the deportation of three foreign priests working with poor Indians in Chiapas.

Through much of 1995, there was rising violence in Mexico, including the arrest, detention, and proven torture of suspected Zapatista sympathizers. In his book *The Other Mexico: The North American Triangle Completed*, John Warnock argued forcefully that in Mexico dissent is controlled through rampant human rights violations, including arrests, torture, and disappearances.

Salutin's article was sparked by the June 28 massacre of a group of peasants on their way to a public protest in Guerrero. The peasants were ambushed by Mexican police. Survivors said the police were intent on preventing the farmers from attending the protest rally in an attempt to crush a militant farmers' organization whose membership was growing in Guerrero state. Eighteen peasant farmers were killed and 22 were wounded. Jorge Madrazo, director of the Mexican government's National Human Rights Commission, said a six-week probe into the June 28 shooting indicates police opened fire "indiscriminately" on the peasants, though they were not armed.

Minimal coverage and the distortion of facts in the Canadian press prompted Salutin to compare the amount of coverage of the Guerrero incident with another "foreign massacre," the bombing on July 24 of an Israeli bus that killed five passengers, along with the bomber. While the Israeli bombing received 1,790 words in *The Globe and Mail*, the Guerrero massacre received only 892.

Amnesty International released a report in November 1995 stating that massive human rights violations, including torture by electric shock and genital mutilation, were continuing in Mexico with "total impunity." The report also shows that nothing has changed with regard to human rights abuses since a similar report was released three years ago.[22]

TRACKING THE COVERAGE

Canada's possible complicity in trading with a rights-abusing nation received little coverage in the mainstream press, although individual incidents that refer to Mexico and its role as a recognized human rights abuser did receive some mention. Through 1995 we found nine articles referring to the massacre in Guerrero (first reporting it as a peasant massacre of police and then as a police massacre of peasants), mostly in *The Globe and Mail* and *The Montreal Gazette*; three stories that referred directly to an Amnesty International report that identified Mexico as a leader in human rights abuses; but very few that commented on Canada's trade relationship and the Mexican state's treatment of its citizens (mostly columns and editorials, and none prominently placed).

In the broadcast media, CBC-Radio reported on several incidents of human rights abuse in Mexico, but did not reflect on the philosophical issues surrounding free trade with countries that have poor human rights records. In addition, CBC-Radio only had one story on the massacre in Guerrero. The primary focus of CBC-Radio coverage of Mexico and human rights in 1995 was on the treatment of Zapatistas.

Between 1995 and 1997, Canadian media carried over 55 stories documenting violence, oppression, and human rights violations in Mexico, including some coverage of Canada's diplomatic moves to aid in Mexican reforms. Much of this discussion in the media, though, was due to Mexican President Zedillo's visit to Canada in June 1996. Although Zedillo himself did not raise the rights issue, his presence prompted more journalists to consider Mexico's human rights record.

Freelance journalist Victor Janoff told us that his nominated story on rights abuses in Mexico "was 'censored' and fits the classic example of how the voices of minority journalists and researchers are often passed over." Janoff notes that he received a CIDA North/South Grant for Journalists and one of the requirements for the grant "was a letter from an editor stating that he or she was interested in publishing his article." An editor of a major Canadian newspaper who had published one of Janoff's articles once before agreed to pay him for a 2,500-word article. Janoff went to Mexico to research and write his story, but when he returned, he claims, the editor seemed much more reticent, and explained that "she was taking a lot of heat for [an article the paper had just run on a gay issue]. She said that there was a feeling at [the paper] that too many gay articles had been running, and that she might have to put mine off for a while."

In the end, Janoff submitted his article and was paid for it, but the editor kept making excuses for the fact that the story never ran. Frustrated, he approached one of the gay newspapers, *Xtra West*, which liked the story but made him shorten it considerably. "Naturally," he concluded, "the circulation [of *Xtra West*] is much lower than the Saturday edition of [the mainstream paper]."

* * *

"FAMILY ENTERTAINMENT" AT CANADA'S ARMS BAZAAR (#8)

Canada has cultivated an image of being the world's peacekeeper. However, it is also one of the largest international suppliers of arms and weapons in the world. In 1995, Canada was the seventh largest exporter of arms and weapons to developing countries, and the tenth largest overall arms exporter in the world. The premiere venue for viewing the military industry's products in this country is Airshow Canada, a biennial exhibition which runs in conjunction with the Abbotsford International Airshow, an annual event widely advertised as family entertainment.

So, while families marvel at these technologies, Canada is hosting an international arms bazaar where representatives from over 70 countries come to buy and sell arms.

Since its inception in 1961, the Abbotsford Airshow had proved a popular family event. It is now the third largest airshow in North America and the largest in Canada, in recent years drawing nearly 300,000 people. Airshow Canada has also grown since its first joint venture in Abbotsford, from 37 military participants in 1989 to 104 in 1995, with 15,000 delegates attending. Representatives from Canada's top military corporations—Bristol Aerospace, Bombardier, Canadian Marconi—display their products alongside those from international military corporations like British Aerospace, McDonnell Douglas, Aerospatiale, Mitsubishi Corp. and Boeing.

Delegates from around the world—including Russia, the United States, and Britain—come to buy, sell and trade arms and weapons. They include representatives from countries with histories of abusing human rights, such as China, Brazil, and Indonesia, all of whom are welcomed by the Canadian government to the Airshow and the trade show. Ray Matty, president of Abbotsford Airshow, states that the airshow's invitation policy is linked to the federal government's foreign policy.

The Abbotsford International Airshow has always had a well-advertised military presence, but the military presence at Airshow Canada goes virtually unnoticed and unreported—as does Canada's role in the international military defense business. Steve Staples, coordinator of End the Arms Race, states that, notwithstanding Canada's self-image as a promoter of international peace, Canada earns more from exporting arms than it spends on peacekeeping.[23]

TRACKING THE COVERAGE

Four articles that reported the corporate trade show (Aerospace Industries Exhibition) connected to the Abbotsford Airshow appeared in 1995 (in *The Vancouver Sun* and *The Financial Post*) but, other than our nominated story, only two stories critical of the military and arms sales appeared. These were in *The Ploughshares Monitor* and *Peace Magazine*. We found no coverage in the broadcast media by either CBC-Radio or CBC-TV.

We found no further coverage of this story in Canada's major news media, although it has received mention in other publications. One article on it appeared in the *Catholic New Times* (Oct. 1996), and one in the *Ploughshares Monitor* (June 1996). The story also received a passing mention in *Peace Magazine* (Nov./Dec. 1996) as the eighth most under-reported story from the 1995 PCC list. Political scientist Ron Dart cites a combination of public relations work and uncritical journalists as the main reason why this story hasn't received more play. "The public relations work of the Air/Trade Show, predictably, projects a media image of benign family entertainment and aerospace technology. Journalists often soak up the message handed to them by the 'image' cabal of the Air/Trade Show...The struggle, even in the local media, to get a substantive counterstory, involves a sustained effort."

*   *   *

HOME-BASED GARMENT WORKERS EXPLOITED (#9)

Doing their homework pays off for most people. For a growing segment of workers in the garment industry in B.C. and across Canada, however, homework does not pay much. Home-based workers, mainly Asian or other Third World immigrant women, work out of their homes on a piecework basis, often for less than the minimum wage. They supply their own machines and electricity and are responsible for any equipment repairs. They earn an average of $4.64 an hour (well below minimum wage in most of Canada) and receive no benefits such as unemployment insurance, Canada Pension Plan benefits, overtime, vacation pay, or workers' compensation.

The Canadian garment industry employs about 60,000 people. Thirty thousand are unionized, the rest are not. B.C.'s garment industry employs approximately 10% of the industry's national workforce, and for the past seven years has had annual sales of $230 million.

Vas Gutnaratna, of the Union of Needle Trades, Industrial and Textile Employees (UNITE) says home-based garment workers in B.C. comprise a further 1,000 to 3,000 members of the workforce—and the numbers are growing. The exact numbers are unknown as the workers are often paid under the table and are not registered as employees of any company.

Home-based workers are generally under contract to one of the many smaller shops in B.C. and are a result of the need for manufacturers to remain competitive against offshore manufacturers, particularly the Southeast Asian and Central American companies. In an effort to keep costs low and to respond quickly to market needs, B.C. manufacturers contract out work that is further sub-contracted, from manufacturer to local factories to home-based workers. The front-end retailers and manufacturers are not responsible for the home workers, since technically they are not the employers. The sub-contractors do not register their employees, thereby evading legal responsibilities. The home-based workers end up being exploited.

Workers are recruited by word of mouth or through ads in ethnic papers. The majority are women of colour from China, India, Vietnam, Korea, and other underdeveloped nations who live and work within their small ethnic communities. Gutnaratna says the women come from countries where they have been oppressed. They generally don't speak English and have little knowledge of their rights. The workers fear they may lose their jobs if they complain or if they try to unionize. As in other provinces, there is an Employment Standards Branch in the provincial government to help non-unionized employees deal with workplace problems. However, any complaints must be made by the workers. The branch does not monitor the garment industry for infractions of the Employment Standards Act.

Attempts to help home workers, either through the unions or the branch, are complicated by the lack of concrete information concerning the workers. The government of B.C., following in the footsteps of Ontario, passed a bill revising the Employment Standards Act in November 1995. Employers must register all home workers. Home-based workers must also be paid the minimum wage, overtime, and vacation pay. Contributions to the Canada Pension Plan and Unemployment Insurance must be made by the employer on behalf of the employees. Penalties of $500 per employee can be levied if an employer does not register a worker.

Kevin Rooney, a spokesman for the Employment Standards Branch, indicates it will hold town hall meetings in conjunction with the Garment Workers Manufacturers' Association and UNITE to inform employers and employees of their rights and responsibilities. However, limited staff means the industry can't be more actively monitored. In the end, the onus is still on the employer to register employees and on the employees to lay complaints. If the branch doesn't know about a problem, it can't deal with it. So home-based workers, while now protected by law, are still open to exploitation.[24]

TRACKING THE COVERAGE

Several stories appeared in the Canadian mainstream media in 1995 that referred to exploitation of garment workers in other countries, but we found only three mentions of the situation of Canadian garment workers working out of their homes in Canada (*The Globe and Mail, The Toronto Star* and *The Montreal Gazette*). None of these stories dealt with the issue extensively. Our nominated story appeared in *The Georgia Straight*. Over the next year, the plight of home-based garment workers began to attract somewhat more media attention. For example, on Jan. 26, 1996, CBC-TV aired a story on the problems faced by home-based garment workers in Canada. In addition, *The Ottawa Citizen* and the *Toronto Star* both carried the same article by Nancy White on the plight of home-based garment workers in Ontario (on Sept. 2 and 21, 1996, respectively), and CBC-TV ran a news piece on Jan. 22, 1996. The issue also received mention as part of the PCC top under-covered story list in the *Toronto Star* (April 20, 1996), and *Briarpatch* published an article in its Dec. 1996/Jan. 1997 issue.

*   *   *

SNAPSHOTS OF OTHER STORIES FROM THE 1995 SHORT LIST

Other notable ranked stories from the 1995 short list include the untold costs (crime, suicide, unemployment, poverty) of New Zealand's approach to public debt, an approach which had been trumpeted by free market fundamentalists in Canada (#5); senior governments' evasion, and ultimately complicity, vis-a-vis lawlessness and the lack of accountability of local government at the Mohawk First Nations community of Kanehsatake near Montreal (#6); and the federal government's waste of money as a result of selling CF-5 training jets cheaply, shortly after spending millions on upgrading them (#10). This last story provoked some debate in the letters pages of *Media* magazine (Winter 1998, Spring 1998, Summer 1998). Journalists at CTV News and the *Ottawa Citizen* argued that, since they had covered this story, it did not deserve to be on our under-reported list; we explained that we were focusing on a particular aspect of this story which, in our judges' view, was under-reported relative to its significance.

Lower-ranked stories for 1995 included Canada's surprisingly high rate of suicide among widowed elderly males (#11); the undemocratic, business-oriented and partisan nature of the Canadian Taxpayers' Federation, contradicting its claims to represent all taxpayers at all economic levels (#12); connections between the Society for Academic Freedom and Scholarship and white supremacist groups (#13); the chronic illness of 140 Canadian soldiers who received large doses of an untested anti-nerve gas agent while serving in the 1991 Gulf War (#14); socially responsible "fair trade" as an alternative to the arguably exploitative North-South trade relations mandated by agreements such as NAFTA (#15); and the unfair competition facing private Canadian businesses from goods made by prisoners in federal penitentiaries (#16).

ENDNOTES:

1. Initially, we used the Canadian Business and Current Affairs periodical index, supplemented by online searches of Infomart and Infoglobe, along with CD-ROM disks of *The Globe & Mail*, and *Maclean's*. We also consulted the Canada News Disk CD-ROM, covering a number of major dailies as well as CBC and CTV national television newscasts, although this data base only became available for our 1995 short-lists of under-reported stories.

2. A further methodological note: we conducted a rough validity test on our lists of under-reported stories, albeit on a small scale, to see whether our project's judgements about the unfamiliarity and newsworthiness of under-reported stories were shared by others. Accordingly, we asked a class of undergraduates at Simon Fraser to rate each of 30 news stories in terms of its familiarity, its significance, its personal interest, and its likely newsworthiness in the dominant media. Unknown to the students, these stories comprised five types: well-covered "junk news" stories low in civic significance, more conventional news stories of greater public import, fictitious stories which were low in news value, fictitious stories high in conventional news value, and stories from our top-ten lists which, of course, we and our national panel had judged to be significant but under-reported. Clearly, the responses of Simon Fraser University students can't be generalized to all Canadians, but our modest efforts at validity testing yielded results that lent support to our assumptions about the significance and lack of audience familiarity with the under-reported stories. Compared to the other clusters of stories, PCC's items were ranked lower in familiarity than well-covered news stories, and only slightly higher than fictional ones. They ranked nearly as high in both public significance and personal interest as the "real" stories, well ahead of the newsworthy fakes, the non-newsworthy fakes, and the

junk news respectively. Nevertheless, the students (quite realistically) ranked the PCC stories, along with the non-newsworthy fakes, as least likely to attract the attention of the dominant media. The average scores for each cluster (based on a scale running from 1 to 5) were as follows. Personal familiarity: junk news, 4.02; "real" news stories, 2.80; PCC under-reported stories, 2.53; non-newsworthy fakes, 2.46; newsworthy fakes, 2.24. Predicted likelihood of coverage in the dominant media: Junk news, 4.02; "real" news, 3.82; newsworthy fakes, 3.72; non-newsworthy fakes, 3.11; PCC under-reported stories, 3.11. Public significance: "real" stories, 4.25; PCC under-reported stories, 4.17; news-worthy fakes, 3.50; non-newsworthy fakes 3.22; junk news, 1.93. Personal interest: "real stories, 4.05; PCC under-reported stories, 3.98; newsworthy fakes, 3.62; non-newsworthy fakes, 2.82; junk news, 2.56.

3.   These updates are based on searches of the Canadian Newsdisk and the Canadian Business and Current Affairs computer databases.

4.   Sources: Mark Fineman, "Oil Firms Hope to Cash in on Somali Peace," *The Toronto Star*, January 20,1993; Geoffrey York, "Why the U.S. Really Cares About Saving Somalia," *The Globe and Mail*, January 27, 1993; Mohammed Urdoh, "The United Nations in Somalia: Is it peacekeeping?" *Peace Magazine*, September October 1993. PCC researcher: Tanya Hamade.

5.   Source: Neil Brooks and Linda McQuaig, "In Tories They Trust," *THIS Magazine*, December 1992. PCC researcher: Tricia Milne.

6.   A check of *Canadian News Disk* revealed 12 articles appearing around the time of Mr. Martin's announcement (Feb.-March, 1995), 6 of which were accounted for by 2 *Canadian Press* reports.

7.   Sources: Robb Cribb, "Canada: One of the Most Hypocritical Countries in the World," *The Ottawa Citizen*, October 18, 1993; East Timor Alert Network (ETAN), "East Timor: Indonesia's Killing Fields," ETAN pamphlet, no date given; Randall Martin, "Educating Indonesia," *The Peak*, February 11, 1993. PCC researcher: Todd Manuel.

8.   Source: Joyce Nelson, "Burson-Marsteller, Pax Trilateral and the Brundtland Gang Versus the Environment," *The New Catalyst*, Summer, 1993. PCC researcher: Robyn Shillito.

9.   Sources: James Winter, "Two Parties in Power," *The Independent*, November 1993; Ian Austin, "Desmarais Seeks Political Capital From Power Links," *The Montreal Gazette*, February 10, 1990. PCC researcher: Magda Szulc.

10.   Source: Paul Webster and Kelly Gallagher-MacKay, "The Hidden Toxic Giant," *Canadian Peace Report*, Spring 1993. PCC researcher: Isaac McEachern.

11.   Source: Phillip Penna, "Cameco and its Weapons Connections," *Briarpatch*, May 1993. PCC researcher: Isaac McEachern.

12.   Sources: Canadian Press, "Auditor general says cleanup likely to burn taxpayers," *The Ottawa Citizen* (This story also ran in *the Winnipeg Free Press* and *Montreal Gazette*), August 9, 1994; Nuclear Awareness Project, "Nuclear nightmare in the Ottawa Valley," Press Release, November 2, 1994. PCC researchers: Cindy Rozeboom and Karen Whale.

13. Sources: Barrie McKenna, "Study says provincial trade deal can wait," *The Globe and Mail*, June 16, 1994; (no listed author), "More borders wiped out," *Pacific Current*, Aug./Sept., 1994; and Valerie Casselton, "Internal trade draft does little to allay labour's fears," *The Vancouver Sun*, May 12, 1994. PCC researchers: Dale Gamble and James Duvall.

14. Sources: Mary Pickering, "Broad patents on basic crops cause alarm," *Alternatives*, Nov/Dec., 1993; Vandana Shiva and Radha HollaBhar, "Intellectual piracy and the Neem tree," *The Ecologist*, Jan./Feb., 1995. PCC researchers: Elizabeth Rains and Carmen Pon.

15. Sources: Doug Fischer, "Investigator fears fraud cases ignored," *The Calgary Herald*, July 9, 1994; Aaron Freeman and Craig Forcese, "Get tough on corporate crime," *The Toronto Star*, Nov. 17, 1994. PCC researcher: Diane Burgess.

16. Sources: Scott Anderson, "Smoking gun," *This Magazine*, March/April 1994; Dr. Jack Micay, "The grim reaper poised to reap windfall," *The Toronto Star*, February 2, 1994; Art Chamberland, "Smuggling means huge profits for tobacco firms," *The Montreal Gazette*, February 1, 1994. PCC researchers: Rita Fromholt and Cindy Rozeboom.

17. Source: Helen Forsey, "Gunning for conservation," *Canadian Forum*, Jan./Feb., 1994. PCC researchers: Elizabeth Rains and Cindy Rozeboom.

18. Sources: Ray Ford, "Breathing May be Hazardous to Your Health," *The Windsor Star*, Nov. 18, 1994; Chris Vander Doelen, "Ozone Rules for Detroit Relaxed," *The Windsor Star*, Feb. 14, 1995; Brian McAndrew, "Copps Attacks U.S. Attempt to Weaken Pollution Laws," *The Toronto Star*, June 3, 1995. PCC Researcher: Christoph Clodius.

19. Sources: Maude Barlow and Bruce Campbell, "Straight Through the Heart," *Canadian Forum*, November 1995; Daniel Tatroff, "Under the Knife in Chilliwack: an American Health Care Program Rides Into Town," *Our Times*, May-June 1995; Joyce Nelson, "Who's Behind Health Cuts?" *Georgia Straight*, Feb. 24-March 3, 1995. PCC Researcher: Susan Wilson Murray.

20. Sources: A book review of Jeane Manning and Nick Begich, *Angels Don't Play This Harp* (Earthpulse Press, 1995); Mark Farmer, "Mystery in Alaska," *Popular Science*, September 1995. PCC Researcher: Nicky de la Roche.

21. Sources: Bruce Campbell, "Why the Right Went Ballistic Over Stats Canada Report," *Canadian Dimension*, April-May 1995; Mary Rowles, "Lies my father-figure told me: debt, deficit, & social spending, *Our Times*, December 1994; George Crowell, "Reforming the Bank of Canada," *Canadian Dimension*, October-November 1995; Buzz Hargrove, "The New Democracy in Canada," *Briarpatch*, Oct. 1995; Maude Barlow and David Robinson, "Martin's 'We Told You So' Budget Serves the Rich," *Pacific Current*, April/May 1995; Mel MacDonald, "Economic Alternatives to the Feds Hack'N'Slash," *Pacific Current*, April/May 1995; Jason Ziedenberg, "Deficit Deception and the War on Truth," *This Magazine*, May 1995. PCC Researchers: Christoph Clodius and Bernie Melanson.

22. Sources: Rick Salutin, "Newsgathering and our Third Amigo," *The Globe and Mail*, August 4, 1995; Linda Diebel, "Mexico a top rights violator, group charges," *Toronto Star*, June 26, 1995; Victor Janoff, "Life Under Siege," *Xtra West*, Oct. 19, 1995; John Warnock, *The Other Mexico: The North American Triangle Completed*, Black Rose Books, 1995. PCC Researcher: Suzanne Maier.

23. Sources: Ron Dart, "Family Entertainment or Mecca of Militarism," *Briarpatch*, September 1995; Kim Bolan, "Airshow 'turning into arms bazaar,'" *Vancouver Sun*, Aug. 10, 1995; Ken Epps, " Airshow Canada," *Ploughshares Monitor*, June 1995. PCC Researchers: Susan Wilson Murray and Angela Austman.

24. Source: Dirk Beck, "The Clothes Behind Closed Doors," *The Georgia Straight*, April 14-21, 1995. PCC Researcher: Susan Wilson Murray.

Chapter Six

Patterns of Omission

Our lists of underreported stories from 1993 to 1995 covered a lot of ground, ranging from the cod fisheries in Newfoundland to forestry giveaways in British Columbia, from the untold costs of NAFTA to the costs and dangers of military pollution, and from the struggles of Canadian garment workers to Brian Mulroney's quest to give the wealthy one last tax break before riding off into his own political sunset. Taken together, the lists of undercovered stories cut a wide swath through the contemporary political and social landscape, and during the last five years they helped to attract much-needed public attention to the issue of blind spots and filters in Canada's news system.

At the same time, there are clear limitations to "top ten" or "top twenty" lists as analytic devices. While the lists are helpful in highlighting some of the specific issues that may deserve more attention from the media, they offer no more than a starting point to help identify general patterns of omission in the news. To find these patterns we needed to explore other research strategies. But first we undertook a review of our short lists of under-reported stories for clues regarding systematic blind spots. We asked ourselves: "What kinds of stories seem to consistently pop up on our short lists of undercovered stories?" and "Why might this be?"

We also began a wide review of media research conducted in Canada and the U.S.—research that might help explain why the media extend wall-to-wall coverage to some issues while allowing others to drop entirely off the public's radar screen. Finally, beginning in 1996, we started to use the technique of content analysis to conduct pilot studies, each focusing on a particular aspect of news coverage.

The next two chapters summarize the initial results of NewsWatch Canada's ongoing search for systematic and pervasive patterns of omission in the Canadian news agenda. As with our surveys of journalists and interest groups, we don't claim that these results are the last word. They are intended to stimulate reflection, debate and further research. Still, we think it is possible to start to identify some of the important social, environmental, and cultural issues that have been largely overlooked by Canada's news system. In this chapter, we sketch the following apparent blind spots:

- The Dark Side of Canadian Militarism
- Environmental Degradation as a Systemic and Ongoing Problem
- The Francophone Perspective in Canada's Language Debates
- Religion and Traditional Social Values
- Human Rights Abuses by Canada's "Friends"
- White-Collar and Corporate Crime
- Public Relations, Private Agendas
- Gender-related Stereotypes

This list of apparent blind spots is by no means exhaustive, and in the next chapter we will narrow our focus and concentrate more closely on what are arguably the most important and debilitating blind spots in the Canadian media: the lack of coverage afforded to Canada's deepening social inequalities, growing corporate power, and alternatives to neo-liberal economic perspectives. Still, when taken together, we believe the research discussed in these two chapters presents a sobering picture of some key blind spots in the mainstream Canadian news media.

THE DARK SIDE OF CANADA'S INVOLVEMENT IN MILITARISM

Canada's image as the world's peacekeeper has without a doubt been an important part of Canadian national identity during the last half century. In fact, some of the respondents in our survey of interest groups (as discussed in Chapter 4), have gone so far as to claim that the "continuing commitment to peace" demonstrated by the Canadian Forces is a big part of "the vision...[which] binds this country together." But this widely celebrated "commitment to peace" has largely concealed a darker side of Canadian militarism—a side revealed by the frequent appearance of critical stories regarding the Canadian arms industry and armed forces on our short-lists of top undercovered stories over the years.

Some of these stories detail the personal, environmental, or fiscal consequences of military priorities and decisions: military pollution (1993, #11), the impact of military life on the wives of armed forces personnel (1994, #17), the federal government's loss of money after upgrading then selling CF-5 training jets (1995, #10), and the apparent cover-up of Canadian soldiers' Gulf War-related illnesses (1995, #14).

Other military-related stories more directly contradict Canada's image as the world's peacekeeper. For example, between 1949 and 1980 the Canadian military's expenditures on peacekeeping missions around the world turns out to have been less than one-half a percent of total military expenditures for the period. As late as 1991-92, the proportion of expenditures devoted to peacekeeping missions was barely 1% of the total military budget, and totalled only about one-third the value of Canadian foreign arms sales (1993, #10).

Meanwhile, NATO's low-level training flights in Labrador threatened the wildlife-dependent economy and culture of the Innu people (1993, #17); and Cameco, a corporation owned mainly by the Saskatchewan and federal governments, was reported to have bypassed the Canadian government's own ban on exporting uranium for military purposes in order to sell the U.S. military "armour piercing" shells (1993, #12). More recently, the Abbotsford International Airshow—an ostensibly "family event"—has become an annual "weapons emporium" where Canadian arms producers mingle with buyers hailing from repressive regimes like Indonesia and China (1995, #8).

Each of these stories raises provocative questions about the nature and role of the military in Canadian life and the role that Canadian arms sales play in sustaining bloody conflicts around the globe. Given the news media's oft-repeated claim to be the nation's "watch dog," you might think that such stories—which contradict the image many Canadians hold of their military—would receive a lot of play. So why have the mainstream Canadian media tended to underplay such stories? In short, what news filters might be operating to limit detailed reporting and analysis on the Canadian military?

Journalists' tendency to fall into habitual work routines may be one reason why military issues get short shrift, according to one reporter we interviewed. "Journalistic ties to the military," this journalist quipped, "are rather pathetic, certainly among this generation." In the past, many journalists working in Canadian newsrooms had served at least at some point in the military and still had contacts or sources within the service. Today, however, relatively few journalists have any real ties to the military, and consequently depend heavily on "official" public relations or news contacts within the government for news about military operations. In the end, this reliance on official sources for military news discourages most journalists from doing the leg-work necessary to uncover stories concerning the hidden consequences of military practices and policies.

Another reason for the lack of coverage extended to the Canadian military perhaps resides in the cultural power that the image of Canadian peacekeeping exerts within the nation's imagination. The image of the peacekeeping soldier in places like Cyprus, Bosnia, and Haiti certainly stands in stark contrast to the more aggressive image of the U.S. military in world affairs—a contrast that was cemented during the 1960s and 1970s by Canada's public refusal to endorse American intervention in Vietnam. In Canada, the image of peacekeeping forms an important sense of who "we" are, as opposed to the more militaristic Americans.

With the image of Canadian peacekeeping fast approaching "sacred cow" status in the national imagination, as former CBC Radio producer Bruce Wark argues, the media have developed a tendency to favour "self-congratulatory stories about 'Canada: the peaceable kingdom'" over more critical stories about the military establishment.

This does not mean that negative coverage of the military never finds its way into the news agenda; the recent scandal over the brutal actions of our "peacekeepers" in Somalia is ample proof of that. What it does mean—barring coverage of occasional disturbing and dramatic events—is that unflattering news about Canada's military policies and practices rarely leak out of the official channels of the defense establishment. We say rarely rather than never because there have been some exceptions to the routine dependence on official channels, such as the recent exposés by *Maclean's* magazine and other media of violent hazing and sexual harassment in the military.

More notably, the lengthy inquiry on the military's apparent cover-up of their actions in Somalia created an unprecedented amount of critical journalism on the Canadian military's inner workings. Even so, the Somalia inquiry itself was ended prematurely by the Liberal government, and within weeks the Canadian press seemed to lose interest in the military. Short of devoting substantial resources to a "military beat" or to a costly investigation of secretive military institutions—an unlikely scenario, in our view—the Canadian media have been quick to return to their old habits. For the most part, reporting on the military simply means attending military press conferences and quoting top military officials.

ENVIRONMENTAL DEGRADATION AS A SYSTEMIC AND ONGOING PROBLEM

In a 1993 article published in the *Utne Reader*, Paul Hawken, an American journalist, describes the current state of the planet's environment with grim precision. The problems facing the global ecology, he writes, are vast and complex. With the world's population at 5.5 billion and counting, fulfilling the wants and needs of the exploding human species "is stripping the Earth of its biotic capacity to produce life." What's worse, Hawken notes, is that the frenzied extraction of natural resources for immediate consumption is so poorly distributed that the top 20% of the world's income earners consume 80% of the world's wealth while the rest of the planet struggles to put food on the table.[1] The reality, Worldwatch Institute's Lester Brown concludes in his annual *State of the World* survey, is that every living system on Earth is in decline.

Whether one agrees or not with the scope of Brown's pessimistic conclusions, there can be little argument that ecosystems around the world are experiencing profound stress. Canada is no exception to the global and systemic problem of environmental degradation. For example, as of this writing, Canada is one of the worst per capita national offenders in overall energy consumption and in carbon dioxide emissions—a key contributor to global warming. Given both the global and national stakes of systemic environmental decline, it is a disappointing surprise that so many stories concerning environmental degradation appeared on our "Most Under-Reported" lists during the 1990s. Examples include:

- Business grabs the environmental agenda (1993, #4)
- Canadian mismanagement and the cod fisheries collapse (1993, #9)
- Is military pollution an overlooked crisis? (1993, #11)
- Does Pickering's nuclear generating station lie in an earthquake zone? (1993, #16)
- Cleaning up after AECL (1994, #1)
- Fish farming: A biological time-bomb? (1994, #9)
- The cost of auto-mobility (1994, #14)
- Proposed U.S. environmental law could harm Canada's air and water (1995, #1)

It is important to make one point right away: we are not alleging that environmental stories never or even rarely make the news. On the contrary, the Canadian media have paid a lot of attention over the past two decades to dramatic environmental crises or "blow-ups" such as the Exxon Valdez oil spill, or to the dramatic confrontations between loggers and environmentalists in British Columbia's forests. Still, we believe that the Canadian media do a rather lacklustre job of covering the systemic and ongoing connections between global environmental degradation and the ordinary every-day workings of the economy, including the pursuit of corporate profit and the promotion of consumerism and materialism as the path to personal fulfilment.

When we began our preliminary investigation into media and the environment, we had a hunch that the news media would choose to play up controversial and dramatic conflicts about environmental issues in lieu of a more sustained engagement with systemic threats to ecological balance. This is one reason why in 1997 NewsWatch Canada chose to study the Canadian news media's coverage of forestry issues in British Columbia. Specifically, by analyzing who the media typically tapped as sources in forestry debates, we sought to determine, at least provisionally, whether the media were presenting a wide range of views regarding the forests or if they were simply playing up the more dramatic "loggers" versus "environmentalists" angle.

From July 1995 to July 1996, NewsWatch researcher Janet Ready collected a sample of 183 print and broadcast stories on logging as an environmental issue from the *Vancouver Sun*, the *Vancouver Province*, the *Globe and Mail*, the *Victoria Times-Colonist*, CBC-TV, and CTV. Overall, she found that these media confined their coverage to three groups of sources: environmental groups, government sources, and timber industry spokespeople. By narrowing their focus to the perspectives of these three groups, the media played up the drama and conflict between "loggers" and "environmentalists" (with government standing in as the "referee"). A host of alternative sources who might have injected some complexity and nuance into the debate—including First Nations, labour and community groups, and independent environmental scientists and academics—were left out in the cold.

South of the border, a study conducted by two American media scholars into the battle over old growth forests in the Pacific Northwest also points to the inclination for the media to play up conflict and drama. In their analysis of four years of news stories broadcast on the three major American television networks (ABC, CBS, NBC), Carol Liebler and Jacob Bendix found that, of all the sources selected to speak about old growth forests in the Pacific Northwest, individual loggers and mill workers appeared most frequently in the news.[2] What's the reason for the popularity of the "mill worker angle" among journalists? Individual loggers and mill workers can speak poignantly about their children's future and the possibility of losing their livelihood. Facing unemployment and dislocation, their highly personal and dramatic stories simply made good TV. On the other hand, environmentalists who seem to promote abstract and intangible interests like "biodiversity" and "habitat protection" were less frequently tapped as sources.

At first sight, this lack of access for environmentalists seems to contradict Janet Ready's findings in selected Canadian media. We suspect, though, that the high media profile of environmental groups challenging B.C.'s forestry practices was a by-product of their confrontational tactics, yielding them media access to talk about their activities, but not necessarily their analyses. Still, while the media on both sides of the 49th parallel generally frame environmental crises in dramatic and personal terms, the more subtle, ongoing, and systemic threats to our ecological survival continue to be under-reported.

One of these threats, according to many ecologically-minded environmentalists, is the continual promotion of hyper-consumption as a way of life. There is a growing sense among many environmental scholars and activists that there are ecological limits to material growth. In this view, the continual promotion of hyper-consumerism in the media (you've seen the ads: "Buy now! No money down! New and improved!") has created a "throw-away" culture—particularly in the industrialized West. Marketing discourse in this culture equates personal happiness with the buying of things. The trap is that there is no end to it: the more we have, the more we want. Unprecedented levels of consumption in the West have provided unrivalled opportunities for material comfort and individual choice, but this hyper-consumption arguably poses a dramatic, pervasive and ongoing threat to the planet's fragile and complex ecosystem.

To discover if this apparent ecological threat was being covered and debated in the Canadian news media, Simon Fraser University researcher Tim Southam (no relation to the newspaper family) analyzed the *Vancouver Sun's* coverage of the environment, recycling programs, and the issue of global warming. Working under the direction of NewsWatch co-director Robert Hackett and SFU Communications professor Stephen Kline, Southam conducted a content analysis of the headlines from all environmental stories published in the *Sun* in 1990 and 1992 (a total sample of 592 stories) to see how many explicitly addressed over-consumption as an environmental concern.[3]

While the *Sun* extended much coverage to environmental protection efforts in Canada and the U.S., the environmental aspects of industry, and the dramatic exploits of environmental activists, not a single headline explicitly mentioned over-consumption as a contributor to environmental decline.

In an effort to look behind the headlines, Southam also selected eight stories from his sample which—judging from the tenor of their headlines—might plausibly address the issue of over-consumption further down in the text. In this analysis, he discovered that two stories did in fact view over-consumption (particularly of energy) as an environmental problem.[4] However, even these stories framed the issue as a matter of individual responsibility and not as a concern for national or international policy-makers. On the whole, Southam concluded, despite the recent prominence of environmental news in the Canadian media agenda, the lack of discussion and debate about over-consumption of consumer goods and resources is notable.

Why do the media continue to focus on isolated if dramatic environmental crises at the expense of a more sustained look at possible systematic links between the consumer economy and environmental decline? We can only speculate at this point, but our initial interviews with both journalists and environmental activists suggest two potential filters. First, as one columnist told us, "The media's interest in the environment ebbs and flows." And, over the past decade, media interest in the environment has begun to ebb. Beginning in the recession years of the early 1990s, many papers reassigned environmental reporters to other news beats—ostensibly in response to reader polls that ranked the environment lower on a list of news priorities than it had been in the late 1980s.

With fewer reporters assigned full-time to environmental coverage, there is a greater tendency simply to cover the most dramatic environmental disasters, such as brush fires in Indonesia or the Exxon Valdez oil spill in Alaska. As a result, systemic and ongoing (and therefore less immediate or sexy) threats to ecological balance are harder to register on the news agenda.

A second filter lies in the media's difficulty with covering the byzantine world of research and science. A reporter we interviewed argued, for example, that "scientists don't speak the same language as the rest of us." As a result, reporters are loath to wade into the morass of contradictory research reports and cutting-edge ecological theory. For some environmental activists, this reluctance to investigate new scientific research into systemic environmental threats can be immensely frustrating. On this point, one environmental activist who responded to our survey argued persuasively that reporters are generally "afraid to tackle [environmental] issues that are not already widely accepted, and unwilling to look for [the] scientific evidence and authoritative opinion required to introduce critical issues." Consequently, the news media tend to focus on the obvious environmental threats—the oil spill, the radiation leak, and the sewage crisis—at the expense of "open-ended issues which are continental and extend over long periods of time."

THE FRANCOPHONE PERSPECTIVE IN UNITY DEBATES

Over 20 years ago, the CRTC's Boyle Committee, which had originally been created to investigate allegations of pro-separatist bias in CBC's French language service, released a stunning indictment of the state of French/English interaction in the Canadian news media. "As presented by the media," their report concluded, "Canada is in a state of deep schizophrenia: if English and French Canadians were on different planets, there could hardly be a greater contrast of views and information."[5] And, as Professor Francois Demers of Laval University has reminded us, NewsWatch Canada is by no means immune from this uniquely Canadian case of media schizophrenia. For example, Demers has noted that some of the stories on our 1995 short-list of "underreported" stories in Canada's anglophone media—including "The Untold Costs of New Zealand's Economic Revolution" and "Canadian Media Mum on Human Rights Abuses in Mexico"—attracted a wealth of coverage in Quebec. The point is well-taken: there are notable particularities of English and French language media, and you can't simply assume that what holds true on one side of the linguistic divide will always be true on the other.

Not surprisingly, this linguistic isolationism seems especially pronounced in the media's coverage of national unity issues. In his survey of the English- and French-language media's coverage of unity debates since the Quiet Revolution in Quebec in the 1960s, Arthur Siegel argues that, far from working to bridge what novelist Hugh MacLennan called the "two solitudes," the English and French press may have actually worked to reinforce the divisions between English and French-speaking Canadians.[6] Siegel points to the sobering possibility that (with certain exceptions, such as major international stories and federal election campaigns) Canadians live in two hermetically sealed media worlds—one English and the other French—which cover the same issues from divergent and often ethnocentric perspectives.

To begin our own exploration into the depth of isolationism in the anglophone media (especially with regard to linguistically and culturally-sensitive issues), we decided to examine if the English-language media apply a double standard in their coverage of minority language rights. More specifically, we sought to discover if the English-language news media play up the concerns of English-speaking residents of Quebec while ignoring or downplaying similar complaints made by francophone communities in the rest of Canada.[7]

To answer these questions, NewsWatch researcher Tricia Wilson conducted a content analysis of five Canadian daily newspapers (*The Halifax Daily News*, *The Montreal Gazette*, *The Toronto Sun*, *The Vancouver Sun*, and *The Globe and Mail*), ultimately collecting a sample of 252 articles on language rights in Canada spanning six months in 1996. What she discovered was that, out of all these stories, a full 68% treated the issue of language rights as a "Quebec issue"—i.e., as an issue relevant only to Quebeckers and Quebec politicians.[8] Conversely, only 28% of the articles discussed language rights as an issue of national concern.

This tendency to frame minority language rights as a "Quebec issue" is also reflected in the sources cited by these stories. For instance, Quebec government officials were tapped as sources in two-thirds of the stories in the sample period, while federal government officials appeared in about one-third of the articles. However, none of the stories quoted, paraphrased, or even mentioned the perspectives of government officials from other provinces, "contributing to the profound under-reporting of minority language issues" in the rest of Canada.

With the debate over language rights framed narrowly as a "Quebec issue," the concerns of the anglophone community in Quebec have accordingly taken centre stage in the English-language media. For example, while nearly 25% of the stories quoted anglophone activists in Quebec, a mere 6% included the views of francophone activists in Quebec or among the Bloc Quebecois in Ottawa. Moreover, 25% of the stories in the sample implied that the rights guaranteed to francophones in Quebec and nationwide were too generous, but only 6% of these stories suggested that the rights guaranteed to anglophones in Quebec were too generous. Finally, 40% of the articles contained allegations that anglophone rights had been violated by the Quebec government's language policies, while only 10% of the stories claimed that francophone rights outside of Quebec had been violated.

In the end, Wilson writes, the amount and overall tone of the coverage afforded to anglophone rights in Quebec suggests a double standard in the story English-language newspapers tell Canadians about national unity. While the problems and concerns of anglophone communities in Quebec receive wide play and much critical commentary, the anglo-Canadian media tend to ignore the perspectives and struggles of francophone communities in places such as Alberta and British Columbia. Concerned primarily with the rights of fellow English-speakers in Quebec, the anglophone media's radar screens don't register the perspectives of francophone communities on national unity perspectives, which might add some much-needed texture and depth to the ongoing debates over Quebec sovereignty.

In our view, this double standard reflected in the coverage of minority language rights may indicate a more fundamental double standard in the English media. Even though the debates over minority language rights are just one small slice of a larger unity pie—a pie that includes, of course, sticky constitutional issues and the omnipresent possibility of Quebec independence—the ethnocentric focus on the concerns of anglophone minorities in Quebec implies an imbalance in the English media's coverage of national unity writ large.

This imbalance lends support to Arthur Siegel's claim that Canadians actually live within two separate media worlds, each mapping the same events using different cultural assumptions and prejudices. We have yet to do any systematic research on the issue at this point, but we suspect that parallel blind spots are likely to be found in the francophone news media as well, as Guy Bertrand, cited in Chapter One, suggests.

The reasons why this linguistic gulf developed in Canada's media are complex and beyond the scope of this book, but a few points deserve mention here. The gap is partly rooted in different traditions of journalism. The francophone press has a stronger history of advocacy and direct involvement in politics, whereas the anglophone press has been more influenced by commercial forces and by U.S. journalism's paradigm of "objectivity." This paradigm of objectivity, however, offers no guarantee that the news media are value-free in some absolute sense. As defined in the work-a-day world of journalism, "objectivity" means handling issues that are contentious within the community in a fair and evenhanded way. It does not mean challenging or rejecting values shared by the whole community. In this respect, both English and French-language media share the contrasting assumptions of their respective communities about the nature of Canada. For most francophone Quebeckers, including journalists, Canada was created as a compact between two "founding peoples," French and English. But for most anglo-Canadians, Canada is a federation with a central government and ten equal provinces, each containing a wide diversity of ethno-cultural groupings.

Thus, for anglos both inside and outside Quebec, the future unity of the Canadian federation is understandably a matter of great concern. As a result, English-language coverage of Quebec politics—including the 1995 sovereignty referendum—usually focuses on one central question: "Will the country hold together?" From this perspective, the anglo media have made no bones about portraying Quebec "separation" as a threat. By contrast—if we take the case of the last referendum as a benchmark—the French-language media were fairly balanced in their coverage of the Yes and No sides in the referendum, aware of the deep divisions within their audiences. More generally, they cover a wider range of stories about Quebec's culture, society and economy—issues that may carry little interest outside the province. The result, once again, is the presentation of two different versions of Quebec and Canadian politics. Our initial research suggests this chasm between the "two solitudes" shows few signs of narrowing any time soon. Some critics fear that the growing influence of Conrad Black in anglo-Canada's press may make it even more difficult to build bridges; his hard-line views on Quebec nationalism are well-documented.[9]

RELIGION AND TRADITIONAL SOCIAL VALUES

Overall, Canadians are a religious people. According to a 1993 StatsCan report, *Religions in Canada*, 87.5% of Canadians hold religious beliefs or affiliations. However, in the view of one church official we interviewed, even though "far more people are involved in religious activities than follow the local sports team," news coverage of religion and faith tends to be "sparse and superficial." Some of the journalists we spoke with also pointed to the overall lack of coverage extended to religion and faith in Canada. "We tend to underestimate the power of religion in people's lives," one journalist told us. "We tend to marginalize it and treat religious people as cranks."

The low priority afforded to religious coverage is also reflected in the paucity of journalists devoted full-time to the religion beat in Canada's major newspapers. For instance, as *Ottawa Citizen* reporter Bob Harvey writes in a recent edition of *Media magazine*, the *Vancouver Sun*, *Calgary Herald*, *Hamilton Spectator*, and the *Citizen* are "probably the only dailies with full-time writers specializing in religion and ethics."[10]

In 1995, NewsWatch researcher Susan Murray conducted a preliminary study of religious reporting in the *Globe and Mail* to see how much attention Canada's first "national" daily was paying to the role of religion and faith in Canadian society. To this end, Murray analyzed all of the stories on religious issues printed in the *Globe and Mail's* front section over a four-month period in 1995 (total sample: 100 articles). The conclusion: religion receives fairly regular coverage, but it tends to play up controversy and sensation at the expense of a sustained engagement with the role of religion in Canada. For example, 52% percent of the stories were coded as "negative," reflecting an emphasis on controversial changes to church policies, child sexual abuse, religious intolerance, and the often bitter debate over the ordination of gays and lesbians in main-line Christian churches. Conversely, only 19% of the stories covered the more positive aspects of faith in Canada, including the role of churches in charities and poverty outreach programs, and a further 29% of the stories were coded as neutral in tone.

The lack of media engagement with the complexity of religious issues may simply reflect the same news values—e.g., negativity, unambiguity and conflict—which journalists apply to other stories. Some observers, however, see a further problem: a "secular bias" among Canadian journalists. For example, one unnamed reporter (identified only as a born-again Christian) argued in the Spring 1998 issue of *Media* that most journalists employ a world view that is predominantly "middle-class, secular, and centrist." For this journalist, the "secular" world view usually "translates into an apathy about faith issues, unless they involve sex or scandal." Many religious conservatives believe that this allegedly "secular" world-view leads journalists to harbour an inherent suspicion of religion and traditional social values. Even worse, they argue, the secular world-view tends to inflect coverage of a whole host of social and cultural issues with a "left-liberal" bias.

With this argument in mind, NewsWatch researcher Christoph Clodius decided to investigate whether or not an institutionalized left-liberal bias in the culture of journalism generates unbalanced coverage of a contentious social issue that has religious implications. Taking the issue of abortion as a test case, he set out to discover if the press coverage extended to this explosive social issue was indeed informed by a "liberal" or "secular" slant toward the "pro-choice" position. Drawing a random sample of 68 articles about abortion from the *Globe and Mail*, the *Winnipeg Free Press*, and the *Victoria Times-Colonist*, Clodius analyzed each story, coding every paragraph as primarily "pro-choice," "pro-life," or "neutral." Out of a total of 528 paragraphs in the study sample, he found that 46% expressed pro-choice perspectives, 19% expressed pro-life perspectives, and 35% were coded as neutral. In short, pro-choice views on abortion appeared more than twice as often as pro-life perspectives in our sample.

On the face of it, these findings are consistent with the claim that the middle-class, secular, and urban world view of contemporary journalists tends to inflect the coverage of religion and social issues with a "left-liberal" slant. Some commentators would take the critique much further. In a rather diverse and lively panel organized by NewsWatch Canada at the 1997 Canadian Association of Journalists' convention, the arch-conservative publisher of *Western Report,* Link Byfield, presented his own list of news stories allegedly buried by the media's left-liberal "group think". His list included the "sociological disaster" of liberalized divorce, the "diseases and dysfunctions" prevalent among homosexuals, the costs of "Indian welfare addiction," the "chokehold" of Quebec politicians on national politics, the "probable connection" between abortion and breast cancer, and the "increasingly successful scientific attack on evolution."[11] (Interestingly, the *Globe & Mail* reprinted Byfield's culturally conservative and arguably eccentric list, but refused to offer equivalent treatment to our own project's work—work that inspired Byfield's musings in the first place.)

Before drifting too far down this well-traveled "liberal media" road, though, we need to qualify any attempt to find a so-called leftist bias in the Canadian media. First and foremost, as noted in Chapter One, and in our survey of journalists discussed in Chapter Three, the issue of "bias" in the media is far more complex than the sweeping notion of "liberal media" suggests. While the media may indeed be inflected toward left-liberal positions on social issues (such as abortion), the Canadian news is heavily laden with market liberal or right-wing perspectives on economic issues (such as government spending and debt).

Moreover, even within the media's coverage of social and cultural issues, the dominance of liberal-left perspectives should not be exaggerated. From politically conservative tabloids such as the *Toronto Sun*, to the free market evangelism of many business columnists and the right-wing populism of many radio talk show hosts, the media overall provide notable space for decidedly non-leftist views.

HUMAN RIGHTS ABUSES BY CANADA'S "FRIENDS"

As violations of some of the basic principles of liberal democracy—freedom from oppression, freedom of speech, freedom of association, and so on—human rights abuses around the world would seem to be inherently newsworthy. Not only do human rights abuses typically meet all the criteria for "newsworthiness" (i.e., drama, deviance, and controversy), but explosions of political oppression—such as those perpetrated in the killing fields of Cambodia or the oil fields of Nigeria—mark particularly dramatic points of departure from such fundamental Canadian notions as personal freedom, human dignity, and social justice. That helps explain why particularly gruesome instances of human rights violations have at least periodically attracted the news media's attention.

However, a quick glance at our undercovered story lists suggests that human rights coverage is uneven. One such neglected story in the early 1990s was Canada's cozy relationship with Indonesia's human rights-violating regime (1993, #3). Aspects of this story, at least, have received greater media attention in more recent years.[12] In 1996, the Nobel Peace Prize was awarded to two activists against the Indonesian occupation of East Timor; in November 1997, protests against the Vancouver APEC summit generated controversy around General Suharto's presence, RCMP actions, and possible Prime Ministerial interference; and soon afterwards, popular unrest in Indonesia itself forced Suharto out of office; and the U.N. intervened in East Timor.

Other human rights stories from our lists, however, continue to languish in the shadows, including the World Bank's funding of forced resettlement in China and elsewhere (1994, #8), the spin doctoring of the Chiapas rebellion and its connection to NAFTA (1994, #10), and other general human rights abuses in Mexico (1995, #7).

Confronted with these important yet undercovered stories, we wanted to find out whether there is any pattern to such omissions. One might speculate that international news coverage in general, and human rights coverage in particular, is especially dependent on the priorities, perspectives and activities of the Canadian government. Such dependence would be reinforced by the media's orientation towards governmental sources, combined with the relatively low priority given to international news by most newspaper organizations and readers. With the exception of the national dailies, newspapers are still regarded as primarily a local medium.

For this reason, it would not be surprising if the media normally tend to take their cues about international politics from the government—particularly when there is a multi-party consensus—and to accord more favourable coverage to "friendly" nations than to "hostile" ones. According to Edward Herman and Noam Chomsky, such a state-oriented double standard in human rights coverage would not be unprecedented. In the U.S., Herman and Chomsky argue, there is a pervasive double standard in news coverage: the U.S. media often attack rights abuses in certain countries, but also tacitly legitimize the U.S. government's foreign policy of supporting repressive right-wing dictatorships that are friendly to U.S. political and economic interests.[13] Exploring this hypothesis in the Canadian context, Robert Hackett studied human rights coverage during the Soviet-American Cold War of the early 1980s. He found that, by and large, the Canadian press (though less consistently than its American counterpart) was generally more likely to cover human rights violations perpetrated by "terrorist" or "pro-Soviet" regimes, compared to those committed by "friendly" or NATO-aligned states.[14] The most consistently negative coverage regarding human rights was reserved for such quintessential Cold War villains as the Soviet Union and Poland's martial law regime, as well as for "the West's" newest enemies—the "terrorist" states of Iran and Libya. By contrast, the comparably dismal human rights records of such pro-Western allies as Saudi Arabia and Turkey received virtually no attention from the Canadian media.

But that was the Cold War—relatively ancient history in today's globalized world. With the collapse of the Soviet Union, and the Berlin Wall reduced to rubble, old geo-political alignments are increasingly irrelevant. What counts now, the pundits tell us, is not a nation's orientation to one of the two former superpowers, but rather its ability to maintain favourable trade and investment relations with nations around the world. Given the priority that governments—including Canada's—place on good relations with important trading partners, we began to wonder whether Canada's news media are applying a new double standard, downplaying human rights violations among Canada's economic partners, in contrast with coverage of other countries.

To begin to answer this question, NewsWatch examined *The Toronto Star's* and *The Globe and Mail's* coverage of human rights violations in six nations tagged as "frequent offenders" by Amnesty International: Nigeria, Burma, Saudi Arabia, Indonesia, China, and South Korea. These six nations comprised three groups, according to the amount of annual trade conducted with Canada: (1) minimal trade (Nigeria and Burma), (2) moderate trade (Saudi Arabia and Indonesia), and (3) extensive trade (China and South Korea). Building on work by NewsWatch researcher Mavis MacMillen, we first searched for the total number of stories written about each nation in both papers during 1995. We then conducted a key-word search within each nation's sample, using the phrase "human rights," thus enabling a comparison of the total amount of coverage of each nation with the number of articles specifically mentioning this theme.

The key-word searches revealed that, of the 6,460 stories published by the two papers about these six countries in 1995, 731 (11.3%) mentioned human rights. But there were substantial differences in the attention given to human rights, on a country-by-country basis. The two smallest traders with Canada, Nigeria and Burma, had the highest proportion of human rights stories (28.6% and 25.6%, respectively, of these countries' coverage). The "moderate" traders were also in the "middle" of human rights coverage: Indonesia (4.9%) and Saudi Arabia (4.8%), while "high" trader South Korea received the fewest human rights items, a mere 2.7%. The one exception to the inverse relationship between trade and attention to rights violations was China, a major trading partner with an average proportion (12.7%) of human rights coverage.

Just how difficult it can be to attract attention to the issue of international human rights was dramatically revealed by the Canadian news media's coverage of the Peruvian hostage crisis in 1996-97. To recapitulate the events that grabbed world headlines at the time: On December 17, 1996, 14 members of the Peruvian People's Revolution (known as the MRTA) stormed the Japanese embassy during a large celebration, taking 500 guests hostage. According to the MRTA, this admittedly desperate and dangerous action was taken to draw international attention to widespread human rights abuses in Peru and to the growing gap between rich and poor. The MRTA is not alone in this criticism of the Peruvian government. Amnesty International reports that the government has been responsible for nearly 1,000 disappearances, hundreds of politically motivated executions, beatings, rapes, and other forms of abuse— perpetrated mostly by Peru's security forces. But if the MRTA's goal was to draw attention to these abuses, concludes NewsWatch researcher Gina Bailey, they generally failed.[15] The press largely bypassed these issues, focusing instead on framing the MRTA as "terrorists" and "Marxist-Leninists."

In her analysis of the coverage extended to this crisis by four newspapers (*The Globe and Mail*, *The Toronto Star*, *The New York Times*, and *The Washington Post*) during the first ten days of this crisis, Bailey discovered that the North American media stuck closely to the Peruvian, U.S., and Canadian government's version of events. Accordingly, the media made little mention of human rights abuses in Peru (in fact the phrase "human rights" appeared in just five out of 76 stories in the total sample) and neglected to detail the Peruvian government's long history of using paramilitary "death squads" to suppress internal dissent. Moreover, the Canadian and American papers selectively covered the demands of MRTA members, playing up the demand to release former MRTA members from prison, but downplaying the MRTA's other demands—including the reinstatement of union rights, the recognition of rural communal lands, and the prosecution of death squads.

Finally, on April 22, 1997, the Peruvian military stormed the embassy, killing all the MRTA members as well as one hostage. There is no doubt that the MRTA members had engaged in an illegal act of political violence, but this does not explain why the North American media presented such a one-sided picture of this hostage crisis. Again, the initial evidence suggests that the Canadian media's reluctance to venture beyond government sources and perspectives—especially those offered by Peruvian officials who would be reluctant to talk openly about human rights—limited the focus of media coverage to the narrow issue of "terrorism." For example, Bailey found that Canadian papers used Peruvian government sources in 34% of their stories (printed in the first 10 days of the crisis), Canadian government sources in 21%, Japanese government in 17%, and the U.S. government in 8%. Conversely, released hostages appeared in 16% of the stories, and MRTA members in just 9%. In short, while journalists amplified the perspectives of government officials, the voices of human rights organizations, MRTA members, and the Peruvian people themselves were relatively muzzled.

A more complex and comprehensive view of these tragic events would have required news organizations to locate reporters full-time in Peru, so that they might be in a position to develop a wider variety of contacts and dig up alternative perspectives. On this occasion, Bailey concludes, the press acted more like a lap-dog than a watchdog of a governments' human rights policies.

It is important to be cautious before concluding that there is an overriding double standard in human rights coverage, or that Cold War ideology has been displaced by other political considerations, such as trade. We need to explore further cases, as well as to take into account other factors that have been shown[16] to influence a country's coverage in the North American media—e.g., population, GNP per capita, the presence of Western news bureaux, and the hard work of human rights advocates themselves in calling public attention to abuses. Moreover, it is possible that trading relations may sometimes trigger, not just inhibit, at least temporary attention to human rights violations. According to one journalist we interviewed, most Canadian news outlets simply forget about human rights, until "the prime minister goes on trade missions to these countries." However, it is clear that such coverage is sporadic and that, without the background that comes from sustained, on-site investigations of human rights issues, reporters on such trade missions are less likely to look behind the official line for alternative perspectives and views.

WHITE-COLLAR AND CORPORATE CRIME

At first glance, it may seem strange to list crime among the Canadian media's most pervasive and systematic blind spots. After all, aren't the nation's airwaves and newspapers constantly splattered with the lurid details of Canada's most wanted violent offenders? Such preoccupation with violent crime, however, is the flip-side of the media's avoidance of other kinds of crime—particularly white-collar and corporate crimes—which may in fact have equally serious social and financial consequences. For example, we have already noted (Chapter Five, story #4, 1994) that the number of workplace deaths due to unsafe or illegal working conditions roughly equals the number of street homicides, and some estimates place the total cost of white-collar crime to Canadian taxpayers and consumers at $20 or even $30 billion a year.

South of the border, the costs of white-collar crime pile up as well. According to investigative writer David Burnham, cited in the U.S. Project Censored's annual report, white-collar crime costs the U.S. 10 to 50 times more money than street crime, and exacts an enormous human toll. For example, in 1987 alone, an estimated 5,070,000 Americans died prematurely from on-the-job exposure to toxins—a figure roughly three times the 21,500 people murdered in the U.S. during the same year.[17] Moreover, from 1970 to 1992, 200,000 Americans died at work, "a significant number from known negligence by the employer."

Despite these figures, the U.S. federal government has continued to look the other way: out of the more than 51,000 federal criminal indictments in 1994, only 250—less than one- half of 1%—involved criminal violations of American environmental, occupational health and safety, and consumer product safety laws. Still, neither the enormous scale of white- collar and corpo-rate crime nor the inaction of the American government has attracted the at-tention of the U.S. media system.

Given these apparent human and financial costs, NewsWatch Canada decided in 1995 to take a closer look into the amount and quality of coverage afforded to white-collar and corporate crime in the Canadian news media. Our hunch was that white-collar crime in Canada was grossly undercovered, especially in comparison to the aggressive and sensational coverage extended to violent crime. To test this hypothesis in a single newspaper, NewsWatch researcher Clayton Jones conducted a content analysis of the *Vancouver Sun's* coverage of white-collar crime during three periods of time: 1977-79, 1985-87, and 1992-94. Using a random sampling procedure, he compiled nine weeks of articles and compared the frequency of white-collar crime coverage to the coverage extended to sexual offenses during the same three time periods.

What he discovered was that the frequency of white-collar crime cover-age actually decreased over the last 15 years. For example, in the 1977-79 period, there were 41 white-collar crime stories, but this figure dropped to 33 items in the 1985-87 period, and then sagged again to 23 items in the 1992-94 period.

This steady decrease in the amount of coverage afforded to white-collar crime stands in stark contrast to the veritable explosion of coverage of sexual offenses over the same period. In the 1977-79 sample, there were only nine news items concerning sexual offenses. This figure jumped by 367% to 33 news stories in 1985-87, and rose a further 52% in the 1992-94 period to 50 items.

At this point, an objection may be raised regarding our singular focus on the *Vancouver Sun*; perhaps other newspapers cover white-collar crime more comprehensively. Fair enough. This is why a later NewsWatch study by Benjamin Letts focused on the amount of white-collar crime coverage in four major Canadian dailies: the *Vancouver Province*, the *Vancouver Sun*, the *To-ronto Star*, and the *Globe and Mail*. In the end, when we compared all of these papers, we found that the *Vancouver Sun* was the paper that had actually devoted the *most* attention to white-collar and corporate crime!

These two studies are far from exhaustive or definitive. Still, they offer some suggestive findings: even when compared to only one category of vio-lent crime—in this case, sexual offenses—white-collar crime still got short shrift in a sample of Canadian newspapers. But if, by all accounts, violent crime constitutes only a small fraction of total reported crimes, then what explains the news media's preoccupation with crime and violence? A full account of this question would require a book in itself, but, briefly, the academic and professional literature suggests two important reasons for the media's addiction to violent crime.

First, to reiterate a point made in earlier chapters, news about street crime is fairly easy to collect. Most newspapers have a specific room where reporters on the "police beat" listen anxiously to a police scanner to hear about the latest rounds of urban mayhem. Some news outlets even assign reporters to stay at police stations full-time (in office space donated by the accommodating constabulary), where they can develop close relationships with police officers and receive "scoops" and leaks before their competitors.[18] In contrast, white-collar crime is more difficult to cover than a "quick hit" of street violence. On this point, one reporter we interviewed quipped, "White-collar crime doesn't come over the police scanner."

Second, violent crime holds particular appeal for television news because it often comes accompanied with dramatic and emotionally charged pictures. As American media critic Lawrence Wallack argues, "Television is a visual medium; it wraps every story in pictures."[19] To get on the air, particularly on commercial networks, news stories must be visual, short, and compelling in order to meet the professional standards for what makes "good TV." For television, then, violent crime typically offers such irresistible imagery as flashing police lights, speeding cars, blood-stained sidewalks, and the agonized faces of grieving family and friends.

By contrast, white-collar crimes like embezzlement or tax fraud offer television or newspapers few opportunities to run dramatic pictures. Instead, such stories often must be told using only a numbing series of charts, graphs, and numbers—story elements that are noticeably short on visual appeal. As one journalist told NewsWatch, white collar crimes are "less dramatic than personal crimes. Corporate crimes are numbers without dramatic appeal...we prefer people stories rather than number stories." In this way, white-collar crime falls off the Canadian media agenda because, as another journalist explained, it is simply "not seen as a sexy issue."

It seems that the need to maximize audiences and minimize costs explains both the Canadian media's preoccupation with street crime and their inability or unwillingness to devote similar resources to white-collar or corporate crime. We also speculate that sustained media attention to corporate crime would, over time, hurt the public image of business in Canada. Such an approach would arguably undermine the ability of news organizations to attract advertising revenue, the lifeblood of most commercial media.

PUBLIC RELATIONS, PRIVATE AGENDAS

The role of the media in the ideal of democracy is simple but powerful. In a democratic society, it is argued, proposals for government and social policy are first subjected to a free and open public debate. In the end, one hopes, government makes political decisions based not on who has the most wealth or power, but rather on which perspective in the debate presents the more persuasive and compelling social vision. This is Civics 101, right? Still, the reality of actually-existing democracy in Canada often deviates from these high-minded ideals. In the daily business of political spin and government lobbying, money talks and, in today's political world, corporate money speaks louder than ever.

At NewsWatch Canada, we have become particularly concerned about the potential influence of the public relations industry in shaping government policy and public opinion. Even more seriously, that influence seems to be escaping the critical scrutiny of the news media. In 1993, for example, we reported on the various public relations strategies deployed by multinational corporations to blunt worldwide criticism of environmental degradation ("Business grabs the environmental agenda," 1993, #4). A year later, one of our most undercovered stories of 1994 reported that, while the Canadian Wildlife Federation markets itself as a conservation group, it is essentially run by those who kill animals for sport, and it promotes a variety of pro-hunting causes (1994, #7). Finally, in 1995 (#12), we discovered that the Canadian Taxpayers' Federation—ostensibly an expression of a "grassroots" Canadian tax revolt—was in fact headed by a board of lawyers, bankers, and business leaders. While each of these stories documents the sophisticated strategies corporate Canada deploys to protect its interests, the mainstream media seem almost completely unconcerned.

South of the border, the news media also seem predisposed to ignore or downplay the behind-the-scenes machinations of corporate PR. For instance, in the U.S., Project Censored has described how the mainline media failed to report on a PR campaign funded by top U.S. corporations and designed to secure "most-favored nation" (MFN) trading status for the People's Republic of China. Their mission: to refute or minimize China's dismal human rights record in hopes of swaying a pliant Congress to give priority to trade with China over a principled stand against political oppression. In the end, this corporate-financed campaign was a smashing success. With MFN status secured, such corporations as AT & T, Boeing, and General Motors were able to move ahead with plans to exploit the burgeoning Chinese market.[20]

In addition to commonplace corporate lobbying, the PR industry sometimes deploys more nefarious tactics. In one case, the chemical industry hired
a PR firm to pose as potential donors interested in contributing to an Oregon-
based campaign that would force anti-freeze makers to add bitterant to their
product (making it less tasty for unwary kids and pets). By pretending to mull
over a donation of $100,000, the PR firm gained access to the activist group's
financial records and its public information game plan for the following year—
information of great value to the chemical industry's fight against such regulations.[21]

The potential power of corporate dollars in shaping Canada's political
agenda is disquieting and, in our view, worthy of ongoing news coverage and
public discussion. Such interests have lobbied government openly for years,
but what is especially disturbing about today's PR industry is the manner in
which corporate alliances plan and execute their lobbying efforts. Increasingly aware that the public is understandably suspicious of big-moneyed special interests seeking government favours, corporate strategists all across North
America have devised a new way to win over public opinion. Instead of
openly and honestly promoting their interests, using their own name and in-
house spin doctors, many wealthy interests, it appears, now hide their PR
efforts behind phony "grassroots" organizations, using these "populist" mouth-
pieces to promote their own hidden and self-interested agendas.

Hiding corporate interests behind a populist mask has become the strategy *du jour* of many U.S. business interests, judging from stories uncovered
by Project Censored. For instance, an alliance of health insurance industry
giants created a phony "activist" group called the Coalition for Health Insurance Choices (CHIC). With the massive resources of the for-profit health
care industry behind it, this "grassroots" organization mounted a massive PR
campaign, ultimately helping to defeat the Clinton Administration's (admittedly half-hearted) attempt at basic health care reform.

As our own "under-covered" lists suggest, this tactic is quickly gaining
converts among Canada's corporate élite. For example, among the 1993 under-reported stories highlighted in Chapter Five was a story that detailed how
the logging industry strategically funded local community groups of loggers,
their families, and townspeople, and advised them on how best to defeat environmental restrictions of logging in old growth forests.

Where is the media coverage of this kind of corporate PR? If the media
system told us the whole story about how politics really works in Canada, an
analysis of the public relations industry would be a notable element. So what
might explain the relative lack of coverage? With the evidence we've accu-

mulated to this point, we can only begin to speculate. One potential source of this blind spot, however, may lie in the news media's own arguably excessive dependence on the public relations industry as a daily source of information and analysis. For example, a 1991 study by Jericho Promotions (a New York PR firm) found that 38 of 2,432 journalists surveyed said they got half of their stories from PR agents, while 17% admitted using PR people for every story.[22]

NewsWatch judge Maggie Siggins has commented wryly that PR organizations such as the Canadian Taxpayers Federation can be "quoted so often in the media that I sometimes feel they are a kind of shadow government." Given this dependence on PR as a daily source of information, it would be surprising if journalists did not feel a certain reluctance to cover the influence of corporate PR in shaping public policy and the news agenda. With deadline pressures and news space to fill, extending critical coverage to the PR industry would be tantamount to biting the hand that feeds them the news every day.

ENGENDERING STEREOTYPES?

As we noted in Chapter Three, close to half of the journalists we surveyed identified "Women's Issues" as a blind spot in the Canadian news agenda. In addition, several stories of particular interest to women popped up on our top under-covered story lists, including the risk to women from using tampons overnight (1994, #15), and the particular hardships of military wives (1994, #17). When the news media do in fact cover issues of specific concern to women—such as domestic violence and sexual assault—they tend to miss the larger social and political forces that underlie such issues, choosing to focus instead on individual histories and personal foibles.[23]

Why might the media not adequately cover the specific challenges and issues faced by over half of the Canadian population? Any answer we could give at this point would be speculative. NewsWatch research has barely tapped the important topic of the media's representation of women, whether as sources, reporters, or newsmakers. (One reason for locating our priorities elsewhere is the very useful research on media and gender already being conducted by MediaWatch, a national non-profit women's organization.)[24] However, our own initial investigations do point to one potential filter on coverage of women's social status in Canada: the lack of access afforded to women as sources of information and expertise in the news.

For example, in an analysis of 15 editions of *The National*— CBC-TV's signature newscast—in April and May of 1996, NewsWatch researcher Angela Austman documented both the gender and occupation of the sources who appeared in each news story. Austman discovered that a full 84% of all sources identified in *The National* were men, who constituted an even greater majority (89%) of sources from élite occupations, such as government officials, professionals, academics, corporate representatives, or interest group spokespersons.

Finally, Austman found that, when women were granted access, they were more likely than their male counterparts to be clustered in stories about "social issues" (e.g., education, religion, family, sexuality, and so on)—the so-called "soft news" topics.

These findings of gender imbalance on *The National* are consistent with MediaWatch's research. In a study of six newspapers across Canada, on a target date for each of four years (1990-93), MediaWatch counted the number of times women were mentioned or referenced in each paper in a single day.[25] MediaWatch discovered that these major Canadian dailies infrequently mentioned women either as sources, experts, or news-makers. In 1993, for instance, their access ranged from a high of 28% of people referenced in the *Toronto Star,* down to just 18% at the *St. John's Evening Telegram.*

Furthermore, when MediaWatch counted the number of female references in each section (Front Section, Business, Sports, Life, and so on) of the papers in the sample, they discovered that, while only 24% of all people appearing in the front section (the domain of "hard" news) were women, female news-makers made up a full 38% of the references in the "Life" or "Entertainment" sections.[26] Again, this demonstrates the tendency for news media to corral women into a "soft news" ghetto, reserving the more prestigious "hard news" (politics, business, international affairs) for their male counterparts.

We do not need to infer a male conspiracy in the media. The gender imbalance in sources is strongly related to the media's long-standing focus on political and institutional authorities, who are still largely male. Still, as MediaWatch concludes, the lack of representation of women in the news can tilt the media's coverage of key social and political issues. For example, consider the issue of violence against women. As the coverage extended to the Paul Bernardo killings demonstrates, the news media often present an impression that violent acts against women are typically committed by deranged strangers or serial killers. However, women's advocacy groups across North America have tried to point out for years that violence against women is, more often than not, a family affair. In fact, of all the female homicides solved in Canada in 1991, 54% of the victims were killed by a family member and another 38% were killed by an acquaintance. Similarly, 80% of all violent crimes against women were committed by individuals known to the victims.

It is not unreasonable to conclude that violence against women is generally not a random or isolated act, but rather a pervasive social and political problem, rooted in the dynamics of largely patriarchal familial and social structures. By referencing a wider range of sources—including the oft-excluded perspectives of women's advocacy groups—it is likely that a more textured and comprehensive view of violence against women (as well as other issues of concern to women in Canada) would emerge in the news.

At the same time, there may be something of a flip-side to this picture. One of our under-reported stories, the high rate of suicide amongst elderly males (1995, #11), alerted us to the possibility that certain types of stories about men as victims of disease, violence, hazards at work, or other social misfortune are also likely to be under-reported. Given the under-representation of women in the media, it may seem odd to highlight men's victimization as a possible blind spot. But this is not necessarily a contradiction; in fact, feminist scholars have long argued that sexist stereotypes of men as powerful and aggressive pigeonhole men in damaging ways. If the image of men as strong and dominant is pervasive, then events or stories that expose the frailties—or even the victimization—of men would seem to contradict contemporary common wisdom.

There is some evidence that such stories are indeed indicative of a media blind spot. Researcher Jim Boyce studied 1,242 headlines in seven major Canadian dailies over three years. He found that, while men and women suffer roughly equal rates of violence (bearing in mind that there is a great deal of male-to-male violence), news headlines were 35 times more likely to refer to female than male victims.[27] More recently, in 1997, the *Globe and Mail* invited its readers to identify stories that the media found "too hot to handle." Interestingly, the most common theme that emerged was apparent male victimization— alleged "gender bias" against fathers and men in family courts, female-originated domestic violence, male fatalities from breast cancer, abuse of elderly men, and male circumcision as a form of sexual abuse.[28]

That same year, NewsWatch conducted its own study. Researcher Kristin Simmons compared twelve months of media coverage of four types of cancer whose victims are gender-specific—breast cancer (mainly female) and ovarian cancer (entirely female), contrasted with the exclusively male ailments of testicular and prostate cancer. In total, men and women fall victim to these diseases in roughly equal numbers. Yet, when Simmons culled 598 health news items which specifically addressed those four types of cancer as well as heart disease from four Canadian dailies and the CBC and CTV national networks, she found a wide discrepancy in media attention to women's and men's health. While heart disease coverage was gender-balanced, almost 46% of the articles in her sample addressed breast cancer, while only 14.2% concerned prostate cancer. In the same sample, a similar imbalance of coverage extended to ovarian cancer (mentioned in 5.4% of the same sample), compared to testicular cancer (only three stories, a mere .5%). We speculate that men's reluctance in our culture to display weakness or to talk about their bodies contributes to this imbalance.

There are other, more controversial, studies that sometimes receive coverage in conservative magazines and publications targeted at men's groups of various types, but are rarely discussed or evaluated in the mainstream media—studies that claim to contradict widely-held stereotypes of women as victims and men as aggressors.[29] These studies, and the debates that often surround them, could certainly be given wider exposure. Still, the difficulty with giving greater media emphasis to topics such as male victimization is the potential political fallout, which may help to explain why conservative publications such as *Alberta Report* promote such topics more vigorously than do middle-market dailies.

Some conservatives are quick to grasp on to virtually any research that can be cited in support of campaigns for a return to more "traditional" gender relations in Canada, and against the use of public funds for such things as, say, shelters for battered women. However, in our view, such campaigns are too often based on highly selective and partisan readings of existing research that overlook the relatively greater economic vulnerability of women across the whole society, and their disproportionate responsibilities for child-rearing.

OTHER BLIND SPOTS?

Most certainly, the list of blind spots in this chapter is far from exhaustive, and our own research suggests that there are probably others. One possibility we have yet to explore thoroughly is under-coverage of the elderly as news-makers. But NewsWatch researchers have done some preliminary work to suggest that a certain amount of "ageism" may be an issue in Canadian news coverage. For example, in a study of coverage of crime victims in the two Vancouver dailies during a three-month period in 1996, Kirsten Simmons and Ben Letts found that, while gender was not a factor, age was: older victims received notably less coverage than younger ones, compared to official statistics.

Another topic deserving of further research is media coverage of technology. While there has been a near-panic surrounding the Y2K problem— the "millennium bug" that may cause computer systems to crash on January

1, 2000—it may well be that the media are more typically boosters of new technology, downplaying critical assessments of its impact or the vested interests behind its development and promotion. Certainly, MicroSoft was able to command global media attention for two months prior to the expensive and flashy unveiling of Windows 95, all of which landed Bill Gates on our "Junk Food News" list of over-hyped stories in 1995.

An exploratory study of a random sample of 45 *Globe & Mail* articles on technology undertaken by NewsWatch researcher Jason Watson found that coverage was twice as likely to be uncritical of technological innovation as critical. Technology stories aside, NewsWatch Canada is always pleased to hear from readers regarding further research on the blind spots we have identified, as well as others you feel deserve further exploration.

ENDNOTES:

1. See Paul Hawken, "A Declaration of Sustainability," *Utne Reader*, September/October (1993), p. 54.
2. Liebler, Carol M. & Bendix, Jacob, "Old-growth forests on network news: news sources and the framing of an environmental controversy," *Journalism and Mass Communication Quarterly* (Spring 1973), pp. 53-65. Cited in Tim Southam, *Social Discourses of the Environment: The Absence of Consumption and Consumerism,* Unpublished M.A. Thesis, (Burnaby: Simon Fraser University, 1995).
3. Southam, *Social Discourses*, p. 52.
4. Southam, *Social Discourses*, pp. 5960.
5. Cited in Arthur Siegel, *Politics and the Media in Canada,* 2nd edition (Toronto: McGrawHill, 1997), p. 227.
6. Siegel, *Politics and the Media*, p. 220.
7. The idea derives from a 1996 syndicated column by Rosemary Speirs: "English Canada's intolerance of French is ignored," *The Toronto Star* (August 20, 1996), p. A13.
8. See Tricia Wilson, "English Papers' Treatment of Unity Issues Unbalanced," *NewsWatch Monitor* (November 1997), p. ii.
9. Maude Barlow and James Winter, *The Big Black Book* (Toronto: Stoddart, 1997).
10. Bob Harvey, "The Ottawa Citizen Mixes the Sacred and the Secular," *Media* (Spring 1998) p. 10.
11. Link Byfield, "Letter from the Publisher," *Western Report* (June 23, 1997); "Some stories are just too hot to handle," *Globe & Mail* (July 19, 1997), p. D3.
12. During 1993, there were 90 stories on "Indonesia and human rights" in the *Ottawa Citizen, Vancouver Sun, Calgary Herald, Toronto Star, Montreal Gazette,* and *Halifax Daily News*, an average of just 15 per paper, according to Canada News Disk; during the first eleven months of 1998, this total had escalated to 279.

13. See Edward S. Herman and Noam Chomsky, *Manufacturing Consent: The Political Economy of the Mass Media* (New York: Pantheon, 1988).

14. Robert Hackett, *News and Dissent* (Norwood, NJ: Ablex Press, 1991), pp. 186-187.

15. For a summary of this study, see Gina Bailey, "Slanted coverage of Peruvian Hostage-taking Incident," *NewsWatch Monitor* (Fall 1997), p. i.

16. James F. Larson, *Television's Window on the World: International Affairs coverage on the U.S. Networks* (Norwood, NJ: Ablex, 1984).

17. Peter Phillips and Project Censored, *Censored 1997: The News That Didn't Make the News* (New York: Seven Stories Press, 1997), p. 39. Burnham's article (from *Covert Action Quarterly*, Summer 1996) is reprinted on pp. 365-369.

18. See Richard Ericson, "Patrolling the Facts: Secrecy and Publicity in Police Work," *British Journal of Sociology*, 40 (1989), p. 209.

19. Lawrence Wallack, Lori Dorfman, David Jernigan, and Makani Themba, *Media Advocacy and Public Health: Power for Prevention* (Newbury Park, CA: Sage, 1993), p. 56.

20. Phillips and Project Censored, *Censored 1997*, p. 76. The original story was reported by Ken Silverstein, Alexander Cockburn, and Jim Hightower.

21. Phillips, *Censored 1997*, p. 37; based on articles by John Stauber and Sheldon Rampton in *CovertAction Quarterly* (Winter 1995/96) and *Earth Island Journal* (Winter 1995/96).

22. Phillips, *Censored 1977*, p. 77.

23. Wallack et al, *Media Advocacy*.

24. For more information on MediaWatch and its recent research, contact them at Suite 204, 517 Wellington Street West, Toronto, Ontario, M5V 1G1; tel. (416) 408-2065.

25. MediaWatch, *Focus on Violence: Survey of Women in Canadian Newspapers* (Toronto: MediaWatch, 1993).

26. MediaWatch, *Focus on Violence*, 1993.

27. J.W. Boyce, *Manufacturing Concern: Worthy and Unworthy Victims — Headline Coverage of Male and Female Victims of Violence* (M.A. thesis, Wilfrid Laurier University, 1994). Abstract supplied to NewsWatch Canada by Mike Jebbett.

28. "More Stories That Are Too Hot to Handle," *Globe and Mail* (August 16, 1997).

29. For one discussion of such studies see Peter Verburg, "The other half of domestic violence," *BC Report* (August 1, 1994), pp. 23-25. One study he cites, for example, was an unpublished Ph.D. dissertation by Reena Sommer (University of Manitoba, 1994). She argued that women and men are equally violent (measured in terms of the number of times arguments escalated into physical violence or threats of violence) in the home. Following Verberg's discussion we undertook an initial scan of article and newspaper databases and turned up only three articles on the topic of violent women over eight years.

Chapter Seven

Blind Spots on Labour, Corporate Power and Social Inequality

One of the most serious blind spots in the Canadian news agenda is the lack of attention given to the consequences of social inequality and unfettered corporate power in Canada. In this chapter we explore this blind spot by focusing on the media's apparent unwillingness or inability to adequately cover issues in four broad areas:

- Exploitation and resistance in the world of work
- Poverty and class inequality
- The neo-liberal agenda: Absent alternatives and hidden consequences
- The power and biases of media corporations themselves

In the media system the voice of corporate Canada speaks loudly and often, but other voices—the poor, labour, and those who present alternatives to an all-against-all free market society are relatively muffled. The problem with this, surely, is that democratic political life works best when a wide diversity of voices and viewpoints are heard within the national media system.

Canada's Labour Scene: Covering (Up) the World of Work

When we think of "business news," we usually think of the daily grind of stock quotes, economic indicators, and investment tips that are part and parcel of TV newscasts across North America. In this way, the voice of business—the entrepreneur, the mutual fund manager, the anxious investor—is a daily and commonplace part of the news on the economy. But is this really all that the world of business and economics is about? What about the people who actually work in the offices and factories, deal with customers, and serve the public? Rarely, it seems, do the voices and perspectives of working people appear in this daily update on the business world. When we do hear from workers or labour organizations, it is usually during times of strife, especially strikes or other dramatic industrial disputes.

The result, many media scholars in the U.S. and U.K. have argued, is a one-sided view of the world of work.[1] While coverage of the business community routinely includes positive coverage over a wide range of topics, coverage of labour typically focuses on confrontational and controversial events such as strikes and contract negotiations. Moreover, labour is typically portrayed as the active and disruptive party. Two Canadian studies in the early 1980s reached similar conclusions.[2] At NewsWatch Canada, we wanted to see if this imbalance in both the amount and tone of coverage attracted by business and labour still holds true in the Canadian media. Are all perspectives on the world of work—from management, to union leaders, to frontline workers—treated fairly?

To address these questions, NewsWatch researchers B. Dianne Birch and Trevor Hughes compiled a sample of news mentioning business and labour topics from the news and business sections of the *Vancouver Sun*.[3] They used two time periods: September-December 1987 and September-December 1997, respectively, before and after Conrad Black's Hollinger Inc. became the controlling owner of the *Sun* and other Southam dailies. To reduce the sample to manageable size, the researchers randomly chose each day of the publishing week three times for both 1987 and 1997, yielding three composite weeks—18 days—for each year. They then selected every fifth article for coding, producing a sample of 168 articles (81 from 1987 and 87 from 1997) that met their criteria for mentioning "business" (i.e., in the business section, written by a business reporter, or dealing with corporate or financial relations) or "labour" (i.e., written by a labour reporter, containing the words "labour" or "union," or dealing with labour relations, union affairs, working conditions, wages, and so forth).

The first part of the analysis concerned the specific themes covered in business and labour stories. For both 1987 and 1997, the *Sun* extended twice as much coverage to business as to labour. In addition, articles about labour tended to focus on disruption—that is, events that interrupt or disturb daily economic life. For example, strikes and contract negotiations accounted for 47.2% of stories about labour while, by comparison, stories about working conditions accounted for a mere 5.7% of labour articles. In contrast, business news covered a wide range of topics, including day-to-day items like financial losses and gains, investments, and financial forecasts. No single category or business topic attracted more than 14 percent of the total coverage afforded to business. What's more, this wide-ranging and routine coverage of business was often augmented by features on "up-and-coming" companies and flattering profiles of business leaders. Rarely, however, were specific unions or union leaders profiled.

Second, the researchers coded the articles according to tone, whether upbeat or positive (e.g., financial gains for business, improved conditions for labour), downbeat or negative (e.g., downsizing for business, lower wages for labour), or neutral in tone. In their analysis, they discovered that *both* business and labour received more downbeat than upbeat coverage in the *Sun*, but news about labour was far *more* likely to be negative or downbeat. For instance, almost 30% of coded items pertaining to business were positive, in contrast to only 6% of labour items. In other words, business news items were five times more likely to be framed positively than were labour items. Moreover, business received nearly one positive article for every negative article, while for every positive labour item, the *Sun* printed five negative ones.

Finally, the study examined the sources quoted in stories about business and labour. How often, in fact, were business sources quoted in relation to labour sources, and how much weight did their perspectives carry within the stories? In particular, the study sought to identify the "defining" sources for each article—those sources, including typically the first one quoted, who set the story's theme and suggest a way for readers to make sense of it. After an initial source has framed the issue, counterbalancing sources are sometimes quoted in the news, but they are "responding" to the issue rather than defining it.[4]

The study found that, in the total sample of 168 articles on business and/ or labour topics, business sources appeared in 56% percent of the stories, and labour sources in just 19%. Moreover, in labour news, business sources were usually present along with labour voices. Business people were sometimes even allowed to define issues in labour stories. In contrast, labour representatives were nearly invisible in business news; the *Sun*, in effect, gave labour neither the opportunity to define nor respond to business issues. In the overall sample, labour voices were tapped as "definers" (i.e., the first source quoted) in only 8.3% of stories, compared to 31.5% for business.

Apart from the imbalance of tone and sources, business topics simply received much more attention than did labour. In 1987, there were 1.7 business-related items for every one about labour issues; by 1997, the ratio had increased to 3 to 1. The declining proportion of labour coverage is doubtless associated with the disappearance of a full-time labour reporter at the *Sun* after 1987.

Is the new Hollinger regime at the *Sun* responsible for the marginalization of labour coverage and labour's voice? It would be too simplistic to make such a direct link. The labour beat has been disappearing in newspapers throughout North America, and the imbalance between labour and business news at the *Sun* certainly predates the Hollinger takeover of 1996. Still, we must conclude, at the very least, that the new regime sees nothing wrong with the lack of balance in labour/business reporting and has allowed it to continue.

The *Sun* went through a remake in 1997 under the marketing slogan "Question everything. We did." It promised readers "incisive, thoughtful writing" on "every subject that matters in your world." Except, that is, the world of work: the *Sun* still has no full-time labour reporter, nor even a reporter who specializes in workplace issues.

Such imbalance, at the *Sun* and throughout Canada's press, is politically and socially significant, in our view. Certainly, many middle- and upper-income Canadians invest in mutual funds or dabble in the stock market, and it is also true that many employee association and union pensions have a vested interest in the performance of funds and stocks. But the reality is that only a small percentage of Canadians make their living through investments, and only slightly more of us have individual investments in the stock market that we monitor or evaluate on a frequent basis. Three-quarters of Canadians are still dependent upon waged or salaried employment for the bulk of their income, so other issues pertaining to the workplace are more directly relevant to most of us than corporate mergers or the daily ins and outs of high finance. By disproportionately emphasizing the voice of business interests—and, typically, the voice of management—the press arguably presents a one-dimensional perspective on the world of work. Meanwhile, issues relevant to labour organizations, employee associations, and most wage earners tend to be marginalized in the mainstream media.

Nowhere is this imbalance more obvious than in the Canadian media's coverage of labour strikes and other organized protests. In 1997, for example, NewsWatch researcher James Compton studied the Toronto newspapers' coverage of the Metro Days of Action—one of the largest political protests ever launched in Canada.[5] On the morning of October 25, 1996, transit workers in Toronto walked off the job to protest the Conservative government's policies of cutting social programs and repealing the previous NDP government's labour law reforms. That same day, teachers, social workers, and other government employees likewise protested by taking the day off work. By October 26, thousands of protesters from all walks of life streamed into downtown Toronto, joining these striking public workers in a broad-based protest, coordinated by a coalition of social justice and labour groups.

How did the Toronto press cover this massive protest against the Tory government? In his analysis of all news articles printed in the *Toronto Star*, the *Toronto Sun*, and *The Globe and Mail* about the protest between October

11 and October 29, Compton found that "the newsworthiness of the Metro Days of Action (for these three papers, at least) lay in its disruption of transit and other government services." The political significance of the demonstrations was indeed covered, but was marginalized by the overwhelming preponderance of stories framed around the immediate and mundane inconveniences caused by the protest.

For example, Compton found that 43% of all articles characterized the Metro Days of Action (MDA) as "disruptive," focusing primarily on actions like the subway shutdown which disturbed the every-day routines of Torontonians. In addition, 18% of the articles described the actions taken by authorities to counter the disruptions caused by the protest, contributing further to the media's overall emphasis on how the protest affected downtown commuters. In contrast, only 39% of the media reports in Compton's sample characterized the MDA as a peaceful political protest. In addition to the dominant theme of disruption, the Toronto dailies' portrayal of the action was generally negative. Nearly three-quarters of the reports were derogatory in tone, while only 24% of them used positive or upbeat language to describe the protests.

The press largely ignored the *breadth* of the protest coalition, focusing instead on the involvement of organized labour. Also missing was much attention to the grievances and purposes underlying the protest. The singular focus on the inconveniences and disruptions sparked by the strike left little opportunity to discuss the Tory government's controversial social and economic policies.

Coverage of the MDA highlighted a more general problem with the media's coverage of labour. While the voice of business is featured prominently as a daily part of social and economic discourse, labour organizations and their leaders and allies are pushed into the background, emerging only during strikes and other disputes to disrupt the smooth functioning of daily life. The result is a distorted view of the world of work, where those who arguably drive the economy—average working people—often find themselves excluded from the media agenda, or, worse still, victimized by it.

Poverty and Class Inequality

Over the last 15 years, most will agree, the political climate in Canada has shifted to the right, and, if you are poor, this has been bad news. Political backlash against the poor has cleared the way for economic policies that have gutted social assistance and welfare programs. Between 1994 and 1996, for example, the federal Liberals slashed cash transfers to support provincial health and social programs by 33% and cut Unemployment Insurance premiums by an average of 11.2% a year.[6] Even the traditionally left-of-centre New Democrats have sometimes followed suit, implementing policies in British Columbia that reduced welfare eligibility for recent out-of-province arrivals, for instance.

Why has this political shift occurred? It is a complex question because, even though the political climate has moved to the right over the past two decades, Canadians have also shown consistently that they do not support the extremes of a conservative free market agenda. Poll after poll for example, has shown strong support for public investments in health care, education, and a viable social safety net. Still, at the same time, many Canadians also say they are having a tougher time making ends meet and feel overtaxed, especially when the quality of existing social programs seems to be eroding. In an atmosphere where people worry about the size of their own family's debt burden, fiscal conservatives have struck a resonant chord with their constant attacks on government deficits and their accompanying arguments about the necessity of having government "live within our means."

Public support for the idea of decreasing the costs of government appears in some instances to be accompanied by a harsher stance toward the poor. In this regard, perhaps the long-running and well-funded campaign by conservative columnists and think tanks to blame the poor for their own poverty has made a dent in public opinion. Certainly, influential conservatives such as Conrad Black and columnist Barbara Amiel share this view. For example, at one point in his autobiography, Black uses the work "unworthy" to refer to "groups, such as strikers and voluntary welfare addicts".[7] Meanwhile, Barbara Amiel, Hollinger's vice-president of editorial, has characterized people in poverty as "a social stratum where...people are simply not competent to lead normal and adequate lives."[8]

Of course, with such a singular focus on poor-bashing and the political hot button of welfare fraud, it is easy to miss how the wealthy often find a way to beat the system, too. In Chapter Five, for example, our #2 "under-covered" story of 1993 detailed how the Mulroney government quietly forgave the wealthiest families in Canada hundreds of millions of dollars in taxes—at the same time as it imposed the GST tax on average Canadians. In the U.S., Project Censored reports that a bill passed in the mid-1990s, ostensibly to raise the minimum wage, also included ten unpublicized provisions which could only be defined as welfare for the rich. Among its other controversial provisions, the bill eliminated a surtax on luxury car purchases and diesel fuel for yachts.[9] It seems, sometimes, that concern with "welfare fraud" is selectively focused on those below the poverty line, rather than those stratospherically above it.

With this idea in mind, we wanted to discover how selected media have covered the issue of poverty over the past decade. How much coverage does a typical daily extend to the poorest members of Canadian society? Has this coverage increased or declined over the past ten years, in light of the shifting political climate, and the increasing influence of Conrad Black in Canada's press system? How are the poor portrayed in this coverage?

To help answer these questions, NewsWatch researchers Scott Uzelman, Louise Barkholt, and Christine Krause examined the coverage of poverty issues in the *Vancouver Sun* in 1988 and 1997, before and after Hollinger's acquisition of the *Sun* and other Southam dailies.[10] For 1988, the researchers used microfilmed editions of the *Sun* and selected every fifth calendar day for analysis, yielding a sample period of 62 publishing days. For 1997 coverage, they used the Canadian News Disk, this time selecting every third day, in order to obtain a similar-sized sample of poverty stories. The researchers coded only those articles that dealt directly with poverty issues, rejecting those that merely mentioned poverty in passing. All in all, they derived a sample of 101 items for 1988 and 106 for 1997.

In the first part of their analysis, Uzelman et al. compared the overall amount of coverage devoted to poverty issues in the two years. They found that the *Sun's* poverty coverage declined from an average of 1.6 items per day in 1988 to 1.0 per day in 1997. To be sure, the average daily total of all news items at the *Sun* dropped by as much as 25%, but the 37.5% decline in poverty coverage outpaced this more general decrease.   Interestingly, the decrease in poverty-related news has taken place at the same time that poverty rates in B.C. and Canada have noticeably increased. For example, according to 1997 Statistics Canada data, the overall percentage of poor in British Columbia—one of Canada's wealthiest provinces—rose from 15% in 1988 to nearly 18% in 1996. Overall, an additional 220,000 joined the ranks of the poor in British Columbia since 1988. So, while the incidence of poverty in B.C. increased by one-fifth, the coverage of poverty in the *Sun* dropped by over one-third.

This decrease in amount was accompanied by other changes in the *Sun's* treatment of poverty issues. For instance, in-depth features on poverty issues declined by nearly two-thirds, from almost 10% of poverty coverage in 1988 to just over 3% in 1997. At the same time, editorials and commentaries on poverty nearly doubled, from just under 8% of poverty coverage in 1988 to 16% in 1997. Why is this shift significant? As several journalists have told NewsWatch, there's a big difference between feature and opinion articles. By

their nature, features—which often include in-depth profiles of everyday people—are more likely to be emotive and sympathetic to the subject of poverty,
while opinion is more likely to be intellectual or critical. Therefore, the *Sun's*
increasing reliance on opinion pieces as opposed to features, we speculate,
distances readers from the everyday lived experience of poverty in Canada.

In addition to charting this decrease in both the overall amount of poverty coverage and the decline in features on poverty, the study also analyzed
the sources cited in the *Sun's* coverage of the poor. Who are the people typically quoted in stories about poverty? Government officials and politicians
were quoted more often than other types of sources, securing almost 41% of
all references in 1988 and 50% in 1997. Business sources also raised their
profile in stories about poverty, appearing in 21% of stories in 1997, up from
12% in 1988. Both of these sources have an institutional stake in downplaying
the severity of poverty, and both increased their presence in poverty stories
over the decade. On the other hand, while advocacy groups who work on
behalf of the poor are still well-accessed, that access declined from a high of
42.7% in 1988 to 37.7% in 1997.

This apparent shift from advocacy groups towards government and business sources may be related to a subtle but significant change in the way the
Sun has portrayed the poor themselves. The researchers coded articles according to whether the poor were cast as "victims" or "threats." For example,
if the poor were depicted as individuals at the mercy of social and economic
circumstances beyond their control, they were coded as victims. In this case,
readers might infer that the poor are deserving of public assistance because
they could not help their situation. On the other hand, if the poor were portrayed as lacking the incentive to work, adding to the nation's fiscal burden, or
threatening the very fabric of Canadian society, they were coded as threats.
With the poor framed as "threats," then, readers may infer that the poor are
undeserving of financial help because—as conservatives like Barbara Amiel
argue—they have only themselves to blame. In this way, distinguishing victims and threats seemed to be a good way to determine whether or not a right-
wing market-liberal perspective has increasingly influenced the *Sun's* coverage of the poor.

Overall, the study found that the vast majority of stories in both 1988
and 1997 portrayed the poor as victims and (implicitly) as deserving of public
assistance. This is still Canada, after all. At the same time, news that portrayed the poor as threats (and therefore, presumably, undeserving of help)
increased noticeably, from 10.9% of stories in 1988 up to 17% in 1997. Overall, this suggests that the *Sun* may be starting to present a less compassionate

perspective of the poor than in the past, despite their increase in numbers across Canada. The *Sun's* chief editor apparently was not surprised by this finding, and argued in a November 27, 1998 talk to Simon Fraser University students that the paper is simply reflecting the perception of many of its readers that the poor are indeed a threat.

We don't want to exaggerate. Our sampled Canadian newspaper has not demonized the poor to the same extent as, say, sex offenders. Still, our research indicates that the *Sun's* coverage of poverty has shifted over the past decade—decreasing in amount, becoming somewhat less sympathetic in tone, less in-depth in treatment, with decreasing access for advocacy groups representing the poor, and more access for business and government sources—sources who potentially have a stake in minimizing the problem of poverty and hunger in Canada. The result of these trends, arguably, is a news media environment that is increasingly unable to capture both the everyday experience of poverty and the role government and corporate policies may play in sustaining it.

THE MARKET LIBERAL AGENDA: ABSENT ALTERNATIVES AND HIDDEN CONSEQUENCES

In the view that is sometimes known as "classical" or "neo-classical" economic theory, it is argued that governments should stay out of the economy entirely, leaving the marketplace alone to do its magic—producing and selling goods, rewarding innovation and productivity, providing jobs, and so on. Drawing on the inspiration of classical liberal economists, such as Adam Smith, large numbers of western intellectuals and policy-makers in the 18th and 19th centuries promoted an economic philosophy of "laissez-faire." Still, while much has been said for the benefits of an unfettered market economy, western societies in the 19th and early 20th centuries learned the downside of "laissez faire"—including environmental pollution, exploitation of workers (including children), and, periodically, agonizing economic panics, crises, and mass unemployment.

Beginning with the Progressive and social democratic movements of a century ago, and firmly entrenched by the 1950s, a general consensus slowly emerged: through labour laws, regulation, public investment, and social programs, government should step in and curb the excesses of business, thereby blunting the most disturbing consequences of completely unregulated markets.

Politics in post-war western societies has often been defined by arguments about the most appropriate balance between free market principles and these forms of public investment and government regulation. Over the past two decades, conservative groups have argued forcefully that the political pendulum swung too far to the political left during the 1960s and 1970s. In response, they have championed a renewed "laissez-faire" market-liberal perspective—a no-holds-barred attack on government regulations, progressive taxation, and universal social programs.

In an ongoing attempt to secure the social and economic conditions more favourable to economic growth and corporate profit, multinational corporations and their allies in political parties and market-liberal policy institutes have worked hard to reverse many of the social reforms of the post-war era. For example, in the interests of "unleashing" market forces, market liberals have sought to minimize tax rates and social programs (which require higher taxation rates), and to dismantle protection for workers, unions, and the environment. For their part, while they sometimes welcome government subsidies, large corporations have adopted much of the market-liberal agenda as their own and have lobbied for lower taxes, a lower ratio of wages to profits, and fewer regulations on how they conduct their operations.

To these traditional market-liberal goals, you can also add a more recent item: the campaign for free trade around the globe. Through arrangements like NAFTA (the North American Free Trade Agreement) and the momentarily shelved Multilateral Agreement on Investment, corporations are free to bypass government regulations merely by voting with their feet. If you don't like labour unions in Europe, move to the U.S. If you don't like paying corporate taxes in Canada, move to the free trade zone in Mexico. If you don't like paying high wages in the U.S., why not locate your shoe factory in Indonesia? In this way, free trade has been a centrepiece of the agenda of large international corporations. As the Canadian Centre for Policy Alternatives argues, free trade "frees" corporations from most restraints on their operations and enables them to pursue profit with little interference from provincial or national governments.[11]

Advocates of free trade and other market-liberal policies argue that, by removing regulations and reducing taxes on businesses, such policies will lead to robust economic growth, better jobs, and rising incomes. It is a debatable assumption, but one increasingly shared within Canada's political establishment. For example, both Brian Mulroney (Progressive Conservative) and his one-time opponent, Jean Chrétien (Liberal), have embraced market-liberal approaches to deficit reduction and free trade. With much of the political élite thus convinced of the necessity for "smaller government" and the benefits of free trade, many critics have argued that the media have simply followed suit, embracing market-liberal assumptions as economic gospel. For example, freelance journalist Richard Starr claimed in a memo to NewsWatch that by 1994 "the triumph of the right-wing economic agenda" was complete, "and any stories that challenged the herd mentality on debt, government spending, trade, social policy, and the role of the state were under-reported."

Frances Russell, a reporter for the *Winnipeg Free Press*, knows how difficult it can be to challenge the market-liberal herd. At the *Free Press* in 1987, Russell started covering the impact on Canada of the bilateral, and then continental, free trade agreements. At one point, she detailed provisions in the agreement that would undermine Canada's ability to pass laws to protect the environment (our 5th-ranked under-reported story in 1993). But, because most of her colleagues "shunned and avoided" looking at the negative consequences of free trade, Russell told us that she often second-guessed herself during her investigation of NAFTA's more obscure provisions. "I have to admit," she wrote to NewsWatch, "that, because all my life I have been distrustful of conspiracy theories, even now I keep asking myself if it is I who is wrong? I who have lost my objectivity? I who have become a political partisan rather than a political analyst?" Despite these doubts, she kept writing because "the bare, bald facts" about the consequences of NAFTA compelled her to keep at it.

Reporters such as Frances Russell are arguably the exception in Canadian journalism. When the journalistic "pack" decides that some perspectives are legitimate and others are not, usually only the most dedicated reporters can go against the crowd. Thus, while the right-wing program of spending cuts, government deregulation, and free trade has seemingly garnered the lion's share of media coverage and commentary, alternative economic perspectives have seemed under-represented in Canada's media environment.

So, beginning in 1995, NewsWatch Canada began to ask: are plausible alternative perspectives on debt reduction, international trade, and economic growth being under-covered by the dominant Canadian media? Or is that claim just sour grapes from left-wingers grumpy about being on the losing end of economic debates in Canada?

NewsWatch researcher Brent Stafford set out to examine one interesting aspect of media coverage of economic policy in Canada's press by comparing the access afforded to right and left-leaning policy institutes.[12] Such institutes (more popularly known as "think tanks") play an important role in helping to shape contemporary public agendas. Typically, they are non-partisan research and advocacy organizations, usually funded by private donations, with a mandate to promote a policy-relevant issue or perspective. Think tanks publish research in support of various social and economic policies, and also generate a considerable amount of PR spin, making them indispensable to journalists looking for quotes on political and economic debates.

To examine whether or not the media were accessing think tanks from a variety of political perspectives, Stafford compiled all references to the leading 15 think tanks in Canada published in 14 major daily newspapers and broadcast on CBC and CTV television newscasts over a six-month period in 1996. Each think tank was then independently classified as "right-wing," "left-wing," or "middle of the road," by a panel of mainstream journalists, yielding seven left-wing, six right-wing, and two centrist institutes. Overall, Stafford reports, right-wing think tanks received 68% of all references, while left-wing think tanks received 19.5%. The hit parade on the right was led by the Conference Board of Canada (317 references), the Fraser Institute (312), and the C.D. Howe Institute (270). By contrast, the leading left-wing think tank—the Council of Canadians—logged in at 121 references, followed by the Canadian Centre for Policy Alternatives (64) and the Canadian Council on Social Development (57).

None of the news organizations in the study gave equal coverage to left and right-wing think tanks, although some were more balanced than others. For example, the *Ottawa Citizen* referenced right-wing groups in 54% of its stories which mentioned think tanks, followed by the *Hamilton Spectator* (62%), and the *Toronto Star* (64%). By comparison, the right-wing think tanks made up almost 97% of all think tank references in the *Toronto Sun*. Close behind the *Sun* in this enthusiastic embrace of the Canadian right were the *Vancouver Province* (84%), the *Calgary Herald* (81%), and the *Financial Post* (80%).

In contrast to their cousins in the print media, the Canadian television networks largely shied away from quoting think tanks of any political stripe. Think tanks were mentioned just 22 times on CTV News and 11 times on CBC's *The National* during the study period.

In a second stage of research, coverage of a leading right-wing institute (the Fraser Institute) and its closest left-wing counterpart (the Canadian Centre for Policy Alternatives) was analyzed for the proportion of supportive coverage they received in the *Vancouver Sun* and the *Globe and Mail* in 1996. When they were covered, both institutes received about the same proportion of supportive sources (sources cited in stories that supported the position of the think tank), and a similar portion of critical or hostile source referencing. While these results seem balanced, it is important to keep in mind that they describe the *tone* of coverage only. In sheer quantity, there were five times more Fraser Institute stories than CCPA ones.

In the following year, NewsWatch did a follow-up study of the two institutes' coverage in the *Vancouver Sun*. Would the CCPA'S new Vancouver office, opened in 1997, improve its access, at least to the local press? Using the full-text Canadian News Disk, researcher Scott Uzelman collected and analyzed all 1997 *Sun* articles printed which contained a substantive reference to either think tank. Indeed, the CCPA had closed the gap, but it still faced a 2.4-to-1 disadvantage: 39 articles compared with 94 for the Fraser Institute.[13] As unbalanced as this may seem, this ratio is a vast improvement over previous years. An earlier search of the *Sun's* database by one of the paper's own reporters found 690 references to the Fraser Institute and only 49 references to the CCPA over the previous decade, yielding an astonishing ratio of 14 to 1.[14]

In addition to this imbalance in the quantity of coverage, the *Sun* treated the two institutes somewhat differently as well. On the one had, both the CCPA and the FI were allowed to define issues (rather than merely responding to them) in most of their appearances in the news. But, on the whole, the *Sun* tapped the Fraser Institute for commentary on a wider range of subjects, *Sun* opinion columnists were far more likely to cite the Fraser Institute than the CCPA, and the FI was quite successful in obtaining coverage for two of its controversial campaigns—redefining poverty and changing environmental priorities.

In summary, while the CCPA enjoyed increased access to the *Sun* in 1997, its right-wing rival still overshadowed it.

This disparity between the access afforded to right and left-wing advocacy groups is not necessarily the product of deliberate media bias. It may well be linked to the greater resources and output of market liberal institutes, compared to their political rivals. More broadly, the imbalance of access both reflects and reinforces the apparent dominance of market- liberal perspectives on economic problems and solutions.

Take the debt and deficit, for example. Throughout the 1990s, the Canadian left has lamented that the mainstream news media have given right-wing perspectives on the debt and deficit more and fuller coverage than alternative perspectives. But is this true? Have the news media promoted the right-wing notion that cutting social programs is the only way to corral the deficit, thereby overlooking alternate ways to manage the problem? To address this question, NewsWatch researcher Jackie Mosdell examined the *Globe and Mail's* economic coverage over a three-month period in 1994-95. The sample comprised all stories in the *Globe's* main news section which contained the words "debt" and/or "deficit" and which specifically concerned the federal budget—

53 articles, including news reports (43), editorials (5), and columns (3).[15] Publications from the Fraser and C.D. Howe institutes were scanned to identify the free market right's preferred solutions to the deficit, namely, cutting social welfare spending, downsizing government, reducing provincial transfer payments, and privatizing public services. For the left's view on the deficit, Mosdell surveyed the CCPA's monthly magazine, The CCPA *Monitor,* and a best-selling book by the progressive writer Linda McQuaig,[16] yielding such prescriptions as increasing government spending (to stimulate the economy), lowering interest rates, and reducing subsidies to corporations (a position that is also embraced by market-liberal purists who oppose government economic intervention in principle).

Overall, Mosdell found that the *Globe and Mail* mentioned market-liberal prescriptions 105 times, while alternative prescriptions were mentioned a mere 29 times, resulting in a ratio of over 3-to-1. One policy strategy—directly cutting social spending—was mentioned 39 times, more often than all left-wing themes combined. Other right-wing prescriptions were also oft-repeated: cutting the size of government 30 times, and reducing provincial transfer payments 28 times. In contrast, the most frequently cited alternative solution to the deficit crisis—slashing subsidies to corporations—appeared in the *Globe* just 14 times.

With progressive voices and perspectives marginalized in the debate over the debt, deficit, and other crucial economic issues, viable alternatives to the market-liberal, slash-and-burn approach to the economy fade into the political background. Consider one left-leaning solution to the debt problem in the 1990s—lowering interest rates. One of the major contributors to the national debt over the last two decades has been the cost of servicing it. According to a controversial 1991 StatsCan draft report, between 1975 and 1989 artificially high interest rates added 44% to the debt (as noted in our 6th ranked under-reported story for 1994, discussed in Chapter Five). However, if Ottawa were to roll over government debt into low-interest loans provided directly by the Bank of Canada (rather than by private investors at higher interest rates), Canada's payments on the debt would be substantially reduced, leaving Ottawa with less reason to cut health care and social programs. This potential alternative to deep cuts in federal support for health care and social assistance—an alternative that would incidentally raise no one's taxes—attracted only three mentions in the *Globe and Mail* during the study period.

With such alternative solutions and perspectives pushed to the margins of debate, the federal Liberals arguably had a freer hand to present their market-liberal program of free trade, deep cuts to social programs, and relaxed regulations on business as the only viable solution to economic recession and the debt crisis. And, as our under-covered story lists of the last few years suggest, the consequences of this market-liberal agenda have only begun to be felt. For example, in response to cuts to federal transfer payments, many provinces are turning over their Medicare systems to private "consultants" hired from the U.S. health industry. Their approach, more often than not, is to slash salaries, cut staff, and replace experienced (and expensive) health professionals with inexperienced (and inexpensive) temps and part-timers (Story #2, 1995).

Moreover, cuts to unemployment insurance and welfare programs open up the possibility that Canada may develop—as long-term poverty cultivates desperation and frustration—what former Health and Welfare deputy minister Richard Splane calls an "American-style angry underclass" (Story #11, 1994). If indeed the market-liberal agenda has produced such changes in the fabric of Canadian society, one would hope to find an open and frank debate in the Canadian media about the merits and drawbacks of laissez faire economics. Unfortunately, our research, preliminary though it be, suggests that a full and varied debate has been one of the missing ingredients in media coverage of economic problems and solutions.

MEDIA CORPORATIONS: COVERING THEMSELVES (UP?)

American media critic Ronald Collins writes, "Independence, in all its many forms, is implicit in the notion of a free press."[17] From public school social studies classes to Hollywood films such as *All the President's Men*, we are schooled in the notion of the media as the Fourth Estate—an independent check on the abuse of government or corporate power in society. This image of a cantankerous and hard-hitting press is a familiar part of our cultural repertoire, one that journalists themselves share. For example, in a defense of his news program's invasive coverage of a police search on B.C. Premier Glen Clark's home in early 1999, BCTV's news director, Steve Wyatt, argued that "It is a basic principle of a free press in a democratic society that we shed light where there might otherwise be darkness...Society is better served when powerful institutions are subject to public scrutiny."[18]

As consumers of the news, however, we are much less familiar with the byzantine corporate structures which own and produce the news in Canada and around the world. For most corporate owners of the media, the news is above all else a business—a commodity to be bought and sold, a source of advertising revenue, and a way to produce a return on an investment. And, like most businesses, news corporations have interests to protect and secrets to guard. Unlike many businesses, however, media companies have considerable potential influence over the public agenda.

So the question arises, who subjects *these* "powerful institutions" to "public scrutiny"? What happens when bottom-line interests of corporate owners (particularly their economic interest in pleasing advertisers) conflict with the ethic of journalistic independence? If our discussions with journalists around Canada are any indication, there is cause for concern. According to one respondent, in today's corporate newsroom "anything that's a direct attack on business is a real hard sell. The people at the top know you won't keep your position if you attack business, even if they won't say it directly." Other journalists agreed, but stressed that few corporate owners directly censor news content. Most choose instead to exert control in more subtle ways—for example, by appointing editors who are on-side with the owner's political views.

This brings us back to a question that we began to explore in Chapter Two: Do the large corporations that own Canada's media influence the news in accordance with their particular political and financial vested interests? If they do, that influence should be detectable in patterns of news coverage in the press. NewsWatch has undertaken initial studies on two potential sources of direct corporate influence on the news: media owners, and advertisers, who account for roughly three-fourths of daily newspapers' revenue.

Our first question concerns the influence that corporate owners exert over the quality and tone of daily news coverage and editorial content. As American media critic Todd Gitlin writes, when most people think of ownership's influence on news, they picture an overweight, cigar-chomping tycoon calling reporters into his office and telling them what and what not to say.[19] The reality of owner influence is much more subtle than this popular image, and thus more difficult to document or prove. For example, as one journalist told NewsWatch, the power of owners to hire and fire often creates an unspoken but still chilling effect in the newsroom. When you know that the ownership typically frowns on particular kinds of stories, he explained, "there's no incentive to make waves, if you want to keep your job." But how do you study "a feeling" or a "sense" that may permeate a newsroom? How do you document the usually implicit influence of ownership on the news?

In our investigations we decided to take a novel approach. If ownership exerts influence, then a change of ownership might be expected to result in a change in the tone or quality of news coverage. So, why not compare the editorial content of the news immediately prior to and then some time after an ownership change? Our first foray into the question of ownership influence compared the Op/Ed page of the *Ottawa Citizen* in 1991, before Conrad Black and Hollinger assumed a controlling share of Southam, to the *Citizen's* Op/Ed page in 1996, immediately after Hollinger's takeover. In this study, NewsWatch researcher Myle Lai compared a two-week sample of op/ed pieces from each of the two years under study. There were certain changes, including a modest decline in the proportion of columns written by *Citizen* staff and a certain rightward shift in the tone of Op/Ed pieces (reinforced by the departure of columnist Christopher Young and managing editor Peter Calamai, and the arrival of Andrew Coyne and Giles Gherson, two of Southam's syndicated writers). But these changes were subtle and could not be attributed directly to the new Hollinger regime.

So, at the *Citizen*, there was insufficient reason to conclude (at least, prior to its revamping under new editor, Neil Reynolds) that the Hollinger takeover had shifted Op/Ed commentary dramatically to the right. But was this true of other Hollinger papers, and what might we find if we looked at news coverage beyond Op/Ed commentary—especially on matters relevant to the vested interests of Conrad Black himself? With these questions in mind, NewsWatch researchers Ilona Jackson, Patsy Kotsopolous, and Darren Seath set out in 1998 to examine the kind of coverage the *Vancouver Sun* gave to Conrad Black and, more broadly, to Black's holding company, Hollinger International.[20] Given the growing influence of Hollinger in Canada's news system, this question should certainly be of interest to Canadians. We felt that self-coverage should be the acid test of the influence of ownership. On the one hand, if a newspaper can cover its own parent company the same way it covers other institutions, readers can reasonably suppose that news decision-making is independent from ownership influence. On the other hand, if there is evidence of a double standard, that raises the possibility that the paper's owners might influence other areas of coverage as well.

To investigate the *Sun's* coverage of its owners, our researchers took a three-pronged approach. First, they compared the *Sun's* recent coverage of Black/Hollinger with its coverage of other major Canadian media tycoons and their companies over the time period. Next, they compared the *Sun's* reporting on Black/Hollinger with that extended by the *Toronto Star*, one of the few major market broadsheets not owned by Conrad Black. Finally, the study compared *Sun* reporting on Black/Hollinger after Black gained majority control of Southam with the *Sun's* coverage before Black assumed the helm. In each of these studies, the researchers coded all articles published in the *Sun* during specific time periods. Avoiding an overly complex process, they studied only the headline and lead sentence of each article in the sample, coding each article for owner/company, subject, location in the paper, story origin (staff or wire service), and tone.

The first part of the study asked the question, "Does a news organization cover its own parent company less critically than it covers other companies in similar industries?" To this end, they examined *Sun* articles printed on four of Canada's largest media corporations: Hollinger, Rogers Communications, Thomson, and Western International Communications (WIC) between May 1996 and April 1997. Excluding articles that merely mentioned the company's name in passing somewhere in the article, the sample comprised 189 articles, with Hollinger attracting the largest amount of coverage (97 articles) and Thomson attracting the least attention (nine articles).

The researchers began by looking at how the article portrayed the companies and owners under question: were the stories supportive, critical, or neutral in tone? They defined articles as being supportive if the headline and lead sentence cast the subject in a positive light or reported profits as increasing. Articles were coded as critical when they hinted at negative developments or reported profits as decreasing. Finally, the research team classified articles as neutral when the lead sentence or headline did not reflect positively or negatively on the company in question.

The study found that the *Sun* was most supportive of Black/Hollinger and least supportive of WIC (owned by the Vancouver-based Griffiths family). Overall, nearly 20% of Hollinger stories were positive in tone, while only 11% of Rogers stories, 11% of Thomson stories, and a mere 7% of WIC articles were coded as supportive. Moreover, while Hollinger received slightly fewer supportive than critical articles (after all, news tends to focus on negative developments), the other three companies received about three times as much critical as supportive coverage.

To be fair, the *Sun* did run stories critical of Black and Hollinger. But every such negative story was located inside the news or business section, whereas the other three media companies, especially WIC, saw much of their critical coverage land on the front page of at least one of the *Sun's* sections. For example, the *Sun* buried an article titled "MP, union want probe of papers' ownership: The purchase of seven more dailies by Conrad Black's Hollinger empire provokes questions about concentration" deep in the middle of the news section. Another unflattering story entitled "Unfair labour practice complaint over Radler talk at *Leader-Post*" appeared in the back of the business section, next to stock quotes and ads for hair replacement formulae.

While the first part of this study suggested differences in the way the *Sun* covered different media organizations, it didn't tell us if these differences were due to the *Sun's* editorial decisions. Perhaps all Canadian media—even Hollinger's competitors—bury bad news about Hollinger in the inside pages. To check this possibility, the research team turned to a major non-Hollinger daily, the *Toronto Star*. How did the *Star's* coverage of Hollinger International compare with the *Sun's*? Collecting 97 articles on Hollinger from the *Sun* and 118 articles from the *Star*, the researchers analyzed the headline and lead sentence for each story in the sample. Overall, they found that, while only 23% of the *Sun's* articles were critical of Hollinger, a full 42% of the *Star's* were critical in tone. Moreover, stories critical of Black/Hollinger had a better chance of appearing on the front page of the *Star*. For instance, 12% of the *Star's* critical coverage of Hollinger appeared on the front page of the news or business sections. Finally, the *Star* published five critical Op/Ed pieces (including letters) for every one supportive of Hollinger. In stark contrast, the *Sun* ran 2.5 supportive Op/Ed pieces for every item critical of Black/ Hollinger.

In addition to its more critical treatment of Hollinger International, the *Toronto Star* also extended more coverage to advocacy groups opposed to Conrad Black's takeover of Southam. Overall, the *Star* printed 15 items detailing opposition to Black's ongoing quest to control much of Canada's news media, while the *Sun* ran only seven such items. But these numbers tell only half the story. Consider the *Star's* and the *Sun's* coverage of the Council of Canadians' legal challenge to block Black's takeover of Southam. While the *Star* and the *Sun* extended roughly the same amount of coverage to the Council's bid to stop the takeover, the *Sun* tended to relegate the Council's main point—that concentrated media ownership is a threat to democratic free expression—to the later paragraphs of the articles, suggesting implicitly that the legal challenge itself was the real story. In fact, the *Sun's* initial story on the Council's law-suit simply failed to mention the Council's fears that freedom of expression would be limited by the Southam purchase. The *Star*, on the other hand, for the most part presented the thrust of the Council's concerns in the opening lines of each article, taking care to mention the Council's belief that concentration of media ownership presents a disturbing threat to Canadian democracy.

Maybe this is just sour grapes from a Hollinger competitor? It is certainly plausible that competitors, such as the *Star,* cover Conrad Black more critically and extend more coverage to his opponents, mainly to gain some kind of advantage. Perhaps, as Black himself might say, the *Star* is simply envious of his success. To account for this possibility, the final phase of this NewsWatch study examined the *Sun's* coverage of Black/Hollinger in two distinct time periods—first, from January 1985 to December 1990 (before Hollinger became an investor in the Southam newspaper chain, including the *Sun*), and second, from May 1996 to April 1997 (after Hollinger assumed full control of Southam). To derive comparable samples, the researchers could not use the Canadian News Disk, which archives no news prior to 1993. Instead, they were forced to use the Canadian Business and Current Affairs (CBCA), a less comprehensive database which indexes articles with "significant reference value." Accordingly, this phase of the study used a smaller sample—14 articles for the first period and 25 for the second—which consequently limits the validity of the study.

Still, the results are suggestive. For example, our researchers discovered that, prior to Black's takeover of the *Sun*, 43% of the *Sun*'s articles on Hollinger were critical. After the takeover, only 28% of the *Sun's* Hollinger stories were critical in tone. In addition, the *Sun's* supportive coverage of Hollinger mushroomed from a pre-takeover low of 7% to 52% after Black took control. In the end, these findings, combined with the other evidence from the same NewsWatch study, suggest a notable imbalance in the way the *Sun* reports on Conrad Black and Hollinger International. Overall, our research suggests that the *Sun's* coverage of Hollinger has been more favourable than its coverage of other media corporations; its coverage of Hollinger has been more favourable than that extended by the *Toronto Star*, a non-Hollinger competitor; and, in fact, its own coverage of Hollinger has become much rosier since Black took over the paper.

The results of our pilot study are consistent with other anecdotal evidence and case studies. The Institute for Alternative Journalism in San Francisco has documented several cases of outright censorship, in which corporate media executives have directly interfered in editorial decisions. They wanted to soften or kill coverage critical of their own company, or of officials whose favours the company was courting.[21] Normally, though, the process is more subtle. As Pulitzer-prize-winning media critic Ben Bagdikian has put it:

> When protection of an owning corporation's private interests intrudes into news decisions, other professionally acceptable reasons are given (such as "Nobody's interested"). The barrier is seldom absolute: there is merely a higher threshold for such stories. News stories that cast doubt on the corporate ethic must be more urgent and melodramatic than stories sustaining that ethic.[22]

Presumably, editors are intelligent enough not to require direct commands from the corporate boardroom to tread carefully in covering their own employer. Two editors at Canadian Press told the 1980/81 Kent Commission on Newspapers that CP edited its news about the media so as to please major media owners. At the time, the Thomson chain had more member newspapers than any other company. The two editors said that CP deliberately shortened a news account of a Thomson paper strike, killed a report about a trade union leader's speech criticizing Thomson, and delayed a story about a government investigation into possible links between birth defects and electronic terminals in Thomson newspaper plants.[23] In Ontario, James Winter has analyzed the biases in newspaper coverage of annual newspaper award ceremonies, an area where each paper has "a blatant self-interest." While self-promotion in this area of coverage is hardly surprising, Winter sensibly suggests that it throws into question "the reporting we get where there are other, perhaps less blatant, examples of self-interest."[24]

ADVERTISERS: CARRYING A BIG STICK

While media owners are one source of influence on news content, other corporate forces, notably advertisers, can also wield potential power in contemporary newsrooms. As we discussed in Chapter Two, most newspapers and broadcasters depend on advertising revenue for their financial survival, and this means that a lot of energy and attention goes into attracting audiences and pleasing advertisers. When advertisers find fault with certain kinds of stories—stories which perhaps portray their industry in a negative light—they can use this power over the media's purse strings to downplay, or even kill, potentially damaging news coverage. For the most part, advertisers do not need to pressure news outlets directly to shape coverage. Instead, newspapers and broadcasters—afraid of alienating their key sources of revenue—will more likely censor themselves and quash stories that might embarrass key advertisers before they ever hit the audience.[25]

We don't want to overstate the case. Many editors and even executives and owners will resist overt pressure from advertisers, and take pride in doing so. Indeed, the credibility of their own product—the news—is potentially threatened by caving in too obviously or frequently to such pressure. Still, in a climate of growing media competition for advertising revenue, there is reason for concern. As a respected American scholar has put it, "the incentive of advertising revenue encourages the media to tailor message content...to treat advertisers' products and their broader interests charitably in both news reports and editorials."[26]

For instance, consider former *Vancouver Sun* reporter Ben Parfitt's claim that pressure from real estate developers led the paper to downplay reports that hundreds, if not thousands, of condominiums in the Vancouver area were leaking and rotting in the incessant West Coast rain. Real estate advertising is a crucial source of revenue for local newspapers. So does a steady supply of real estate advertising revenue buy developers good will in local newspapers? Ben Parfitt thinks so. During February of 1993, Parfitt wrote a series of articles on the growing leaky condo problem for the *Vancouver Sun*, and, once his series started to run, angry condo owners began to phone him "in droves" with their horror stories about rotting walls, ruined carpets, and massive repair bills.[27] Years later, Parfitt noted in the *Georgia Straight*, an independently owned urban weekly, that he had just begun to document what would eventually turn into a major housing crisis.

According to Parfitt, however, the more compelling the story became, the less play the *Sun's* editors appeared to give it. His first leaky condo story debuted on the front page, but then later stories were moved back in the paper, ending up near the back of the B section by week's end. Coincidentally, this week was also Parfitt's last at the *Sun*. Electing to take an employee-buyout offer from Southam, he left the *Sun's* news desk with a stack of suggestions on follow-up "leaky condo" stories before moving on. However, it took five years before leaky condos again exploded into major local and indeed national news. Between his 1993 exposés and the 1998 "big news" story, Parfitt claims that "the *Sun* did little to influence public discourse on this major health and safety issue." In neglecting this story for so long, Parfitt concludes, the *Sun* put the "interests of advertisers...ahead of those of its readers."

Writing in the *Georgia Straight*, Parfitt describes how, after his first stories ran, developers associated with two of the leaky projects met then editor-in-chief Ian Haysom, publisher Don Babick, and marketing direct Ron Clarke. He alleges that some developers threatened to pull their ads from the *Sun*'s "New Homes" section, a cash cow which brought in $4 million a year in advertising dollars. In the end, Parfitt claims, "we have a market filled with rotting buildings and a mainstream press...whose conspicuous silence on the issue helped make a terrible problem even worse."

Following up Parfitt's revelations, NewsWatch co-founder Donald Gutstein evaluated the leaky condo stories that appeared in the *Sun* between the initial Parfitt series in 1993 and October 22, 1997—a date preceding the explosion of the story in the early part of 1998.[28] In his analysis, Gutstein found only 20 stories addressing the leaky condo issue during the entire four-and-a-half-year study period. The minimal coverage that did find its way into the *Sun* often did its best to downplay the severity of the problem. For example, during 1996, the *Sun*'s main channel of information to its readers about leaky condos was the "New Homes" section. Four out of the five items printed during that year appeared in this developer-supported section. Not surprisingly, these stories emphasized the good job being done by developers to deal with the problem. Not one tenant's advocate or other critical voice appeared in these stories.

The high water mark for leaky condo coverage during the study period actually came a year earlier in 1995. Of the eight items that appeared in 1995, five were columns by Elizabeth Aird outlining the shoddy, even illegal, practices of builders and developers throwing projects together willy-nilly to cash in on a booming housing market. Aird revealed in a later column that she was a victim of a leaky condo project. For its part, the *Sun*'s editors countered with an editorial coinciding with the last of Aird's columns on the condo issue. The *Sun*'s view was that the problem was caused by "fly-by-nighters," not reputable builders. Correcting this problem only required tinkering with the system— for example, defining areas of responsibility more clearly, licensing builders, and simplifying regulations. Ultimately, though, the *Sun* cautioned, it was "buyer beware." This arguably toothless statement was the only *Sun* editorial on the subject between the Parfitt series and February 1998, when the leaky condo story flooded into the local and national media.

So, Gutstein concludes, it's not that the *Sun* did not know about the crisis during those intervening four-and-a-half years. Parfitt suggested follow-up stories, and the Aird columns should have alerted *Sun* editors. Moreover, in April 1996, Canadian Press printed a hard-hitting wire story about "a flood of leaky condos," but the *Sun* did not publish this either.[29] Instead, the *Sun*'s editors chose to run such promotional stories as "House hunter has big choice as prices fall, realtor says,"[30] and "Condomania! It's a buyer's market!"[31] During this time, good news stories and advertiser-friendly fluff continued to outweigh and overwhelm solid, balanced reporting on the leaky condo crisis.

Finally, when the leaky condo story began to take off in early 1998, the *Sun* dutifully extended coverage to the crisis, but by then it was merely following a story already "out there" in the media, rather than leading or uncovering the story through hard-nosed investigative reporting. Prior to 1998, the *Sun* seemed content to rake in real estate advertising and to allow the story to languish in obscurity.

Did the *Sun* pull its punches when faced with a possible advertising boycott from angry developers? Ultimately, we cannot answer this question without further evidence about what may have happened behind closed doors. The

Sun's chief editor told NewsWatch that the potential of libel suits from developers and condo strata councils worried about diminishing property values was a more important factor that led not only his paper, but all Vancouver media, including the less commercially-dependent CBC, to approach the leaky condo story cautiously. This is a useful caveat, which suggests two points. First, we are talking not of the shortcomings of a single newspaper, but of structural pressures that affect all news media. Second, the point does not contradict our argument about the potential influence of advertisers on the news; indeed, it suggests that, through their access to undoubtedly high-priced lawyers, major corporate interests have additional weapons to influence the media.

In the end, our research suggests that the unwillingness or inability of Canada's dominant media corporations to cover themselves critically or to disclose their own interests may be the biggest blind spot of all. Corporate-owned media are willing —at least, sometimes, and arguably more often—to promote their corporate image or to protect key advertisers from unflattering news coverage. This can potentially undermine the expression of a diversity of viewpoints in the press on some relevant issues. But, if corporate self-interest may play a role in reducing the diversity of stories, voices, opinions, and perspectives in the press, the question is: what can we do about it? In a word: plenty. Our next chapter details some suggestions for public policy and grassroots action—in short, the collective first steps we can take to create a news system that strengthens, rather than restricts, a diverse and democratic public sphere.

ENDNOTES

1. See, for example, Glasgow University Media Group, *Really Bad News* (London: Writers and Readers, 1982).
2. Graham Knight, "Strike Talk: A Case Study of News;" and Robert A. Hackett, "The Depiction of Labour and Business on National Television News," both in Marc Grenier (ed.), *Critical Studies of Canadian Mass Media* (Toronto: Butterworths, 1992). Both articles were originally published in the *Canadian Journal of Communication*, in 1982 and 1983 respectively.
3. Summarized in Donald Gutstein, with Robert Hackett and NewsWatch Canada, *Question the Sun! A Content Analysis of Diversity in the Vancouver Sun Before and After the Hollinger Takeover* (Burnaby: NewsWatch Canada, 1998).
4. The distinction between defining and responding sources derives from Michael

Clow with Susan Machum, *Stifling Debate: Canadian Newspapers and Nuclear Power* (Halifax: Fernwood Books, 1993).

5. James Compton, "Toronto Papers Misrepresented Last Year's Days of Action," *NewsWatch Monitor* (November 1997), p. iv.

6. Matt Sanger, "Federal, Provincial Downloading Hurting Municipalities,"*CCPA Monitor* (May 1998). See also the NewsWatch web site for 1994's #11 underreported story, "Federal Welfare Cuts Will Mean Crueler Canada".

7. Conrad Black, *A Life in Progress* (Toronto: Key Porter, 1993), p. 420.

8. Quoted in *Maclean's* (August 22, 1988).

9. Peter Phillips and Project Censored, *Censored 1997: The News That Didn't Make the News* (New York: Seven Stories Press), p. 36.

10. See Gutstein et al, *Question the Sun!*, pp. 31-38.

11. Editorial, *CCPA Monitor* (October 1997), p. 2.

12. Brent Stafford, "Rightwing Research Agencies Quoted Much More Often," *NewsWatch Monitor* (Summer 1997), p. i.

13. Gutstein et al, *Question the Sun!*, pp. 16-18.

14. Robert Sarti, "New Competitor Challenges Fraser Insitute's Influence," *Vancouver Sun* (February 8, 1997), p. A18.

15. Jackie Mosdell, "The Globe and Mail has the 'Right Stuff,' all Right," *NewsWatch Monitor* (Summer 1997), p. iv.

16. Linda McQuaig, *Shooting the Hippo: Death by Deficit and Other Canadian Myths* (Toronto: Viking, 1995).

17. Ronald Collins, *Dictating Content: How Advertising Pressure Can Corrupt a Free Press* (Washington, D.C.: Center for the Study of Commercialism), p. 1.

18. Steve Wyatt, "BCTV Defends Warrant Coverage," *Vancouver Sun* (March 12, 1999), p. A19.

19. Todd Gitlin, "Foreword" to Collins, *Dictating Content*, p. xixii.

20. Summarized in Gutstein et al., *Question the Sun!*, pp. 39-44; and Donald Gutstein, "Vancouver Sun's Coverage Acid Test of Owner's Influence," *NewsWatch Monitor*, vol. 1, no. 4 (Fall 1998), pp. i-iii.

21. Institute for Alternative Journalism, *Bottom Line vs. Top Story: The Synergy Report* (San Francisco: IAJ, October 1997), pp. 1-13.

22. Ben Bagdikian, *The Media Monopoly* (Boston: Beacon Press, 5th edition, 1997), p. 16.

23. Bagdikian, *The Media Monopoly*, p. 94.

24. Winter, *Democracy's Oxygen*, p. 108.

25. See Collins, *Dictating Content*, p. 4.

26. C. Edwin Baker, *Advertising and a Democratic Press* (Princeton, NJ: Princeton University Press, 1994), p. 44.

27. Ben Parfitt, *The Georgia Straight* (May 21-28, 1998), p. 23-24.

28. Gutstein et al., *Question the Sun!*, pp. 68.

29. See Canadian Press, "Leaky Condos major BC Consumer Issue," (28 April, 1996).

30. *Vancouver Sun* (2 April, 1996), p. D1.

31. *Vancouver Sun* (21 June 1996), p. D6.

Chapter Eight

Beyond the Blind Spots

Students of media inevitably confront an apparent paradox. On the one hand, criticism of the media and its negative effects abound. Highbrow culture critics complain about the degeneration of "serious news" into "infotainment;" political conservatives complain about an alleged liberal bias among journalists, and left-leaning critics see the media as little more than a vast propaganda machine expressing dominant economic and political interests.

On the other hand, in the midst of all this suspicion and media bashing, a significant number of people—some say a majority—regularly trust the mainstream television news stations and newspapers to convey the information and diverse perspectives they need to act as informed citizens.

One corollary of this trust is a widespread reluctance to believe that there are systematic blind spots in our country's media. In today's age of information abundance, the argument typically runs: how could there be blind spots in the media? The media system is not only a vast web encompassing television, newspapers, periodicals and, now, the Internet; it is also highly competitive and complex, involving a diverse system of checks and balances. Seemingly everything gets reported somewhere, even if only on obscure Internet web sites. Moreover, in a media environment increasingly catering to "narrowcasting" (for example, through cable television and the Internet) and "segmented" markets, there seems to be a diversity of news for just about everybody—including much that counters "official" views. If you think that there are important stories "missing" from the news, it's only because you haven't been paying close enough attention.[1]

Lazy you. This argument conveniently downplays the fact that most of us, academics included, don't have the time or inclination to do in-depth media searches on all the important (and often hidden) forces that affect our lives. We still depend heavily on the kind of information that is readily and conveniently available to the average, hard-pressed, gotta-pay-the-bills-this-week citizen. When we look at this information of convenience—the information we consume while sitting on our couches after a long day, or sample quickly over coffee—we find that the same kinds of issues, events and perspectives get presented to us day in and day out. Not surprisingly, the issues and points of view the mainstream media highlight on a day-to-day basis tend to become those which the public also perceive as important.

While the influences of news media in society are very complex and interactive, and news media research is often notoriously inconclusive, there is widespread agreement with Bernard Cohen's classic argument that the press "may not be successful much of the time in telling people what to think, but it is stunningly successful in telling readers what to think about."[2]

This does not mean that media audiences are unreflective dupes, passively accepting whatever messages the mainstream media convey. But it does mean that the press (and other media) have the ability to focus public attention on some people, events or issues, and away from others. By doing that, mainstream media help to set the agenda for both public discussion and government's policy decisions. As York University professor Arthur Siegel notes, that agenda-setting role of the media has a flip-side: "The media exert influence not merely through their choice of certain issues for emphasis in news presentation and editorial comment, but also through the omission of others."[3] One notable theory of such omissions proposes that the media can contribute to a "spiral of silence:" people who hold viewpoints that are excluded in the media tend to become reluctant to express them for fear of social isolation or ridicule. The result is that "those views which are perceived to be dominant gain even more ground and alternatives retreat still further."[4] Therefore, from the viewpoint of democratic values, it's not good enough to say that, if you find the news media inadequate, you can simply turn off the TV, cancel your subscription, and look elsewhere for alternative information: It matters greatly to the kind of society we live in what kind of information is (or is not) readily available to your friends, neighbours, and fellow workers.

That is why interest groups and parties struggle so strenuously for media access, because in the end news blind spots are about cultural and political power. Information itself is never completely neutral, and organizing it into narrative formats—forms of story-telling—makes information even more socially-determined. For example, journalism, like any way of processing and telling stories about the world, is inherently connected to social values, interests and assumptions. You can't tell stories without making some assumptions about how the world works and who your audience is. To paraphrase one of America's leading communication scholars, the news constructs pictures of the world which tell us about what exists, what is important, what is good or bad, and what is related to what.[5]

Our search for blind spots in the news has been motivated by a desire to understand how this complex process works. In doing this, we have struggled to answer two key questions: By presenting some information and opinions and excluding others, does Canada's press privilege certain values and interests while marginalizing or excluding others? And, if so, what values and what interests? Answers to these question do not come easily: the issues are immensely complex and difficult, inherent with controversy and differing interpretations. Still, recognizing that NewsWatch itself is a work in progress, we offer the following observations as provisional conclusions based on our work to date.

In the first place, our research findings invite a modestly favourable comparison of Canada with our southern neighbour. For example, judging from our list of under-reported stories from the mid-1990s, Canada's press is not overlooking jaw-dropping infamy on the scale uncovered by Project Censored in the United States. Compare our list of under-reported news for 1995 (highlighted in Chapter Five), with Project Censored's "top ten" list for the same year:

1. The Telecommunications Deregulation Bill stealthily passed through Congress, paving the way for huge new concentrations of media power.

2. Wealthy corporations benefit from $167.2 billion annually in tax subsidies, potentially enabling a balanced budget without slashing aid to the poor, according to a policy instiute report.

3. Child labour in the U.S. is worse now than in the 1930s.

4. The Internet infrastructure is being massively privatized, benefiting companies like IBM and MCI.

5. Even as the U.S. pushes a treaty to work toward elimination of nuclear weapons, it spends billions to resume production of a radioactive gas used to enhance the explosive power of nuclear warheads.

6. Newt Gingrich's think tank has a radical plan to privatize much of the Food and Drug Administration's supervision of drugs and medical devices.

7. For more than three decades, the Soviet Union secretly pumped billions of gallons of atomic waste directly into the Earth, and according to Russian scientists, the practice continues.

8. Medical fraud by health care providers costs the U.S.
$100 billion or more annually.

9. America's chemical industry is fighting to prevent the banning of methyl bromide, a pesticide 50 times per unit more destructive to the ozone layer than CFCs.

10. Members of a pro-NAFTA business coalition are breaking their own promises to create U.S. jobs and promote labour and environmental standards in Mexico.[6]

If our project, with a few exceptions, has not uncovered similarly significant stories of self-interest on the part of business, government and the military, there are at least three possible reasons. All of them may be valid; they are not mutually incompatible.

First, Canada does not have a military-industrial complex with huge budgets and international connections on anything like the U.S. scale. Second, Canada's alternative press, from which many of our under-covered stories derive, is much weaker than its American counterpart. With smaller circulations and fewer foundation grants, Canada's alternative magazines have difficulty financing the time-consuming research needed to undertake groundbreaking journalism. Third, it may just be that Canada's news media system is less constrained and monolithic than is America's corporate press. After all, Canada's Parliament has five political parties representing a much broader ideological range than America's Republican/Democrat duopoly. Moreover, in the CBC, Canada has a much stronger public broadcaster. Those factors do contribute to diversity in Canada's media system.

Still, Canada's press has its own important blind spots including those we've summarized in Chapters Six and Seven. Why might whole areas of publicly significant news be filtered out? It's not simply a matter of too little space in the paper. After all, the media find plenty of room for celebrity gossip and other forms of infotainment—stories of people and events that are so grossly over-reported, sensationalized, and hyped out of proportion to their significance that it becomes difficult to differentiate between tabloid and the so-called mainstream forms of media.

To illustrate the point that it's not simply lack of time or space that keeps more substantive food off our media plates, our project group released a Canadian junk food news list for 1995. The stories were rank-ordered by a national panel of publishers and journalists, and compiled by James Winter at the University of Windsor. In Winter's view, the list broke down into several types: an important story covered in a sensational manner, with minimal exploration of the underlying issues (the O.J. Simpson and Paul Bernardo trials); a trivial story that received more coverage than it deserves (actor Hugh Grant nabbed with a prostitute); a superficial approach to an important issue, ignoring more complete information about the subject (the information high-way); or an advertisement dressed up as news (the release of Microsoft's Windows 95).[7]

There's nothing any more wrong with a little junk food in our news coverage than in our diets—and there's an argument to be made that many human interest news stories resonate with timeless themes of human experience, the stuff of myth and drama. That's the basis for their popular appeal. But, really—Windows 95? If there's plenty of space for junk food news, then we need to ask what other factors might filter out a "healthier" diet of citizen-relevant information.

Throughout this book we have argued that a range of media filters are at work. For instance, ethnocentrism and nationalism tend to filter out news that upsets our collective sense of who we are (consider the blind spots of francophone perspectives on language rights, or Canada's role as an international arms trader). Complexity is another factor that may sideline some stories (like white-collar crime). Moreover, news is about events, not trends or processes; and in identifying events, the news is anchored on institutions and their spokespeople, rather than on unorganized, unaffiliated individuals. Routinely, news is about the event, not the condition; the conflict, not the consensus; the fact that advances the story, not the one that explains it.[8] News is about what went wrong today, not what goes wrong every day.

Acting together, these two filters—the reliance on events and on institutional sources—combined with the decline of investigative journalism, result in news that generally legitimizes established institutions and their core agendas. Individual personalities may be attacked, particular scandals may emerge, sometimes an entire political party or corporation may come under sustained media fire. Still, unless institutions are internally divided or blatantly incompetent, the media usually pay little attention to the negative consequences of the normal day-to-day functioning of those institutions, or to perspectives that challenge the core agendas around which institutional élites are reasonably unified—such as fighting government deficits through slashing social programs.

There's more to it than that, however. Not all institutions are equal. Some have much more money, power, credibility, or "cultural capital" than others. Our research suggests that the business community gets consistently better press—or less critical attention—than several other major institutions, notably government and organized labour. Problems such as environmental degradation or poor working conditions (two of our blind spots) may be covered, but rarely are they interpreted as consequences of a market-driven business system. Impressionistically, this is by contrast with the sustained critical attention given to the public sector, where government inefficiency and red tape is a frequent interpretive theme.

Why might there be little media scrutiny of the negative consequences of the business system? Three possible explanations come to mind.   First, perhaps the free enterprise system runs so smoothly that it doesn't qualify as news. After all, it's the plane that crashes that is newsworthy, not the thousands that land safely. But, recurring global economic crises, such as the "Asian flu" of 1997, render perfection an unlikely explanation for the relatively less critical coverage of business as an institution—not to mention widespread unemployment and the growing gap between the world's richest and poorest people. One could look closer to home, and ask where was the media's skepticism before the Bre-X "gold find" in Indonesia was revealed as a spectacular hoax—or, for that matter, leaky condominiums in Vancouver.

A second explanation would suggest that, while business is as subject to human shortcomings as any other institution, it's less newsworthy than political scandals because its problems are considered to be private rather than public matters. There is something to this explanation. The "watchdog" function of the press has traditionally been directed at government and public authorities, not the private sector. In the libertarian tradition, government has been seen as the main potential threat to civil liberties and press freedom. Governments spend public money, which taxpayers are legally compelled to provide. By contrast, business has supposedly earned its money in the marketplace, through the voluntary purchases of their products by consumers.

Given these libertarian assumptions, it's understandable that journalism's watchdogs have barked much louder at government than at private capital.

Still, there are many good reasons today for rethinking the traditional boundaries between public and private. In banking, communications, and other economic sectors, mergers and takeovers are producing national and global monopolies that dwarf most national governments. Fifty-one of the world's largest 100 economies are corporations; only 49 are countries. The world's largest 200 corporations, with a combined revenue of $7.1 trillion, have far more economic clout than the poorest four-fifths of humanity ($3.9 trillion).[9] Moreover, deregulation and international trade agreements like NAFTA have given the corporate sector more political clout vis-a-vis national governments. Corporate practices have significant impact on labour, the environment, politics and society at large. For these reasons, it would be appropriate to expand journalism's search for institutional accountability to the private sector.

There is a third explanation for the kinder, gentler news treatment of business—an explanation we reviewed in Chapters One and Two. This explanation focuses on the media themselves, calling attention to power and ideology, from the relatively direct influence of advertising and corporate ownership, to the more subtle ways in which free market ideology has come to dominate public discourse. This interpretation is consistent with a good deal of media theory, which suggests that the dominant media are so highly integrated into the economic system that, crudely put, they do not want to bite the hands that feed them.

An interpretation much like that was offered by James Winter, who helped to compile our project's initial under-reported news lists. In his view, these lists appear to support political/economic perspectives in the academic literature, which regard ownership and corporate concentration as primary explanations for news media content. The simple fact that, with few exceptions, the news media are owned by large corporations, may be reason enough to expect the systematic exclusion of material that presents "free market economics" and "private enterprise" in a negative light. The NewsWatch research may well suggest that the news media overall tend to offer "support of corporate capitalism," as American sociologist Gaye Tuchman put it.[10]

Still, there is a wrinkle in the research. Our project's more recent research on religion and abortion news suggests that "traditional" or conservative mores are not heavily represented in the urban press. In turn, this suggests an uneasy accommodation between the secular, largely urban, "liberal" views of many journalists and the economically-conservative interests of media owners. In other words, journalists are often "permitted" to express liberal views on social or moral questions so long as they do not fundamentally or repeatedly challenge the core political and economic interests of media owners and the rest of the corporate élite.[11]

A similar interpretation was offered in the very pages (to its credit) of the Hollinger-owned *Edmonton Journal*. Having observed the press first hand in ten foreign countries, retired Canadian diplomat Harry Sterling has concluded that the media everywhere "ultimately end up reflecting the value system of those who control the real levers of power in any particular country." In yesterday's Soviet Union or today's China, the Communist Party decrees what is news. In Western countries, the press may on the surface appear to be free to cover what it likes, but in practice, argues Sterling, "such freedom exists only so long as journalists do not seriously challenge the basic foundations of the existing socioeconomic system and the vested interests that dominate market economies...especially the business community and the wealthy."

Sterling then goes on to challenge Conrad Black's oft-stated view that Canadian journalists are leftists who fill the press with "envious pap":

We fail to detect many journalists in Canada who could qualify for the label of leftists by traditional standards...Perhaps by "left" Black means those who collectively stumble over each other in their eagerness to support every politically correct cause or motherhood issue while ignoring the real forces shaping society. However, these journalists represent no serious threat to those who control the real levers of power. Admittedly, they occasionally go through the motions of appearing to challenge the establishment, nipping a few ankles, but this in turn helps propagate the illusion that the press and media are not beholden to anyone. But if critical journalists were as radical as portrayed, they'd be demanding a higher progressive income tax, an end to tax shelters, and nationalization of profit-loaded banks and petroleum companies. But they don't.[12]

Though Sterling perhaps oversimplifies and trivializes journalists' political views, his general argument fits the NewsWatch findings. We do not subscribe to a one-dimensional view of the media; news production is a complex process, with certain openings for diversity and dissent.[13] Still, we believe that there is enough evidence to conclude that Canada's press has significant blind spots that are not simply the product of chance, the biases or laziness of individual journalists, or haphazard manipulation by particular sources. Rather, something more systematic is at work—certainly not a conspiracy, but rather the institutional "logic" of a press system dominated by large private sector corporations. The dominant press corporations have little real competition as agenda-setting sources of information, and their essential business is selling audience attention to advertisers. News is produced within a system of limits and possibilities whose parameters are set by this institutional logic.

THE ISSUE OF CENSORSHIP—AGAIN

If there are significant blind spots, and if they are systemic rather than haphazard, then perhaps it's time to revisit the question of censorship that was raised at the outset of this book. More and more, media theorists talk of "structural censorship"—the systematic exclusion of information as a by-product of the very structure of the media system. Is it appropriate to call these omissions "censorship"? Or is that just rhetorical excess?

It is a difficult question. But at NewsWatch Canada we believe that there is something to be said for expanding the traditional notion of censorship in two ways. First, private centres of power, as well as governments, can prevent or punish the dissemination of "taboo" topics. Second, we don't need to have an absolutist conception of censorship. That is, to be effective, structural censorship doesn't need to suppress all traces of a "forbidden" topic; it may be sufficient simply to marginalize it. Such counter-information might be formally reported somewhere, but it's buried so deeply in the back pages of the media system that it doesn't really matter.

While we need to allow for the possibility of structural censorship, it would hardly be ethically fair or analytically useful to label all forms of editorial decision-making as "censorship." When it is guided by criteria of public service, editorial filtering is arguably both inevitable and desirable. Accordingly, we have adopted a view of censorship that includes the following elements:

1. marginalization or suppression of publicly relevant information;

2. a conscious decision or policy—for example, to avoid covering a particular topic, or to assign news-gathering resources in such a way that the exclusion of certain kinds of news is almost inevitable;

3. imbalance of power relations: that is, those whose actions or decisions result in the omission have the power to enforce their preferences;

4. sanctions or penalties against those who dare to violate the censorship by placing the counter-information in the public domain.

Conscious exclusion backed by power and penalties—these are surely the hallmarks of censorship. Reconsidering some of the cases discussed in Chapter One, we believe that this definition would apply to many of them— actions not only by government, but by private sector actors as well, such as commercial distributors' refusal to carry a given film.

Of course, gray areas abound. If a reporter herself decides not to pursue a newsworthy story that would likely be spiked because it treads on powerful toes, is that (self)censorship? Perhaps. But what if the reporter is genuinely persuaded that the story really isn't newsworthy, after all? What counts as "publicly relevant" information, as a genuinely significant and newsworthy story, or as an idea that deserves to be in the public domain? If a letter to the editor is tossed into the wastebasket because it is poorly written or incites hatred against an ethnic group, is that censorship? What if all letters on an apparently public topic are rejected? What if a newspaper doubles its business section and transfers its last remaining labour reporter, making the positive contributions of trade unions even less likely to make the news?

Food for thought. You can debate the concept of censorship and its boundaries endlessly. They are especially murky when no clear decision to exclude a particular story or topic has been made, and yet the possibility exists that the very criteria that news media use to decide what is newsworthy themselves rest upon ideological assumptions and relations of power. (As one important example, consider the traditional libertarian distinction between private and public, noted above.) To pursue this question adequately, we would need to address the complex question of ideology, and the ways that power relations can influence institutional routines and the very consciousness of news producers and news consumers—a question much discussed by media scholars.[14]

That discussion takes us beyond the scope of NewsWatch's initial mandate, which seeks primarily to research and call attention to the presence of blind spots in Canada's press. Our analysis certainly does not lead us to a blanket indictment of working journalists, who after all initially covered some of our under-reported stories. The worrying question is whether they have enough encouragement and resources from the news organizations that employ them, to continue providing Canadians with the full range of relevant information which a democracy needs. We close this book by asking what concerned Canadians can do to offset the institutional biases and blind spots of the press.

WHERE TO GO FROM HERE?

What follows is not a recipe for reform or a blueprint for action. These would be premature, to say the least; and it is hardly our place to offer action plans that other people would have to carry out. What we offer are simply some suggestions about where to begin the important but necessarily long-term and broad-ranging project of diversifying the press system.

News organizations, if they wished, could re-allocate resources and beats to provide better coverage of the blind spots. For instance, what about more attention to global economic institutions like the IMF, World Bank or NAFTA—news written from the viewpoint of citizens in different countries rather than investors, focusing on the implications of globalization for democracy and the environment, not just the economy?

Why not more sustained coverage of politics and human rights in Canada's major APEC and NAFTA partners, like Indonesia and Mexico? What about risking a transfer of some resources from sports and life-styles to, say, environmental coverage? What about having fewer police beats and business reporters, and more coverage of the advocacy groups and social movements that are trying to promote democratic values in an increasingly global context? What about restoring and renewing the labour beat, to help give a voice to younger, minority, part-time, and women workers, as well as traditional trade unions?

The discussion of news filters in the first several chapters, however, suggests some of the reasons why news organizations are unlikely to chose to move in these directions. And, to be fair, many news consumers themselves are either satisfied with the political and media status quo, or they have given up on the possibilities of change through civic action. For some people, it seems, the satisfactions to be derived from news about personalities, sports, entertainment and life-styles are good enough. Everyday life is simply too frenzied and too exhausting to handle much more.

That doesn't mean the rest of us need to sink into apathy and despair about the possibility of revitalizing the public sphere of debate on which democracy depends. Journalists themselves could work through professional associations, like the CAJ, to promote the ethos of public service in newsrooms. Individual reporters could consciously seek to broaden the range of sources they quote, to try to ensure that those with the most money and the biggest staffs are not consistently over-accessed. When the next Fraser Institute report rolls off the corporate-funded assembly line, phone the Canadian Centre for Policy Alternatives for a counterbalancing opinion. And, of course, vice versa—though our research suggests that "vice versa" is less likely to be a problem.

If they chose, newsworkers' unions could also place the issues of editorial autonomy from management and owners higher on their collective bargaining agendas, along with stronger guarantees of balance and diversity in news reporting and commentary. A good principle to launch discussion is the clause in the Broadcasting Act which obliges broadcasters, as holders of a public trust, to "provide a reasonable opportunity for the public to be exposed to the expression of differing views on matters of public concern." Journalists could even try to democratize newsrooms from within—for example, by following the practice of some outstanding European dailies where senior editors are elected by their workplace colleagues, rather than appointed by owners. We also invite journalism and communication students and academic researchers across the country to join us in the huge task of monitoring media output. NewsWatch Canada has only begun to make small slices into the media cake in order to sample its flavour.

To the extent that moral conservatism is a blind spot in the urban, secular, "liberal" press, the media system has moved significantly in recent years to fill it. Through the *Sun Media* chain of newspapers, increasingly in Southam, and through the newsmagazine *Alberta/B.C. Report*, the traditionalist right has a significant presence. The same is not yet true of the left, as defined by Harry Sterling above. Challenges to "the corporate agenda" more direct than "politically correct" identity politics, or alternatives to the business system that look beyond liberal defences of the existing welfare state, are being articulated by various advocacy groups, but they are nearly absent in the corporate press. A serious and successful initiative by the labour movement to finance an institutional basis for independent, progressive and ground-breaking journalism would be a huge step towards removing the blind spots.

In the meantime, progressive advocacy groups could make more effective use of the openings in the press that are available for "alternative" viewpoints. From her experience co-hosting the CBC television program *FaceOff*, in which spokespeople from the Left and the Right debate a public issue, Judy Rebick complains that left-wing groups lack media savvy and are less likely to take advantage of the opportunity for access. If so, then progressive groups are in part the authors of their own exclusion.

Newspaper readers who think of themselves not just as consumers but as citizens could invest in informing themselves about the marginalized viewpoints and issues. The alternative magazines that were the source of some of our under-reported stories, magazines such as *Canadian Forum, Canadian Dimension* and *This Magazine*, would be one starting point, notwithstanding their limited resources. And of course there's always the Net. One Canadian web site specializing in an alternative take on the news is James Winter's *Flipside* at the University of Windsor—irreverent, idiosyncratic, but never boring.

Similarly, media consumers-*cum*-citizens could become more informed about the institutions that select and construct news for mass audiences. A widespread process of media education could in itself contribute to an evolutionary shift in the press. There are some very good journalism reviews, especially the *Columbia Journalism Review* in the U.S. Canada's counterparts, notably *Media* magazine and the *Ryerson Review of Journalism*, may be less professionally sophisticated, but they offer a useful home-grown forum for debate. And don't overlook the books mentioned in the footnotes to this book.

At the same time, for the reasons outlined in Chapter Two, we are skeptical that consumer action in the marketplace alone will fundamentally diversify the news system. In some ways, the pressures of the marketplace themselves contribute to the blind spots we have discussed. Many advertisers seek media that will deliver up-scale consumers, not the great unwashed masses. The logic of the market is not one person, one vote, but rather one dollar, one vote.

That means that there is a role for public policy to help level the media playing field.

Traditional libertarians and many journalists understandably shudder at the thought of state intervention in the press. We are certainly not advocating anything like government censorship or regulation of press content. Rather, we see a role for government to promote structural pluralism within the media system. The underlying idea is that every institution (including, we would hasten to add, universities) has its strengths and weaknesses. Every media organization is a system of power as well as of communication—it is institutionally "wired" or programmed to produce certain kinds of information easily, and to ignore or marginalize others. If that's the case, and if a democratic public sphere needs "diverse and antagonistic" sources of information, then we need to ensure that there are different kinds of media, financed and controlled in different ways.

One proposal has been put forward by Free Marketeers such as former *Globe and Mail* (now *National Post*) columnist Terence Corcoran, and Hollinger executive Peter Atkinson. They suggest that, if press concentration is indeed a problem, then the federal government should amend the Income Tax Act in order to allow foreign companies to start or to buy Canadian newspaper franchises. In this view, foreign media conglomerates could provide more diversity and competition between newspaper chains in Canada.

One problem with this scenario is that it does nothing to reduce the blind spots associated with commercial pressures and corporate ownership, as such. Moreover, while it might encourage a certain amount of competition in the short term, in the long run the logic of newspaper economics would lead to the same kind of industry domination by one or a few chains—only they'd be foreign rather than Canadian-based. Would we really be better off if Rupert Murdoch replaced Conrad Black?

If we look to other liberal/democratic countries, and to some important public enquiries on the press here in Canada, we can find some better ideas on how to reconcile the economic logic of concentration with the democratic requirement of diversity.[15] One kind of measure seeks to limit the degree of corporate concentration in the press. Some European countries have adopted legislative measures to limit the degree of market dominance enjoyed by single media companies. Sweden has a press subsidy system designed to help smaller papers survive. Even the free enterprise United States has stronger anti-trust legislation than Canada does. The Competition Act could be amended to require Canada's sleepy (or tightly leashed) competition watchdogs to take into account the impact of media mergers on editorial independence and diversity.

An extension of this approach would try not only to increase the number of corporate owners, but to encourage more diverse kinds of ownership in the media system. Stable and adequate financing for non-commercial public broadcasting would be one aspect. A fund to support new community-based or non-profit media could be another. Possibly, this fund could be financed by a tax on advertising; certainly, it would need to be administered at arm's length from the government, to prevent political interference. Precedents for this approach can be found in how the federal government has nurtured Canada's film industry without turning bureaucrats into movie producers.

Even without changes in media ownership, public policy could promote greater diversity in press content. We could take a look at France's right-of-reply legislation, which mandates the press to provide space for groups it has attacked. Canada's 1981 Royal Commission on Newspapers suggested measures to protect the editors of chains and conglomerates from ownership interference. But we are a long way from a legislative press policy in Canada. Politicians, governments and parties are frequently angry and frustrated with the media, and they may try to exert pressure, including defamation suits, complaints to press councils or ombudsmen, the withdrawal of government advertising, and even a cabinet directive to launch a CRTC enquiry in 1977. Still, a government attempting to move beyond particular cases of coverage to diversify the very structure of the media system would have to have be willing to endure immense pressure. It is an unlikely prospect, because no government is likely to want to invoke the wrath of media owners and the legions of free marketeers. That's why effective media reform will come about only with sustained public pressure. For example, Conrad Black's takeover of Southam in 1996 has spawned an effort to build such a movement: the Campaign for Press and Broadcasting Freedom was launched by the Council of Canadians and several labour organizations to research and advocate media diversity and accountability.

This initiative is still at an embryonic stage. It needs the energies of a coalition of various progressive groups who feel excluded from the media, each devoting a small portion of its resources to changing the media landscape within which they work. The Campaign has at least taken the very important first step of putting the question of media power, accountability and reform on the political agenda. It is an issue that needs an even broader, more wide-ranging public debate. At the same time, there is parallel work to be done, by carefully monitoring how well the press is fulfilling its function of democratic public communication. That's the underlying purpose of

NewsWatch Canada, and we hope that, through this book, many other Canadians, including working journalists and news consumers, will join in this project.

ENDNOTES

1. See an elaboration of this point by one of NewsWatch Canada's initial critics, Chris Dornan. "If it's News to You, You Haven't Been Paying Attention," *Globe and Mail* (April 22, 1994).
2. Bernard C. Cohen, *The Press and Foreign Policy* (Princeton, NJ: Princeton University Press, 1963), p. 13.
3. Arthur Siegel, *Politics and the Media in Canada*, 2nd edition (Toronto: McGrawHill Ryerson), p. 22.
4. Denis McQuail, *Mass Communication Theory*, 3rd edition (London: Sage, 1994), p. 362.
5. George Gerbner, "Toward 'Cultural Indicators': The Analysis of Mass Mediated Public Message Systems," in George Gerbner, Ole R. Holsti, Klaus Krippendorff, William J. Paisley, and Philip J. Stone, eds., *The Analysis of Communication Content* (New York: John Wiley, 1969), pp. 123-32.
6. Carl Jensen and Project Censored, *20 Years of Censored News* (New York: Seven Stories Press, 1997), pp. 320-34.
7. James Winter, *Democracy's Oxygen* (Montreal: Black Rose, 1997), p. 136.
8. On this point see Todd Gitlin, *The Whole World is Watching* (Berkeley: University of California Press, 1980), pp. 122-23.
9. Data cited in Maude Barlow and James Winter, *The Big Black Book* (Toronto: Stoddart, 1997), pp. 209-210.
10. Gaye Tuchman, *Making News: A Study in the Construction of Reality* (New York: The Free Press, 1978), pp. 162-164, 120; cited in Winter, *Democracy's Oxygen*, p. 132.
11. Conrad Winn and John McMenemy, *Political Parties in Canada* (Toronto: McGraw-Hill. Ryerson, 1976), p. 132.
12. Harry Sterling, "There's no Real Left for Black to Silence," *Edmonton Journal* (Nov. 10, 1996), p. F2.
13. See, for example, Robert A. Hackett, *News and Dissent: The Press and the Politics of Peace in Canada* (Norwood, NJ: Ablex, 1991), chapter 12.
14. See, for example, John B. Thompson, *Ideology in Modern Culture: Critical Social Theory in the Era of Mass Communication* (Cambridge: Polity Press, 1991). For a recent Canadian example, see Robert Hackett and Yuezhi Zhao, *Sustaining Democracy? Journalism and the Politics of Objectivity* (Toronto: Garamond, 1998).
15. For a discussion of some of these, see Barlow and Winter, *The Big Black Book*, pp. 212-224.

The Missing News

Index

A

D

E

Eagleson, Alan, 87-88

Edges, 140

editorial concentration. See: concentration of ownership, implications for journalism; media corporations, as blind spots

Eldorado Resources, 134

environmental degradation, 146, 150-151, 166, 168-172, 185, 201, 223

- complexity of environmental issues, 172
- ebb and flow of media interest, 172
- promotion of hyper-consumerism, 171
- structural connection to global economy, 170

Ericson, Richard, 99

Exxon, 141

Exxon Valdez, 169, 172

F

FaceOff, 230

Farmer, Mark, 151-152

Fifth Estate, 113

filters, news

- advertisers, 213-216
- corporate media ownership, 38-39, 207-213
- defined, 26
- government constraints, 40-43
- legal constraints, 42
- official sources, 167, 173, 223
- reliance on events, 223
- trade relations, 182
- work routines, 167

See also: advertising; government sources; journalists; media ownership; 'new class'; news values

Financial Post, 23, 53, 132, 150, 152-153, 158, 204

Fineman, Mark, 126

Fishman, Mark, 82

Forcese, Craig, 141-142

Forsey, Helen, 144

N

S

T

U